MEI structured mathematics

Statistics 5 & 6

**ALEC CRYER
MICHAEL DAVIES
BOB FRANCIS
GERALD GOODALL**

Series Editor: Roger Porkess

MEI Structured Mathematics is supported by industry:
BNFL, Casio, GEC, Intercity, JCB, Lucas, The National Grid Company,
Sharp Texas Instruments, Thorn EMI

Acknowledgements

The authors and publishers would like to thank the following companies, institutions and individuals who have given permission to reproduce copyright material. Every effort has been made to acknowledge ownership of copyright. The publishers will be happy to make arrangements with any copyright holders whom it has not been possible to contact.

The illustrations were drawn by Jeff Edwards.

Photograph: Emma Lee/Life File (page 1).

The Associated Examining Board
The University of Cambridge Local Examinations Syndicate
The University of London Examinations and Assessment Council
The University of Oxford Delegacy of Local Examinations

The above examination boards cannot accept any responsibility for the accuracy or method or working in the answers given.

Orders: please contact Bookpoint Ltd, 39 Milton Park, Abingdon, Oxon OX14 4TD. Telephone: (44) 01235 400414, Fax: (44) 01235 400454. Lines are open from 9.00–6.00, Monday to Saturday, with a 24 hour message answering service. Email address: orders@bookprint.co.uk

British Library Cataloguing in Publication Data
A catalogue record for this title is available from The British Library

ISBN 0 340 701 323

First published 1998
Impression number   10 9 8 7 6 5 4 3 2 1
Year   2004 2003 2002 2001 2000 1999 1998

Copyright © 1998 Alec Cryer, Michael Davies, Bob Francis, Gerald Goodall

Typeset by the Alden Group, Oxford.
Printed in Great Britain for Hodder & Stoughton Educational, a division of Hodder Headline PLC, 338 Euston Road, London NW1 3BH by Scotprint Ltd, Musselburgh, Scotland.

MEI Structured Mathematics

Mathematics is not only a beautiful and exciting subject in its own right but also one that underpins many other branches of learning. It is consequently fundamental to the success of a modern economy.

MEI Structured Mathematics is designed to increase substantially the number of people taking the subject post-GCSE, by making it accessible, interesting and relevant to a wide range of students.

It is a credit accumulation scheme based on 45-hour Components which may be taken individually or aggregated to give:

3 Components	AS Mathematics
6 Components	A Level Mathematics
9 Components	A Level Mathematics + AS Further Mathematics
12 Components	A Level Mathematics + A Level Further Mathematics

Components may alternatively be combined to give other A or AS certifications (in Statistics, for example) or they may be used to obtain credit towards other types of qualification.

The course is examined by OCR (previously OCEAC), with examinations held in January and June each year.

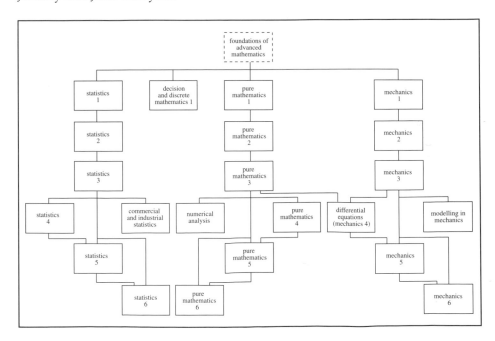

This is one of the series of books written to support the course. Its position within the whole scheme can be seen in the diagram above.

Mathematics in Education and Industry is a curriculum development body which aims to promote the links between Education and Industry in Mathematics, and to produce relevant examination and teaching syllabuses and support material. Since its foundation in the 1960s, MEI has provided syllabuses for GCSE (or previously O Level), Additional Mathematics and A Level.

For more information about MEI Structured Mathematics or other syllabuses and materials, write to MEI Office, 11 Market Street, Bradford-on-Avon BA15 1LL.

Contents

1

Tests for proportion

What happens to the hole when the cheese is gone?

Berthold Brecht

Try rolling your tongue, as in the photograph below.

Most people are unable to roll their tongues, but the ability to do so, which is an inherited characteristic and so cannot be learned, is possessed by a certain proportion of the population.

It has been suggested that 30% of the population of Britain are tongue rollers.

Collect your own sample of people and determine how many are tongue rollers. Use your data to repeat the steps in the following example.

A sample of size 23 was collected from two statistics classes: three of them could roll their tongues.

We are going to test the hypotheses:

H_0: the proportion of the population who can roll their tongues is 0.3;

H_1: the proportion of the population who can roll their tongues is different from 0.3.

How many or few of a sample of size 23 would have to be tongue rollers in order to reject the null hypothesis? If H_0 is true, the probability of each possible number of tongue rollers can be calculated, using the binomial distribution. For instance,

$$P(5 \text{ tongue rollers out of } 23) = {}^{23}C_5(0.7)^{18}(0.3)^5 = 0.133$$

The complete set of probabilities and cumulative totals is given below: R is the variable 'number of tongue rollers'.

r	$P(R = r)$	$P(R \leqslant r)$	r	$P(R = r)$	$P(R \leqslant r)$	r	$P(R = r)$	$P(R \leqslant r)$
0	0.000 27	0.000 27	8	0.152 73	0.770 86	16	0.000 09	0.999 98
1	0.002 70	0.002 97	9	0.109 09	0.879 95	17	0.000 02	1.000 00
2	0.012 72	0.015 69	10	0.065 45	0.945 40	18	0.000 00	1.000 00
3	0.038 15	0.053 84	11	0.033 15	0.978 55	19	0.000 00	1.000 00
4	0.081 76	0.135 60	12	0.014 21	0.992 76	20	0.000 00	1.000 00
5	0.133 15	0.268 75	13	0.005 15	0.997 91	21	0.000 00	1.000 00
6	0.171 19	0.439 95	14	0.001 58	0.999 49	22	0.000 00	1.000 00
7	0.178 18	0.618 13	15	0.000 41	0.999 90	23	0.000 00	1.000 00

NOTE *You should note that, provided that your sample size was no larger than 20, the Student's Handbook will provide the equivalent figures for you.*

If we are to test at the 5% level, the critical region is $\{R \leqslant 2\} \cup \{R \geqslant 12\}$. This is because:

$$P(R \leqslant 2) = 0.015 69 \text{ which is less than 2.5%};$$

but $\qquad P(R \leqslant 3) = 0.053 84 \text{ which is greater than 2.5%};$

and because:

$$P(R \geqslant 12) = 1 - 0.978 55 = 0.021 45 \text{ which is less than 2.5%};$$

but $\qquad P(R \geqslant 11) = 1 - 0.945 40 = 0.054 60 \text{ which is greater than 2.5%}.$

The sample of size 23 contained three tongue rollers. This figure does not lie in the critical region so the null hypothesis is accepted.

Confidence intervals

We could also use this sample to construct a confidence interval for the proportion, π, of tongue rollers in the population.

In previous work you have seen that a confidence interval gives the range of values of a population parameter which would make the actual experimental result look reasonably plausible. In this context that means that you are trying to determine the range of values of π which would *not* put the sample proportion of three out of 23 within either the lower or the upper tail of the critical region. If you are looking for a 95% confidence interval, that means the values for π for which:

3 out of 23 is not in the lower 2.5% tail, so $P(R \leqslant 3) > 0.025$;

and   3 out of 23 is not in the upper 2.5% tail, so $P(R \geqslant 3) > 0.025$;

which is more conveniently expressed as $P(R \leqslant 2) < 0.975$.

Algebraically, therefore, we want the values of π for which:

sample proportion not in the lower tail:

$$^{23}C_0(1-\pi)^{23} + {}^{23}C_1(1-\pi)^{22}\pi + {}^{23}C_2(1-\pi)^{21}\pi^2 + {}^{23}C_3(1-\pi)^{20}\pi^3 > 0.025;$$

and sample proportion not in the upper tail:

$$^{23}C_0(1-\pi)^{23} + {}^{23}C_1(1-\pi)^{22}\pi + {}^{23}C_2(1-\pi)^{21}\pi^2 < 0.975.$$

These equations can only be solved numerically, with results $\pi < 0.336$ and $\pi > 0.028$.

Thus the 95% confidence interval for π is $0.028 < \pi < 0.336$.

EXAMPLE

Apples sold as class B may not have more than 10% of the fruit bruised. A retailer who buys a consignment of apples labelled class B suspects that his wholesaler has supplied inferior apples and checks a random sample of 16 apples, five of which are bruised. Is there evidence at the 5% level that his suspicion is correct?

Solution:

The hypotheses are:

H_0:   proportion of apples bruised $= 0.1$;

H_1:   proportion of apples bruised > 0.1.

Using the binomial tables in the *Student's Handbook* for n $= 16$ and p $= 0.1$, we find

$P(R \geqslant 4) = 1 - P(R \leqslant 3) = 1 - 0.9316 = 0.0684$ which is greater than 0.05;

but $P(R \geqslant 5) = 1 - P(R \leqslant 4) = 1 - 0.9830 = 0.0170$ which is less than 0.05;

so that the (one-tailed) critical region at the 5% level is $\{R \geqslant 5\}$.

As the experimental result lies in this critical region, the null hypothesis is rejected; that is, there is evidence for his suspicion.

EXAMPLE

In a group of 17 students, one has blue eyes. Assuming that the students constitute a random sample from the population, show that $[0, 0.25)$, is an approximate one-sided 95% confidence interval for the proportion of blue-eyed people in the population.

Solution:

The confidence interval $[0, \pi)$ for the true proportion of blue-eyed people in the population is the set of values of p for which the outcome 'one student out of 17 has blue eyes' is not in the lower tail of the distribution of outcomes, that is for which:

P(1 or fewer students out of 17 has blue eyes if the

population proportion is p) > 0.05.

The tables in the *Student's Handbook* with $n = 17$ and $r = 1$ give the result that, if $p = 0.25$, then

P(1 or fewer students out of 17 has blue eyes) $= 0.0501$.

so that 0.25 is the required upper limit of the confidence interval.

Exercise 1A

1. It is claimed that 40% of heavy lorries on the road are not roadworthy. The police in one county stop a sample of 15 heavy lorries and find that two of them are not roadworthy. Are the police justified in disputing the claimed figure?

2. The Andean flea is found in the pelts of llamas. A sample of 14 llamas from a flock is inspected and five are found to be infested with the flea. Show that $(0.15, 0.75)$ is an approximate symmetrical 2% confidence interval for the proportion of llamas in the flock which is infected.

3. Approximately one in 20 people is left-handed. A writer for *Wisden* suspects that good cricketers are more likely than this to be left-handed. He looks at one county squad and finds that, of the 19 players, three are left handed. Test the writer's hypothesis. Suggest why his sampling procedure may be unsatisfactory.

4. In a survey within a firm to determine the popularity of the National Lottery, a sample of 16 employees is questioned, and 14 say that they purchase tickets every week. Show that $(0.7, 1]$ is a one-sided 90% confidence interval for the proportion of employees in the firm who purchase tickets every week.

5. A sample of 12 nuts is taken from a large batch and four are found to have cracked shells. Show that $(0.1, 0.65)$ is an approximate symmetrical 95% confidence interval for the proportion of nuts in the batch with cracked shells.

6. It is claimed that at least 70% of doctors are overweight. In a random sample of 18 doctors, only nine are overweight. Show that the null hypothesis is rejected at the 10% level, but accepted at the 5% level.

Large-sample approximation

In most of the examples and exercises in the last section, the sample size was small enough so that you could use prepared tables. When this is not possible, the testing of hypotheses about confidence intervals and the finding of confidence intervals for the proportion of a population with a given characteristic could involve a considerable amount of calculation.

Fortunately, for large sample sizes, an approximation can be used to find results relatively painlessly: let us go back to our tongue-rolling example on page 1.

If π is the population proportion of tongue rollers, the number, R, of tongue rollers found in a sample of size n has the binomial distribution $B(n, \pi)$. Thus, if n is large, by Normal approximation:

$$R \approx N(n\pi, n\pi(1 - \pi))$$

as $n\pi$ is the mean and $n\pi(1 - \pi)$ is the variance of the binomial distribution. Then the sample proportion, P, has the approximate distribution:

$$P = \frac{R}{n} \approx N\left(\frac{n\pi}{n}, \frac{n\pi(1 - \pi)}{n^2}\right) = N\left(\pi, \frac{\pi(1 - \pi)}{n}\right)$$

That is, in large samples the sample proportion is distributed approximately Normally, with mean π and standard deviation $\sqrt{\dfrac{\pi(1 - \pi)}{n}}$

Finally, therefore, the test statistic:

$$\frac{P - \pi}{\sqrt{\dfrac{\pi(1 - \pi)}{n}}}$$

has approximately a standard Normal distribution, $N(0, 1)$.

EXAMPLE

In a sample of size 60, 13 people were found to have double-jointed thumbs. At the 5% level, test the one-tailed hypotheses:

H_0 the proportion of the population with double-jointed thumbs is 0.3;
H_1 the proportion of the population with double-jointed thumbs is less than 0.3.

Solution:

The test statistic which you saw above has approximately a standard Normal distribution and has, for the data given, the value:

$$\frac{p - \pi}{\sqrt{\dfrac{\pi(1 - \pi)}{n}}} = \frac{\frac{13}{60} - 0.3}{\sqrt{\dfrac{0.3(1 - 0.3)}{60}}} = -1.4086$$

The critical value of the standard Normal distribution at the one-tailed 5% level is 1.645. As $-1.645 < -1.4086$, we accept the null hypothesis at this significance level.

Confidence intervals

Finding a confidence interval for the population proportion using this large-sample approximation, means, as before, looking for the values of π for which the sample proportion is not in the critical region. For instance, in the case of a 95% two-sided confidence interval, that is the values of π for which:

$$-1.960 < \frac{\frac{13}{60} - \pi}{\sqrt{\dfrac{\pi(1 - \pi)}{60}}} < 1.960$$

(as 1.960 is the two-tailed 5% significance level for the standard Normal distribution).

However, the rearrangement of this inequality to obtain limits on π, while possible, is tedious and it is therefore conventional to replace π in the denominator with its unbiased estimate from the sample, p, which we would expect to introduce very little error for large n. Thus the confidence interval is:

$$-1.960 < \frac{\frac{13}{60} - \pi}{\sqrt{\frac{\frac{13}{60}\left(1 - \frac{13}{60}\right)}{60}}} < 1.960$$

This rearranges to:

$$\frac{13}{60} - 1.960\sqrt{\frac{\frac{13}{60}\left(1 - \frac{13}{60}\right)}{60}} < \pi < \frac{13}{60} + 1.960\sqrt{\frac{\frac{13}{60}\left(1 - \frac{13}{60}\right)}{60}}$$

or, finally:

$$0.112\,42 < \pi < 0.320\,91$$

The range of values of n for which this large-sample approximation is appropriate depends on π. A rule of thumb is that both $n\pi$ and $n(1 - \pi)$ (or np and $n(1 - p)$ for a confidence interval, where π needs to be estimated) should be greater than about 5. You have met this criterion before when approximating binomial by Normal distributions.

Summary

To test the hypothesis that the population proportion with a particular characteristic is π, using the sample proportion p in a sample of size n, the test statistic is:

$$\frac{p - \pi}{\sqrt{\frac{\pi(1 - \pi)}{n}}}$$

which has approximately a standard Normal distribution for large n.

Given the sample proportion p in a sample of size n, an approximate $a\%$ confidence interval for the population proportion is:

$$p - \tau_a\sqrt{\frac{p(1 - p)}{n}} < \pi < p + \tau_a\sqrt{\frac{p(1 - p)}{n}}$$

where τ_a is the two-sided $(100 - a)\%$ critical value for the standard Normal distribution.

Investigation

The approximation of a binomial by a Normal distribution can be improved using a continuity correction. How does this affect the formulae for the test statistic and confidence interval? How much difference does this correction make for different values of n?

Exercise 1B

1. The proportion of winning tickets in a large charity raffle is claimed to be $\frac{1}{4}$. Jake bought 40 tickets and won four prizes. Is there evidence at the 5% level that the claimed proportion is incorrect?

2. The seeds of a new variety of crocus are being tested. The experimenter plants 55 seeds and 37 of them germinate.

   (i) Give a 95% two-sided confidence interval for the proportion of the seeds of this new variety that germinate.

   (ii) What assumptions are you making in your analysis?

3. Rat-o-kill claims that an 80% success rate in eliminating rats can be achieved with their product. A firm of pest exterminators believes that this claim is exaggerated. When the product is used in 36 properties, the rats are eliminated in 22 of them. Is there good evidence for the pest exterminators' suspicions?

4. Of the 11 234 babies born in a Health Authority's area during one year, 13 of them have a particular birth defect.

   (i) Give a one-sided upper 99% confidence bound for the proportion of babies born with this defect in the population.

   (ii) Discuss carefully the assumptions underlying your calculation.

5. A given coin is tossed N times. The true probability of a head on each toss is π and, in the sample, a fraction, p, of the tosses shows a head.

   (i) What is the two-tailed critical region, at the 95% level, for the test $\pi = \frac{1}{2}$?

   (ii) For what range of values of p does $\frac{1}{2}$ lie in the two-sided 95% confidence interval for π?

   (iii) Comment on your answers to (i) and (ii). What happens as $N \rightarrow \infty$?

6. In an opinion poll voters are asked whether they would vote for the Conservative or Labour Party.

   Of the 326 voters expressing preference, 147 preferred the Conservatives, 179 the Labour party.

   (i) Test the hypothesis that voters are equally likely to prefer either party.

   (ii) Give a 95% two-sided confidence interval for the proportion of voters preferring the Labour party.

   (iii) When you are justified in ignoring those questioned who did not express a preference?

   (iv) How many voters would have to be questioned in order to detect reliably a difference of 3% in the support for the two parties?

   (v) What other problems affect real opinion polls of this type? Why do they not always correctly predict the results of elections?

Differences in proportions

Like tongue rolling, colour blindness is also an inherited characteristic.

In a sample of 230 men and 410 women, 15 men and 4 women are found to have colour blindness of a particular type. Is there evidence that the proportions of men and women who have this type of colour blindness differ?

We want to test the hypotheses:

H_0: the proportions of men and women having this type of colour blindness are equal;

H_1: the proportions of men and women having this type of colour blindness are different.

If R_m and R_w are the numbers of men and women having this type of colour blindness in samples of size 230 and 410, then their distributions are:

$$R_m \sim B(230, \pi_m) \text{ and } R_w \sim B(410, \pi_w)$$

where π_m and π_w are the proportions of the whole population of men and women, respectively, who are colour blind.

As the sample sizes are large, we can make Normal approximations:

$$R_m \approx N(230\pi_m, 230\pi_m(1 - \pi_m)) \text{ and } R_w \approx N(410\pi_w, 410\pi_w(1 - \pi_w))$$

and so the sample proportions P_m and P_w of men and women who are colour blind have the distributions:

$$P_m \approx \frac{R_m}{230} = N\left(\pi_m, \frac{\pi_m(1 - \pi_m)}{230}\right) \text{ and } P_w = \frac{R_w}{410} \approx N\left(\pi_w, \frac{\pi_w(1 - \pi_w)}{410}\right)$$

The difference in sample proportions then has distribution:

$$P_m - P_w \approx N\left(\pi_m - \pi_w, \frac{\pi_m(1 - \pi_m)}{230} + \frac{\pi_w(1 - \pi_w)}{410}\right)$$

If the null hypothesis (that the proportions of men and women having this type of colour blindness are the same) is true, $\pi_m = \pi_w = \pi$, say, then:

$$P_m - P_w \approx N(0, \pi(1 - \pi)(\tfrac{1}{230} + \tfrac{1}{410}))$$

and so:

$$\frac{P_m - P_w}{\sqrt{\pi(1 - \pi)(\tfrac{1}{230} + \tfrac{1}{410})}} \approx N(0, 1)$$

As π is unknown, we replace it with the obvious sample estimate based on both the men's and women's samples (as it is supposed under the null hypothesis to be equal in both populations):

$$\hat{\pi} = \frac{R_m + R_w}{230 + 410}$$

Thus the final test statistic is:

$$\frac{P_m - P_w}{\sqrt{\hat{\pi}(1 - \hat{\pi})(\tfrac{1}{230} + \tfrac{1}{410})}}$$

This also has approximately a standard Normal distribution because, as n is large, we would expect the change in distribution made by replacing π with its sample estimate to be small.

With the data given, the estimate of π is:

$$\hat{\pi} = \frac{15 + 4}{230 + 410} = \frac{19}{640}$$

so the test statistic is:

$$\frac{\frac{15}{230} - \frac{4}{410}}{\sqrt{\frac{19}{640}\left(1 - \frac{19}{640}\right)\left(\frac{1}{230} + \frac{1}{410}\right)}} = 3.96655$$

This is much larger than the two-tailed 5% significance level for the standard Normal distribution, 1.960, so the null hypothesis is rejected in favour of the alternative, that the proportions of men and women who are colour blind differ.

We can use the same data to find a one-sided confidence interval giving a lower limit for the difference in proportions.

The result:

$$P_{\mathrm{m}} - P_{\mathrm{w}} \approx \mathrm{N}\left(\pi_{\mathrm{m}} - \pi_{\mathrm{w}}, \frac{\pi_{\mathrm{m}}(1 - \pi_{\mathrm{m}})}{230} + \frac{\pi_{\mathrm{w}}(1 - \pi_{\mathrm{w}})}{410}\right)$$

was derived above, and implies that:

$$\frac{(P_{\mathrm{m}} - P_{\mathrm{w}}) - (\pi_{\mathrm{m}} - \pi_{\mathrm{w}})}{\sqrt{\left(\dfrac{\pi_{\mathrm{m}}(1 - \pi_{\mathrm{m}})}{230} + \dfrac{\pi_{\mathrm{w}}(1 - \pi_{\mathrm{w}})}{410}\right)}} \approx \mathrm{N}(0, 1)$$

As previously, we shall use the fact that n is large to replace π_{m} and π_{w}, by their sample estimates P_{m} and P_{w} (where, in this case, we should certainly not assume that these are equal) so that:

$$\frac{(P_{\mathrm{m}} - P_{\mathrm{w}}) - (\pi_{\mathrm{m}} - \pi_{\mathrm{w}})}{\sqrt{\left(\dfrac{P_{\mathrm{m}}(1 - P_{\mathrm{m}})}{230} + \dfrac{P_{\mathrm{w}}(1 - P_{\mathrm{w}})}{410}\right)}} \approx \mathrm{N}(0, 1)$$

A 95% one-sided confidence interval is then given by:

$$\frac{(P_{\mathrm{m}} - P_{\mathrm{w}}) - (\pi_{\mathrm{m}} - \pi_{\mathrm{w}})}{\sqrt{\left(\dfrac{P_{\mathrm{m}}(1 - P_{\mathrm{m}})}{230} + \dfrac{P_{\mathrm{w}}(1 - P_{\mathrm{w}})}{410}\right)}} \leqslant 1.645$$

as the one-tailed critical value at the 5% level for a standard Normal distribution is 1.645. Rearranging gives:

$$(P_{\mathrm{m}} - P_{\mathrm{w}}) - 1.645\sqrt{\left(\frac{P_{\mathrm{m}}(1 - P_{\mathrm{m}})}{230} + \frac{P_{\mathrm{w}}(1 - P_{\mathrm{w}})}{410}\right)} < \pi_{\mathrm{m}} - \pi_{\mathrm{w}}$$

or, substituting:

$$\left(\tfrac{15}{230} - \tfrac{4}{410}\right) - 1.645\sqrt{\frac{\tfrac{15}{230}\left(1 - \tfrac{15}{230}\right)}{230} + \frac{\tfrac{4}{410}\left(1 - \tfrac{4}{410}\right)}{410}} < \pi_{\mathrm{m}} - \pi_{\mathrm{w}}$$

i.e.

$$\pi_{\mathrm{m}} - \pi_{\mathrm{w}} > 0.027\,51$$

EXAMPLE

A newspaper claims that Scotsmen are more likely than Englishmen to enjoy fried breakfasts. Of 312 Scotsmen, 220 enjoy fried breakfasts, while 186 of 298 Englishmen do so. Test an appropriate hypothesis at the 1% level.

Solution:

Appropriate hypotheses are:

H_0: equal proportions of Scots and English men enjoy fried breakfasts;
H_1: a greater proportion of Scots than English men enjoys fried breakfasts.

The test statistic is:

$$\frac{P_S - P_E}{\sqrt{\hat{\pi}(1-\hat{\pi})(\frac{1}{312} + \frac{1}{298})}}$$

where $P_S = \frac{220}{312}$ is the proportion of Scotsmen who enjoy fried breakfasts, $P_E = \frac{186}{298}$ is the corresponding proportion of Englishmen and $\hat{\pi} = \frac{220+186}{312+298} = \frac{406}{610}$ is the overall estimate of the proportion of Scots and English men who enjoy fried breakfasts. The test statistic is therefore:

$$\frac{\frac{220}{312} - \frac{186}{298}}{\sqrt{\frac{406}{610}\left(1 - \frac{406}{610}\right)\left(\frac{1}{312} + \frac{1}{298}\right)}} = 2.119$$

The one-tailed 1% significance level for the standard Normal distribution is 2.326 and $2.119 < 2.326$, so we accept the null hypothesis.

EXAMPLE

In a boys' school 67 of the 186 fifth-year pupils pass GCSE maths, whereas, in a girls' school in the same town, 55 of the 118 fifth-years pass. Give a 99% confidence interval for the difference in pass rates between the two schools. Comment on the assumptions underlying this calculation.

Solution:

If the girls' pass rate is π_g and the boys' pass rate is π_b, then a confidence interval for the difference in pass rates is:

$$(p_g - p_b) - 2.576\sqrt{\left(\frac{p_g(1-p_g)}{118} + \frac{p_b(1-p_b)}{186}\right)}$$

$$< (\pi_g - \pi_b) < (p_g - p_b) + 2.576\sqrt{\left(\frac{p_g(1-p_g)}{118} + \frac{p_b(1-p_b)}{186}\right)}$$

where p_b, p_g are the sample proportions of boys and girls passing and 2.576 is the two-tailed 1% significance level for the standard Normal distribution.

The data provided give:

$$p_g = \frac{55}{118}, \qquad p_b = \frac{67}{186}$$

so that the confidence interval is:

$$-0.043 < \pi_g - \pi_b < 0.255$$

The calculation assumes that the pupils in this year are a random sample of the intake of the school.

Summary

To test the hypothesis that there is no difference in proportions with a particular characteristic in two populations, we use the sample proportions p_1 and p_2 with that characteristic in samples of size n_1 and n_2 drawn from the two populations. The test statistic is then:

$$\frac{p_1 - p_2}{\sqrt{\hat{\pi}(1 - \hat{\pi})\left(\dfrac{1}{n_1} + \dfrac{1}{n_2}\right)}}$$

which has approximately a standard Normal distribution for large n, where:

$$\hat{\pi} = \frac{n_1 p_1 + n_2 p_2}{n_1 + n_2}$$

is an estimate from the two samples of the common proportion with the characteristic.

Given the sample proportions p_1 and p_2, with a particular characteristic in samples of sizes n_1 and n_2, an approximate $a\%$ confidence interval for the difference $\pi_1 - \pi_2$ in proportions with that characteristic in the populations from which the samples are drawn is:

$$(p_1 - p_2) - \tau_a\sqrt{\frac{p_1(1 - p_1)}{n_1} + \frac{p_2(1 - p_2)}{n_2}}$$

$$< \pi_1 - \pi_2 < (p_1 - p_2) + \tau_a\sqrt{\frac{p_1(1 - p_1)}{n_1} + \frac{p_2(1 - p_2)}{n_2}}$$

where τ_a is the two-sided $(100 - a)\%$ critical value for the standard Normal distribution.

Investigation

Use a χ^2 test to investigate whether the prevalence of the type of colour blindness discussed earlier is independent of sex. Use the data given there, in the form of a contingency table:

	Men	Women	Row totals
Colour blind	15	4	19
Not colour blind	215	406	621
Column totals	230	410	640

You should find that the χ^2 value you calculate is the square of the test statistic 3.966 55 which we calculated for the test of equality of proportions. This is, in fact, true in general because the chi-squared distribution with one degree of freedom is just the distribution of the square of a standard Normal variable.

You can show this algebraically if you are ambitious. The strategy is as follows.

1. Set up a table with algebraic entries:

	Men	Women	Row totals
Colour blind	a	b	$a + b$
Not colour blind	c	d	$c + d$
Column totals	$a + c$	$b + d$	$a + b + c + d$

2. Now set up a table of expected values. The marginal totals will be the same, of course. Explain why the entry in the top left-hand (colour-blind men) cell will be:

$$\frac{(a+b)(a+c)}{a+b+c+d}$$

and complete the table.

3. You should find that the squared difference (observed − expected)^2 which appears in the calculation of the χ^2 value is the same for each cell and equal to:

$$\left(\frac{ad-bc}{a+b+c+d}\right)^2$$

so that you obtain an expression for χ^2 which begins:

$$\chi^2 = \frac{(ad-bc)^2}{a+b+c+d}\left\{\frac{1}{(a+b)(a+c)} + \cdots\right\}$$

where there are four terms in the braces.

4. Show that your expression for χ^2 simplifies to:

$$\chi^2 = \frac{(ad-bc)^2}{a+b+c+d}\left\{\frac{(a+b+c+d)^2}{(a+b)(a+c)(b+d)(c+d)}\right\} = \frac{(ad-bc)^2(a+b+c+d)}{(a+b)(a+c)(b+d)(c+d)}$$

5. Explain why, in the test for a difference of two proportions, you should take

$$p_1 = \frac{a}{a+c}, \ p_2 = \frac{b}{b+d}, n_1 = a+c, n_2 = b+d \text{ and } \hat{\pi} = \frac{a+b}{a+b+c+d}$$

and show that, by substituting these expressions into the formula:

$$\frac{(p_1-p_2)^2}{\hat{\pi}(1-\hat{\pi})\left(\dfrac{1}{n_1}+\dfrac{1}{n_2}\right)}$$

for the square of the test statistic, you obtain the same result as for the χ^2 test.

Exercise 1C

1. When trying to decide between two suppliers of rheostats, a company tests 100 from each supplier and determines how many fail the test. If one rheostat from company A and three rheostats from company B fail the test, is this evidence that the suppliers differ in the proportions of their rheostats which would fail the test?

2. Construct a 98% symmetrical confidence interval for the difference in proportions of male births in China and Britain, given the data:

873 live births in China produced 471 males;

726 live births in Britain produced 372 males.

3. It is claimed that male rats are quicker learners than female rats. In a maze-running experiment, after seven training runs, 23 of the 40 male rats and 8 of the 30 female rats being used had met the criterion for success at the task. Is this good evidence for the claim?

4. The prevalence of the inherited disease sickle-cell anaemia is greater amongst black than white Americans. Random samples of both racial groups were tested for the disease. Of the 78 blacks tested, six had anaemia, while only one of the 130 whites tested had the disease. Construct a one-sided 95% confidence bound for the least

amount by which the proportions of sufferers in the two groups might differ.

5. In a railway efficiency monitoring exercise, it was found that 176 of a random sample of 243 Network South East services were on time, whereas 82 of a sample of 107 Great Western services were on time. Is there evidence at the 5% level that the proportion of trains on time in the two regions differ? Discuss carefully the problems involved in constructing a random sample of trains for these purposes.

6. In an opinion survey, 86 of a sample of 130 Conservative Party members and 21 of a sample of 117 Labour Party members favour selective state schools. Find a 90% two-sided confidence interval for the difference in the proportions of each party in favour of the policy.

7. How many times would you have to toss two coins and count the number of heads occurring before you could expect reliably to detect the difference in their probabilities of showing a head, when this probability was 0.49 on one and 0.51 on the other?

8. It is said that men are three times as likely as women to die of a heart attack. What test statistic would you use to test this hypothesis, and what would its distribution be?

K E Y   P O I N T S

- To test the hypothesis that the population proportion with a particular characteristic is π, use the sample proportion, p, in a sample of size n. The test statistic is then:

$$\frac{p - \pi}{\sqrt{\dfrac{\pi(1 - \pi)}{n}}}$$

which has approximately a standard Normal distribution for large n.

- Given the sample proportion p in a sample of size n, an approximate $a\%$ confidence interval for the population proportion is:

$$p - \tau_a\sqrt{\frac{p(1 - p)}{n}} < \pi < p + \tau_a\sqrt{\frac{p(1 - p)}{n}}$$

where τ_a is the two-sided $(100 - a)\%$ critical value for the standard Normal distribution.

- To test the hypothesis that there is no difference in the proportions of a particular characteristic in two populations, we use the sample proportions p_1 and p_2 with that characteristic in samples of size n_1 and n_2 drawn from the two populations. The test statistic is then:

$$\frac{p_1 - p_2}{\sqrt{\hat{\pi}(1 - \hat{\pi})\left(\dfrac{1}{n_1} + \dfrac{1}{n_2}\right)}}$$

where $\hat{\pi} = \dfrac{n_1 p_1 + n_2 p_2}{n_1 + n_2}$

which has approximately a standard Normal distribution for large n.

- Given the sample proportions p_1 and p_2 with a particular characteristic in samples of size n_1 and n_2, an approximate $a\%$

confidence interval for the difference $\pi_1 - \pi_2$ in proportions with that characteristic in the populations from which the samples are drawn is:

$$(p_1 - p_2) - \tau_a \sqrt{\frac{p_1(1-p_1)}{n_1} + \frac{p_2(1-p_2)}{n_2}} < \pi_1 - \pi_2$$

$$< (p_1 - p_2) + \tau_a \sqrt{\frac{p_1(1-p_1)}{n_1} + \frac{p_2(1-p_2)}{n_2}}$$

where τ_a is the two-sided $(100 - a)\%$ critical value for the standard Normal distribution.

2 Variance tests

Have you noticed that the astronomers and mathematicians are much the most cheerful people of the lot? I suppose that perpetually contemplating things on so vast a scale makes them feel that it doesn't matter a hoot anyway, or that anything so large and elaborate must have some sense in it somewhere.

Dorothy Sayers

There is currently a great deal of debate about possible changes to the climate of the Earth through 'global warming'. The climate of the planet is governed by many factors and, as a result, is extremely complicated. We may receive the first indication that the climate has changed significantly from a change in variability rather than from a change in the mean. In this chapter we will develop ways of testing to see if the variance has changed.

In *Statistics 3* you learnt about hypothesis tests for the mean of a Normally distributed random variable. In order to do this you had to know the sampling distribution of $\bar{X}$, the sample mean.

Because $\mathrm{E}[\bar{X}] = \mu$ and $\mathrm{Var}\,[\bar{X}] = \sigma^2/n$ when sampling from $\mathrm{N}(\mu, \sigma^2)$, then you get $z = \dfrac{\bar{X} - \mu}{\sigma/\sqrt{n}} \sim \mathrm{N}(0, 1)$ if the population variance is known,

or, if the population variance is unknown:

$$t_{n-1} = \frac{\bar{X} - \mu}{\hat{\sigma}/\sqrt{n}}$$

This information enables you to carry out hypothesis tests for the population mean.

In this section you will learn similar tests for the population variance and, to do this, you will need to know the sampling distribution of $S^2 = \dfrac{\sum\limits_{i=1}^{n}(X - \bar{X})^2}{n - 1}$ the unbiased estimate of the population variance. Before doing this you need to take a closer look at the χ^2 distribution.

The χ^2 distribution

In *Statistics 3* and *Statistics 4* you met the χ^2 test in which you used the χ^2 statistic. We are now going to take a closer look at how the χ^2 statistic is distributed.

If Z is a random variable with distribution N(0, 1), then the distribution of Z^2 is called the χ^2 distribution with 1 degree of freedom. Similarly, if $Z_1, Z_2, Z_3, \ldots Z_n$ are independent random variables each with distribution N(0, 1), then the distribution of $Y = Z_1^2 + Z_2^2 + Z_3^2 + \cdots + Z_n^2$ is called the χ^2 distribution with n degrees of freedom and is written χ_n^2.

It is not too difficult to derive the probability density function for χ_1^2 by using distribution functions.

$$\text{If } Y = Z^2 \text{ where } Z \sim N(0, 1)$$

$$\text{then } f(z) = \frac{1}{\sqrt{2\pi}} e^{-\frac{1}{2}z^2} \text{ for } -\infty < z < \infty$$

The distribution function of Y is given by $G(y) = P(Y < y)$

$$= P(Z^2 < y)$$
$$= P(-\sqrt{y} < Z < \sqrt{y})$$
$$= F(\sqrt{y}) - F(-\sqrt{y})$$

But the probability density function of Y is given by $g(y) = G'(y)$

$$\text{Therefore } g(y) = \frac{1}{2\sqrt{y}} f(y) + \frac{1}{2\sqrt{y}} f(-y)$$

$$= \frac{1}{2\sqrt{y}} \left(\frac{1}{\sqrt{2\pi}} e^{-\frac{1}{2}y} + \frac{1}{\sqrt{2\pi}} e^{-\frac{1}{2}y} \right)$$

$$\text{and so } g(y) = \frac{1}{\sqrt{2\pi}} y^{-\frac{1}{2}} e^{-\frac{1}{2}y} \text{ for } 0 < y < \infty$$

For χ_n^2 we will simply state the pdf $f(x) = K_n x^{(n/2)-1} e^{-\frac{1}{2}x}$ for $0 < x < \infty$ where K_n is a constant dependent on the degrees of freedom.

In fact $K_n = \dfrac{1}{(n-2)(n-4)\cdots} \left(\dfrac{1}{\sqrt{2\pi}} \right)$ if n is odd;

and $\quad K_n = \dfrac{1}{(n-2)(n-4)\cdots} \left(\dfrac{1}{2} \right)$ if n is even.

The products in the denominator continue as long as the terms are positive and so, for example, if $n = 11$ the terms are 9.7.5.3.1.

Thus for χ_6^2 the pdf is given by $f(x) = \frac{1}{16} x^2 e^{-\frac{1}{2}x}$ which is shown below.

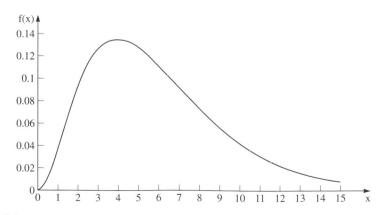

Figure 2.1

Activity

Show that $\int_0^{12.59} \frac{1}{16} x^2 e^{-(x/2)} dx \approx 0.95$ and that $\int_0^{16.81} \frac{1}{16} x^2 e^{-(x/2)} dx \approx 0.99$

In this particular case the pdf of the distribution is not too difficult to integrate and so we could find the critical values of the χ^2 statistic at the 5% and the 1% levels. In general, however, this is not the case and so we use the χ^2 tables in the MEI handbook.

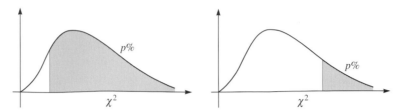

Figure 2.2

$p\%$	99	97.5	95	90	10	5.0	2.5	1.0	0.5
$\nu = 1$	0.0001	0.0010	0.0039	0.0158	2.706	3.841	5.024	6.635	7.879
2	0.0201	0.0506	0.103	0.211	4.605	5.991	7.378	9.210	10.60
3	0.115	0.216	0.352	0.584	6.251	7.815	9.348	11.34	12.85
4	0.297	0.484	0.711	1.064	7.779	9.488	11.14	13.28	14.86
5	0.554	0.831	1.145	1.610	9.236	11.07	12.83	15.09	16.75
6	0.872	1.237	1.635	2.204	10.64	12.59	14.45	16.81	18.55
7	1.239	1.690	2.167	2.833	12.02	14.07	16.01	18.48	20.28
8	1.646	2.180	2.733	3.490	13.36	15.51	17.53	20.09	21.95
9	2.088	2.700	3.325	4.168	14.68	16.92	19.02	21.67	23.59

The distribution of S^2

At the beginning of the chapter we said that in order to do any tests on the population variance you will need to know the distribution of S^2.

Throughout this section $S^2 = \dfrac{\sum(X - \bar{X})^2}{n - 1}$

S^2 is an unbiased estimate of the population variance σ^2 (S^2 is often denoted by $\hat{\sigma}^2$).

It can be shown that $\dfrac{(n-1)S^2}{\sigma^2} \sim \chi^2_{n-1}$

The proof of this is not needed at a first reading and so is included as an appendix at the end of the chapter (see page 29).

Hypothesis test for the population variance

Now that you know the sampling distribution of S^2 you are able to carry out hypothesis tests on the population variance. To see how this is done consider two examples.

The nominal weight of a bag of crisps is 25 grams. A machine is set to fill bags with a quantity of crisps which is distributed $N(26, \frac{1}{9})$. This will ensure that only about one bag per thousand will contain less than the nominal amount. After a number of complaints about underweight bags, a sample of ten bags is taken and weighed. The results, in grams, are: 26.1, 26.2, 25.4, 26.6, 26.0, 25.7, 26.4, 26.7, 26.8, 26.1. Does this sample provide evidence at the 5% level that the variance of the weights is now greater than $\frac{1}{9}$?

Solution:

The hypotheses are:
$$H_0: \ \sigma^2 = \frac{1}{9}$$
$$H_1: \ \sigma^2 > \frac{1}{9}$$

This is a one-tailed test at the 5% level.

We know that $\dfrac{(n-1)S^2}{\sigma^2} \sim \chi^2_{n-1}$ and, in this case, $n = 10$. Under H_0: $\sigma^2 = \frac{1}{9}$

So $S^2 \sim \frac{1}{81} \chi^2_9$

Looking at your tables, in the column headed 5.0 and the row $\nu = 9$ you can see that the critical value of χ^2_9 is 16.92

$p\%$	99	97.5	95	90	10	5.0	2.5	1.0	0.5
$\nu = 1$	0.0001	0.0010	0.0039	0.0158	2.706	3.841	5.024	6.635	7.879
2	0.0201	0.0506	0.103	0.211	4.605	5.991	7.378	9.210	10.60
3	0.115	0.216	0.352	0.584	6.251	7.815	9.348	11.34	12.84
4	0.297	0.484	0.711	1.064	7.779	9.488	11.14	13.28	14.86
5	0.554	0.831	1.145	1.610	9.236	11.07	12.83	15.09	16.75
6	0.872	1.237	1.635	2.204	10.64	12.59	14.45	16.81	18.55
7	1.239	1.690	2.167	2.833	12.02	14.07	16.01	18.48	20.28
8	1.646	2.180	2.733	3.490	13.36	15.51	17.53	20.09	21.95
9	2.088	2.700	3.325	4.168	14.68	16.92	19.02	21.67	23.59

So your critical value for S^2 is $\frac{16.92}{81} = 0.2089$

Hence we reject H_0 if S^2 exceeds this value.

From our sample above, $S^2 = 0.1956$

As $0.1956 < 0.2089$ there is insufficient evidence at the 5% level to reject H_0 and the conclusion is that the machine is behaving as intended and that the variance is still $\frac{1}{9}$.

After an extensive overhaul, the crisp machine in the first example continues to fill bags with a quantity of crisps which is Normally distributed with mean 26 g. However, it is not clear whether or not the variance is still $\frac{1}{9}$. To test this, a sample of 15 bags were weighed and the results were:

26.3, 26.2, 25.6, 25.6, 26.0, 26.1, 26.9, 25.6,
25.1, 25.9, 26.4, 26.9, 26.4, 25.4, 26.9

Does this provide evidence at the 5% level that the variance is no longer $\frac{1}{9}$?

Solution:

In this case the hypotheses are: $H_0: \sigma^2 = \frac{1}{9}$
$H_1: \sigma^2 \neq \frac{1}{9}$

This is a two-tailed test at the 5% level.

We know that $\dfrac{(n-1)S^2}{\sigma^2} \sim \chi^2_{n-1}$, $n = 15$ and that $H_0: \sigma^2 = \frac{1}{9}$

So $S^2 \sim \frac{1}{126}\chi^2_{14}$

From your tables in the row $\nu = 14$ in the columns headed 2.5 and 97.5 you can see that the critical values of χ^2_{14} are 5.629 and 26.12.

$p\%$	99	97.5	95	90	10	5.0	2.5	1.0	0.5
$\nu = 1$	0.0001	0.0010	0.0039	0.0158	2.706	3.841	5.024	6.635	7.879
2	0.0201	0.0506	0.103	0.211	4.605	5.991	7.378	9.210	10.60
3	0.115	0.216	0.352	0.584	6.251	7.815	9.348	11.34	12.84
4	0.297	0.484	0.711	1.064	7.779	9.488	11.14	13.28	14.86
5	0.554	0.831	1.145	1.610	9.236	11.07	12.83	15.09	16.75
6	0.872	1.237	1.635	2.204	10.64	12.59	14.45	16.81	18.55
7	1.239	1.690	2.167	2.833	12.02	14.07	16.01	18.48	20.28
8	1.646	2.180	2.733	3.490	13.36	15.51	17.53	20.09	21.95
9	2.088	2.700	3.325	4.168	14.68	16.92	19.02	21.67	23.59
10	2.558	3.247	3.940	4.865	15.99	18.31	20.48	23.21	25.19
11	3.053	3.816	4.575	5.578	17.28	19.68	21.92	24.72	26.76
12	3.571	4.404	5.226	6.304	18.55	21.03	23.34	26.22	28.30
13	4.107	5.009	5.892	7.042	19.81	22.36	24.74	27.69	29.82
14	4.660	5.629	6.571	7.790	21.06	23.68	26.12	29.14	31.32

Hence the critical values of S^2 are $\frac{5.629}{126}$ and $\frac{26.12}{126}$ i.e. 0.045 and 0.207.

So reject H_0 if the value of S^2 is outside the interval (0.045, 0.207).

For this sample $S^2 = 0.31$.

0.317 is outside the interval (0.045, 0.207) and so reject H_0 and conclude that the variance is no longer $\frac{1}{9}$.

Exercise 2A

1. A random sample of size 16 from a Normal population gave $S^2 = 28.6$

Test the hypothesis at the 5% level that the population variance is 14.8

2. A random sample of size 10 from a Normal population gave $S^2 = 1.08$

Test the hypothesis at the 10% level that the population variance is 2.

3. Nine observations of a random variable X were:

10.4   11.2   10.7   10.3   9.9   10.6
11.0   11.1   10.5

Assuming that X is Normally distributed, test, at the 5% level, the hypothesis that the population variance is 0.08.

4. Over a long period of cycling to college, a student had found that the standard deviation of his journey time was 9.3 minutes. After the opening of a new cycle path he recorded the following journey times (in minutes) for a

Exercise 2A continued

random sample of eight journeys:

48.6 39.9 61.2 50.3 44.7 46.6 51.2 38.3

Test at the 5% level of significance whether there has been a change in the variability of the journey time.

5. The management of an airline are concerned about the day-to-day variability in the number of passengers using a certain flight. Over a long period of time, the standard deviation of the number of passengers had been found to be 18.4. In an attempt to reduce this, a simplified fares structure has been introduced, since when the numbers of passengers on this flight on ten randomly chosen days were:

87 64 52 73 81 65 73 80 49 70

(i) Does this constitute evidence at the 5% level that the variance has been reduced?

(ii) What assumptions do you make in applying the hypothesis test?

6. A sample of 14 from a certain population gives the results:

9.1   14.3   11.2   8.4   8.5   14.0   9.9
8.9   11.0   10.2   10.8   11.4   13.0   9.9

(i) Test at the 5% level whether the sample could have been drawn from a parent population with variance 2.

(ii) Test at the 5% level whether the sample could have been drawn from a Normal population with a variance greater than 2.

7. Three samples are taken from a Normal population and the population variance estimated. The estimates were:

6.03 from a sample of size 7;
7.11 from a sample of size 6;
6.82 from a sample of size 12.

(i) Pool the sample variances to form an unbiased estimate of the population variance.

(ii) Does this provide evidence at the 5% level to support the hypothesis that the population variance is:

(a) 10;

(b) 4?

Confidence intervals for the population variance

As with the population mean, once you have developed a hypothesis test for the population variance, little extra work is required to derive a confidence interval.

You now know that $\dfrac{(n-1)S^2}{\sigma^2} \sim \chi^2_{n-1}$ and so you can use the fact that:

$$P\left(\chi^2_{n-1}(97.5\%) < \frac{(n-1)S^2}{\sigma^2} < \chi^2_{n-1}(2.5\%)\right) = 0.95$$

to get a 95% confidence interval.

Rearranging gives $P\left(\dfrac{(n-1)S^2}{\chi^2_{n-1}(2.5\%)} < \sigma^2 < \dfrac{(n-1)S^2}{\chi^2_{n-1}(97.5\%)}\right) = 0.95$

So the values $\dfrac{(n-1)S^2}{\chi^2_{n-1}(2.5\%)}$ and $\dfrac{(n-1)S^2}{\chi^2_{n-1}(97.5\%)}$

are the limits of a 95% confidence interval for σ^2.

EXAMPLE

Assuming that the distribution of marks scored in an examination follow a Normal distribution, find a symmetrical 95% confidence interval for the population variance σ^2 if a random sample of 12 marks gave:

51, 60, 50, 65, 64, 50, 60, 66, 71, 62, 62, 68

Solution:

With $\nu = 11$ the values of $\chi_{11}^2(2.5\%)$ and $\chi_{11}^2(97.5\%)$ are 21.92 and 3.82

For this sample $S^2 = 49.48$

So the limits of the confidence interval are $\dfrac{(11)(49.48)}{21.92}$ and $\dfrac{(11)(49.48)}{3.82}$

And so the 95% confidence interval for σ^2 is (24.83, 142.47)

Interpretation

It is important to realise that this does *not* mean that the probability of σ^2 lying in this interval is 0.95. The population variance, σ^2, has a fixed value which either lies in this interval or not and so the probability that σ^2 is in the interval is either 0 or 1. The correct interpretation is that each sample of size 12 will lead to a different confidence interval and that σ^2 will lie in 95% of these intervals.

In the example above it was specified that a symmetrical confidence interval was required. This means that the probability in each tail has to be equal and so we looked at $\chi^2(2.5\%)$ and $\chi^2(97.5\%)$. As you saw in *Statistics 4*, it is also possible to have confidence intervals which are not symmetrical. Possible non-symmetrical 95% confidence intervals could use, for example, $\chi^2(1\%)$ and $\chi^2(96\%)$. For a one-sided 95% confidence interval you would use either $\chi^2(5\%)$ or $\chi^2(95\%)$, whichever is appropriate.

Confidence intervals for σ^2 when more than one sample is available

If two samples of size n_1 and n_2 are available from a Normal population where

$$S_1^2 = \frac{\displaystyle\sum_{i=1}^{n_1}(X_{1i} - \bar{X}_1)^2}{n_1 - 1} \quad \text{and} \quad S_2^2 = \frac{\displaystyle\sum_{i=1}^{n_2}(X_{2i} - \bar{X}_2)^2}{n_2 - 1}$$

then:

$$\frac{(n_1 - 1)S_1^2}{\sigma^2} \sim \chi_{n_1-1}^2 \quad \text{and} \quad \frac{(n_2 - 1)S_2^2}{\sigma^2} \sim \chi_{n_2-1}^2$$

Now, as $\chi_{n_1-1}^2$ is the sum of the squares of $n_1 - 1$ independent standard Normal variables and, similarly, $\chi_{n_2-1}^2$ is the sum of the squares of $n_2 - 1$ independent standard Normal variables then $\chi_{n_1-1}^2 + \chi_{n_2-1}^2$ is the sum of the squares of $n_1 + n_2 - 2$ independent standard Normal variables.

Therefore we have $\dfrac{(n_1 - 1)S_1^2 + (n_2 - 1)S_2^2}{\sigma^2} \sim \chi_{n_1+n_2-2}^2$

This can clearly be extended to any number of samples.

EXAMPLE

Assuming that the weights of newborn babies in a certain county is a Normally distributed random variable, calculate a one-sided 95% confidence interval giving an upper bound for the population variance using the two random samples below which were taken on different days (all measurements are in kg).

Day 1 : 4.8, 3.2, 3.1, 3.8, 3.7, 3.5, 3.7

Day 2 : 3.9, 4.4, 3.8, 3.6, 4.8, 3.3, 4.1, 4.6, 4.0

Solution:

From the data $n_1 = 7$ and $S_1^2 = 0.311$

$n_2 = 9$ and $S_2^2 = 0.230$

So $\dfrac{6S_1^2 + 8S_2^2}{\sigma^2} \sim \chi_{14}^2$ and so $\dfrac{3.71}{\sigma^2} \sim \chi_{14}^2$

From your tables you can see that $\chi_{14}^2(95\%) = 6.571$

So $P\left(\dfrac{3.71}{\sigma^2} > 6.571\right) = 0.95$ and so $P(0.565 > \sigma^2) = 0.95$

This gives the one-sided confidence interval (0, 0.565)

Exercise 2B

1. A random sample of size 30 from a Normal population has a variance of 11.5. Construct:

   (i) a 95% confidence interval;

   (ii) a 98% confidence interval;

   for the population variance.

2. Ten bags of fertiliser supplied to a garden centre were found to have the following masses:

   2.57 2.05 1.65 2.62 2.44 1.48 2.31
   1.58 2.60 1.85

   Find a 95% confidence interval for the population variance, assuming that the population distribution is Normal.

3. Nine observations of a random variable X were:

   10.4 11.2 10.7 10.3 9.9 10.6
   11.0 11.1 10.5

   (i) Assuming that X is Normally distributed, find a 90% confidence interval for the population variance.

   (ii) Deduce a 90% confidence interval for the population standard deviation.

4. Over a long period of driving to work, a man had found that the standard deviation of his journey time was 9.3 minutes. After the opening of a new stretch of motorway, he recorded the following

   journey times (in minutes) for a random sample of ten journeys:

   37.4 48.6 39.9 61.2 50.3 44.7 46.6
   51.2 38.3 45.9

   Construct a 90% confidence interval for the population variance.

5. The management of an airline are concerned about the day-to-day variability in the number of passengers using a certain flight. Over a long period of time, the standard deviation of the number of passengers had been found to be 18.4. In an attempt to reduce this, a simplified fares structure has been introduced, since when the number of passengers on this flight on ten randomly chosen days was:

   67 64 52 73 81 65 73 80 69 70

   (i) Construct a 95% confidence interval for the population standard deviation.

   (ii) What conclusion would you come to in the light of your answer to (i)?

6. Over a long period of driving to work, a commuter had found that the standard deviation of her journey time was 6.8 minutes. After the opening of a new stretch of motorway, the journey times (in minutes) for a random sample of ten journeys were found to be:

34.2   41.6   56.0   32.1   52.8   44.5   45.1
68.7   48.3   45.4

(i)   Test at the 5% level of significance whether there has been a change in the variability of the journey time, stating carefully your null and alternative hypotheses.

(ii)   Provide a two-sided 90% confidence interval for the new variance.

(iii)   What underlying distributional assumption is required for your analysis to be satisfactory?

[O&C MEI Statistics 5, June 1992]

Hypothesis test for the difference in population variances

In this section we are going to develop a method to determine whether or not two samples could have come from populations with equal variances. Possibly one of the most common abuses in statistical analysis is the indiscriminate use of the unpaired *t*-test to compare two population means. For this test to be valid it is necessary for the variances of the two populations to be equal. This means that you need to test the two samples to see if it is reasonable to assume that they come from populations with the same variance.

The *F*-distribution

A test for the difference between two variances is based on a distribution called the *F*-distribution which is defined in the following way:

$$F_{\nu_1, \nu_2} = \frac{\chi^2_{\nu_1}/\nu_1}{\chi^2_{\nu_2}/\nu_2}$$

where ν_1 and ν_2 are the degrees of freedom of two independent χ^2 distributions.

The pdf for F_{ν_1, ν_2} is given by:

$$f(x) = \frac{Kx^{(\nu_1/2)-1}}{(\nu_1 x + \nu_2)^{\frac{1}{2}(\nu_1 + \nu_2)}} \qquad 0 < x < \infty$$

where K is a constant such that $\int_0^\infty f(x)\,dx = 1$

If you look at the relatively simple case with $\nu_1 = 4$ and $\nu_2 = 2$ then you get:

$$f(x) = \frac{kx}{(4x+2)^3}$$

Using the fact that $\int_0^\infty \frac{kx}{(4x+2)^3}\,dx = 1$ you can find that $k = 64$.

The graph of $y = \frac{64x}{(4x+2)^3}$ is shown below.

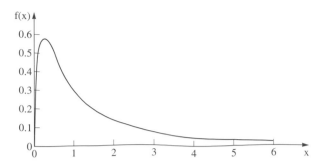

Figure 2.3

In this particular case it is now possible to find values of x such that

$$\int_x^\infty f(x)\, dx = \frac{p}{100}$$

However, for larger values of ν_1 and ν_2 this becomes increasingly difficult and we have to rely on printed tables.

Below is a portion of the 5% points of the F-distribution. This table gives the x value which is the boundary of a 5% right-hand tail. For the example earlier, with $\nu_1 = 4$ and $\nu_2 = 2$, you can see that this value is 19.2.

This means that $\displaystyle\int_{19.2}^\infty \frac{64x}{(4x+2)^3}\, dx = 0.05$

You can check this result yourself.

Also provided in your handbook are tables for 2.5%, 1% and 0.1%.

5% points of the F-distribution

ν_2 \ ν_1	1	2	3	4	5	6	7	8	10	12	24	∞
1	161.4	199.5	215.7	224.6	230.2	234.0	236.8	238.9	241.9	243.9	249.0	254.3
2	18.5	19.0	19.2	19.2	19.3	19.3	19.4	19.4	19.4	19.4	19.5	19.5
3	10.13	9.55	9.28	9.12	9.01	8.94	8.89	8.85	8.79	8.74	8.64	8.53
4	7.71	6.94	6.59	6.39	6.26	6.16	6.09	6.04	5.96	5.91	5.77	5.63
5	6.61	5.79	5.41	5.19	5.05	4.95	4.88	4.82	4.74	4.68	4.53	4.36
6	5.99	5.14	4.76	4.53	4.39	4.28	4.21	4.15	4.06	4.00	3.84	3.67
7	5.59	4.74	4.35	4.12	3.97	3.87	3.79	3.73	3.64	3.57	3.41	3.23
8	5.32	4.46	4.07	3.84	3.69	3.58	3.50	3.44	3.35	3.28	3.12	2.93
9	5.12	4.26	3.86	3.63	3.48	3.37	3.29	3.23	3.14	3.07	2.90	2.71

Using the *F*-distribution to test the equality of two variances

To test the equality of the variances, σ_1^2 and σ_2^2, of two Normal distributions, you need to take an independent random sample from each distribution, of size n_1 and n_2, and to calculate unbiased estimates, S_1^2 and S_2^2, of σ_1^2 and σ_2^2.

The hypotheses will be H_0: $\sigma_1^2 = \sigma_2^2 = \sigma^2$
                        H_1: $\sigma_1^2 \neq \sigma_2^2$

So under H_0 $\quad \dfrac{(n_1 - 1)S_1^2}{\sigma^2} \sim \chi^2_{n_1-1}$ and $\dfrac{(n_2 - 1)S_2^2}{\sigma^2} \sim \chi^2_{n_2-1}$

So from the definition of the F-distribution $F_{\nu_1, \nu_2} = \dfrac{\chi^2_{\nu_1}/\nu_1}{\chi^2_{\nu_2}/\nu_2}$

you can deduce that

$$F_{n_1-1, n_2-1} = \dfrac{(n_1 - 1)S_1^2}{\sigma^2(n_1 - 1)} \bigg/ \dfrac{(n_2 - 1)S_2^2}{\sigma^2(n_2 - 1)}$$

Which cancels nicely to give $F_{n_1-1, n_2-1} = \dfrac{S_1^2}{S_2^2}$

This ratio can now be compared with the critical values from the F-tables. In order to reduce the amount of tabulation required this ratio is always calculated with the largest of the two values in the numerator and so you will always get a value of $F > 1$. This means that only the right-hand tail of F is of interest. A value of F which is close to 1 would suggest that the two population variances are equal. The further F differs from 1, the more likely it is that the variances are not equal. The critical values of F are given in the tables.

You are now in a position to carry out a test for the equality of two variances.

EXAMPLE

Angela and Bryony are members of Ascot Golf Club. They are both applicants for the post of Club Captain. One of the criteria involved in making the selection between the applicants is golfing ability. In order to examine whether there is any difference between Angela and Bryony in terms of golfing ability, a random sample of eight scores achieved by Angela and a random sample of 12 scores achieved by Bryony were taken. The scores are recorded below.

Angela: 75 77 71 73 73 79 81 74
Bryony: 74 74 79 80 72 72 75 76 74 79 74 77

(i)   State formally the null and alternative hypotheses that are to be tested.

(ii) State an appropriate assumption concerning underlying Normality.

(iii) State a further necessary assumption concerning the underlying distributions.

(iv) Carry out the test, using a 5% level of significance.

Solution:

(i)   First define μ_A and μ_B to be the population means of the scores obtained by Angela and Bryony respectively.

The hypotheses are: H_0: $\mu_A = \mu_B$
$\qquad\qquad\qquad\qquad\quad$ H_1: $\mu_A \neq \mu_B$

(ii) The underlying distributions of the scores obtained by Angela and Bryony must both be Normal.

(iii) The variances of the two distributions, σ_A^2 and σ_B^2 must be equal. You can now test this.

From the two samples you should find: $n_A = 8$ and $n_B = 12$
$\qquad\qquad\qquad\qquad\qquad\qquad\qquad\qquad$ also $S_A^2 = 11.41$ and $S_B^2 = 7.36$

The hypotheses are: H_0: $\sigma_A^2 = \sigma_B^2 = \sigma^2$

H_1: $\sigma_A^2 \neq \sigma_B^2$

This is a two-tailed test at the 5% level, so use the 2.5% points of the F-distribution.

As $11.41 > 7.36$ the relevant F-distribution is $F_{7,11}$

From your tables you can see that the critical value of F is 3.76 and so you should reject H_0 if $\dfrac{S_A^2}{S_B^2}$ is greater than this value.

In fact $\dfrac{S_A^2}{S_B^2} = \frac{11.41}{7.36} = 1.55$ and so H_0 cannot be rejected and you can assume that the population variances are equal.

(iv) Now you can carry out the two-sample t-test with a clear conscience.

The hypotheses are: H_0: $\mu_A = \mu_B$

H_1: $\mu_A \neq \mu_B$

This is a two-tailed test at the 5% level and the appropriate t-distribution is t_{18}
As t_{18} is not tabulated you will need to interpolate between t_{15} and t_{20}
The value you should get is $t_{18} = 2.104$ and so reject H_0 if $|t_{calc}| > 2.104$

From the two samples $\overline{x_A} = 75.375$ and $\overline{x_B} = 75.5$

The pooled, unbiased estimate of the common variance is given by

$$\hat{\sigma}^2 = \frac{7(11.41) + 11(7.36)}{18} = 8.94$$

and so $t_{calc} = \dfrac{75.375 - 75.5}{\sqrt{8.94(\frac{1}{8} + \frac{1}{12})}} = -0.092$

$0.094 < 2.104$ and so we cannot reject H_0. Hence we conclude that the mean scores obtained by Angela and Bryony are not significantly different.

EXAMPLE

The captain of the first team at Fisher Cricket Club wishes to promote one of two promising batsmen, Alan and Brian, from the second team. He wants to make his decision in a statistically meaningful way. To do this he takes a random sample from each player's previous scores for the second team. The samples were:

Alan: 23, 27, 48, 13, 34, 64, 19, 22, 64, 43, 12, 20
Brian: 0, 7, 98, 66, 11, 17, 113, 1, 2, 9

Their mean scores are very similar, but it seems that Alan is more consistent.

Test at the 5% level to see if the population variance of Alan's scores is less than that of Brian.

Solution:

The hypotheses are: H_0: $\sigma_A^2 = \sigma_B^2 = \sigma^2$

H_1: $\sigma_A^2 < \sigma_B^2$

This is a one-tailed test at the 5% level, so use the 5% points of the F-distribution.

For these samples $n_A = 12$, $S_A^2 = 336.99$ and $n_B = 10$, $S_B^2 = 1864.04$

As $1864.04 > 336.99$ the appropriate F-distribution is $F_{9,11}$

$F_{9,11}$ is not tabulated so interpolate between $F_{8,11}$ and $F_{10,11}$

From the tables you can see that the values are 2.95 and 2.85 respectively, therefore take $F_{9,11}$ to have a critical value of 2.90 and reject H_0 if the calculated value of $\dfrac{S_B^2}{S_A^2}$ is greater than this value.

But $\dfrac{S_B^2}{S_A^2} = \dfrac{1864.04}{336.99} = 5.53$ and so you should reject H_0 and conclude that Alan is more consistent than Brian.

Exercise 2C

1. At the 5% level, test if it is reasonable to suppose that a random sample of size 25, which gives an unbiased population variance estimate of 5.17, could be from the Normal population as a random sample of size 20 which gives an unbiased population variance estimate of 3.92.

2. A sample of size 10 gave an unbiased population variance estimate of 3.44. Another sample of size 8 gave an unbiased population variance estimate of 6.62. Test at the 2% level to see if it is reasonable to assume that both samples are from the same Normal population.

3. Two independent samples of size 25 are taken from a Normal population. The first gave an unbiased population variance estimate of 28.36. Calculate how large the unbiased population variance estimate of the second sample would have to be before the two samples will be accepted as from different populations at the 5% level, although they are from the same population. (You may recognise this as the probability of making a type I error.)

4. Two apprentices were tested by being asked to make 60 identical components on the same machine. Each batch of 60 was measured and the mean and standard deviation *of the sample* calculated.

	Mean in mm	Standard deviation in mm
Apprentice A	14.71	0.017
Apprentice B	14.74	0.037

Does this provide evidence at the 5% level that Apprentice B is less consistent?

5. In an experiment on the reaction time in seconds of two individuals, A and B, measured under identical conditions, the following results were obtained:

Person A: 0.41 0.38 0.37 0.42 0.35
0.38
Person B: 0.32 0.36 0.38 0.33 0.38

(i) Show that there is no significant difference between the samples in terms of variance.

(ii) What assumptions have you made?

6. The masses (in grams) of two samples of eggs, one sample from species A and one sample from a related species, B, are given below:

Species A: 12.3 13.7 10.4 11.4 14.9
12.6
Species B: 15.7 10.3 12.6 14.5 12.6
13.8 11.9

(i) Test whether there is a significant difference between the two samples in terms of variability and then, if appropriate, test if there is any difference in the mean masses of the two populations.

(ii) What assumptions have you made?

7. In order to test the effectiveness of a new rust-proofing treatment for steel, the times until rust started to appear were recorded for two samples, one being given the standard treatment and the other the new treatment. The table below gives the times (in units of 100 days):

Exercise 2C continued

New: 22.0 23.9 20.9 23.8 25.0
24.0 21.7 22.8 23.1 23.5
23.0

Standard: 23.2 22.0 22.2 21.2 21.6
21.9 22.9 22.8

(i) Test at the 5% level the hypothesis that the population variances for the new and the standard treatments are the same.

(ii) Test at the 5% level whether the mean time for the new treatment is significantly greater than the mean time for the standard treatment.

(iii) Clearly state the assumptions you needed to make in order to carry out the tests in (i) and (ii).

8. (i) The data below are the number of hours of labour per hectare required for planting winter wheat on a random sample of 15 farms:

2.2 2.5 1.9 2.3 2.6 2.7 1.8 2.0
2.5 2.6 3.4 2.9 3.1 2.7 2.3

Obtain a 95% confidence interval for the variance of the population underlying this data. What assumptions about the statistical nature of this population are necessary for your analysis to be valid?

(ii) It is thought that the variability in the number of hours of labour per hectare for planting *spring* wheat may be greater than that for winter wheat. A random sample of nine farms gave the following number of hours of labour per hectare for planting spring wheat:

2.7 2.8 3.1 3.8 2.1 2.3 2.9
3.7 2.2

(a) At the 5% level of significance, test whether there is greater variability in the number of hours of labour per hectare for planting spring wheat than for planting winter wheat.

(b) State carefully the null and alternative hypotheses you are testing.

(c) What further assumptions are necessary for your analysis to be valid?

[O&C MEI, Statistics 5, June 1993]

9. In a chemical plant, a certain product is made by two processes. The product always contains a small amount of impurity and it is necessary to know whether the processes are equally variable in terms of the percentage of impurity in the product. The percentages of impurity in a random sample of ten batches of the product made by one process were:

4.4 3.6 4.8 2.8 4.4 4.1 3.9 4.2
4.5 5.1

and the percentages of impurity in a random sample of eight batches of the product made by the other process were:

3.5 4.7 4.1 5.6 4.8 3.4 5.4 4.7

(i) At the 5% level of significance, test whether it is reasonable to assume that the underlying population variances are equal. State your null and alternative hypotheses and the critical value of your test statistic at the 5% level of significance.

(ii) State the assumptions about the underlying distributions that are required for your analysis to be satisfactory.

(iii) In the light of your test, would you be prepared to use a t-test to examine whether the underlying population means are equal? Explain your answer.

[O&C MEI, Statistics 5, June 1995]

10. An orchestra performs a weekly series of concerts. Some of these concerts consist wholly or mainly of works that are established as part of the normal concert repertoire; these are referred to as 'traditional' concerts. The other concerts consist mainly of unfamiliar works; these are referred to as 'innovative' concerts. The orchestra managers accept that, on the whole, the audiences for the 'innovative' concerts may be smaller than those for the 'traditional' ones, but are concerned about the variability in the audience sizes for the two types of concert.

The next 18 concerts consist of eight 'innovative' and ten 'traditional' concerts. Regard these as random samples. For the eight 'innovative' concerts, the usual unbiased estimate of the population variance of audience size is found to be 818. For the ten 'traditional' concerts, the corresponding estimate is found to be 384.

(i) At the 5% level, test whether the population variances of audience size for the two types of concert may be assumed to be equal.

(ii) Produce a two-sided 80% confidence interval for the population variance of audience size for the 'traditional' concerts.

(iii) Denoting the lower and upper limits of this confidence interval by l and u respectively, a manager states that the probability that the population variance is between l and u is 80%. Explain why this interpretation is incorrect. Give the correct interpretation.

Appendix

In the chapter it was stated that the distribution of S^2, the unbiased estimator of the population variance, is given by $\dfrac{(n-1)S^2}{\sigma^2} \sim \chi^2_{n-1}$. We will now prove this.

Proof:

$$S^2 = \frac{\sum(X - \bar{X})^2}{(n-1)} \rightarrow (n-1)S^2 = \sum(X - \bar{X})^2$$

Dividing by σ^2 leads to $\dfrac{(n-1)S^2}{\sigma^2} = \dfrac{\sum(X - \bar{X})^2}{\sigma^2}$

Now we have need of a very important result:

$$\sum_{i=1}^{n}(X - \bar{X})^2 = \sum_{i=1}^{n}(X - \mu)^2 - n(\bar{X} - \mu)^2$$

Proof:

Left-hand side $= \sum(X - \mu + \mu - \bar{X})^2$

$\qquad\qquad = \sum[(X - \mu) - (\bar{X} - \mu)]^2$

$\qquad\qquad = \sum(X - \mu)^2 - 2\sum(X - \mu)(\bar{X} - \mu) + \sum(\bar{X} - \mu)^2$

But $\bar{X}$ and μ are both constant and so:

$$\sum(X - \mu)^2 - 2(\bar{X} - \mu)\sum(X - \mu) + n(\bar{X} - \mu)^2$$
$$= \sum(X - \mu)^2 - 2(\bar{X} - \mu)(\sum X - n\mu) + n(\bar{X} - \mu)^2$$

But $\sum X = n\bar{X}$ and so:

left-hand side $= \sum(X - \mu)^2 - 2n(\bar{X} - \mu)^2 + n(\bar{X} - \mu)^2$

$\qquad\qquad = \sum(X - \mu)^2 - n(\bar{X} - \mu)^2$ which equals the right-hand side.

So we have proved the identity $\sum(X - \bar{X})^2 \equiv \sum(X - \mu)^2 - n(\bar{X} - \mu)^2$

So, returning to our argument above:

$$\frac{(n-1)S^2}{\sigma^2} = \frac{\sum(X - \mu)^2}{\sigma^2} - \frac{n(\bar{X} - \mu)^2}{\sigma^2}$$

$$= \sum\left(\frac{X - \mu}{\sigma}\right)^2 - \left(\frac{\bar{X} - \mu}{\sigma/\sqrt{n}}\right)^2$$

But $Z_i = \dfrac{X_i - \mu}{\sigma}$ is distributed $N(0, 1)$ and so $\left(\dfrac{X_i - \mu}{\sigma}\right)^2 = Z_i^2$ is distributed χ_1^2

Therefore $\sum\left(\dfrac{X_i - \mu}{\sigma}\right)^2$ is the sum of n independent Z_i^2 variables.

Therefore $\sum\left(\dfrac{X_i - \mu}{\sigma}\right)^2$ is distributed χ_n^2

Notice that $\sum\left(\dfrac{X - \mu}{\sigma/\sqrt{n}}\right)$ is also distributed $N(0, 1)$ and so $\left(\dfrac{\bar{X} - \mu}{\sigma/\sqrt{n}}\right)^2$ is distributed χ_1^2

And so $\sum\left(\dfrac{X - \mu}{\sigma}\right)^2 - \left(\dfrac{\bar{X} - \mu}{\sigma/\sqrt{n}}\right)^2$ is distributed χ_{n-1}^2

Therefore $\dfrac{(n-1)S^2}{\sigma^2} \sim \chi_{n-1}^2$

KEY POINTS

- The distribution of S^2, the unbiased estimate of the variance of a Normal population is given by $\dfrac{(n-1)S^2}{\sigma^2} \sim \chi_{n-1}^2$

- The limits of a 95% confidence interval for σ^2, based on a sample of size n, are

$$\frac{(n-1)S^2}{\chi_{n-1}^2(2.5\%)} \quad \text{and} \quad \frac{(n-1)S^2}{\chi_{n-1}^2(97.5\%)}$$

- To test the equality of the variances of two Normal populations.

    (i)   Collect a random sample from each population of sizes n_1 and n_2

    (ii) Calculate S_1^2 and S_2^2, unbiased estimates of the variance of each population.

    (iii) Calculate $\dfrac{S_1^2}{S_2^2}$ (assuming $S_1^2 > S_2^2$)

    (iv) Compare your value of $\dfrac{S_1^2}{S_2^2}$ with the critical value of F_{n_1-1, n_2-1}

3 Errors in hypothesis testing

Errors using inadequate data are much less than those using no data at all.

Charles Babbage

When the Chartbuster video hire chain decides to stock a title, it orders about four hundred copies of the video to send out to its many shops from a distributor who mass-produces copies under licence from the movie company. Before accepting the delivery and paying the distributor, the Chartbuster quality control department views a small number of the videos to make sure that the copying has been carried out to an acceptable standard. How should this testing be carried out?

Chartbuster's contract with the distributor states that no more than 3% of the video copies may be blemished on delivery and so the company has decided on the following procedure:

● Select 12 copies of the title at random from the batch.

● View each of the 12 copies, counting those which have a serious blemish.

● Reject the batch if more than one copy in the sample is blemished.

In this chapter we are going to look at how effective different statistical testing procedures are, and how this effectiveness depends on the sample size used and the criterion adopted for making the decision involved.

Types of errors in hypothesis testing

Ideally, Chartbuster would like this procedure to produce the results:

● If 3% (or fewer) of the copies are seriously blemished, the batch will be accepted.

● If more than 3% of the copies are seriously blemished, the batch will be rejected but, as their procedure involves testing only a small sample of the batch, they cannot hope to discriminate so precisely.

(I) One possible error is that Chartbuster will reject a perfectly acceptable batch. The probability of this happening can be calculated using the binomial distribution, as the sample is small compared to the entire batch and we assume that we are choosing 12 copies at random.

In the worst case where the batch is still acceptable, 3% of the copies will be seriously blemished and so:

P(batch is erroneously rejected)

$$= \text{P(more than one copy in the sample is blemished)}$$
$$= 1 - \text{P(zero or one copy is blemished)}$$
$$= 1 - \left((1 - 0.03)^{12} + \binom{12}{1} 0.03 \cdot (1 - 0.03)^{11} \right)$$
$$= 0.048\,65 \approx 5\%$$

Of course, if fewer than 3% of the copies are seriously blemished – that is, the batch is better than just acceptable – the probability that the batch is erroneously rejected will be less than this.

(II) Another possible error is that Chartbuster will accept a poorly copied batch: if as many as 10% of the copies were blemished, for instance, we would have:

P(batch is erroneously accepted)

$$= \text{P(at most one copy in the sample is blemished)}$$
$$= (1 - 0.1)^{12} + \binom{12}{1} 0.1 \cdot (1 - 0.1)^{11}$$
$$= 0.659 \approx 66\%$$

This seems rather high so we could reverse this question and ask what proportion, p, of the copies would have to be blemished before there was at most, say, a 5% chance of erroneously accepting them:

P(batch is erroneously accepted) $= 5\%$

i.e. P(at most one copy in the sample is blemished) $= 5\%$

i.e. $(1 - p)^{12} + \binom{12}{1} p(1 - p)^{11} = 0.05$

i.e. $(1 - p)^{11}(1 + 11p) = 0.05$

This equation needs to be solved numerically (for instance, by the Newton–Raphson method) to give:

$$p = 0.3387 \approx 34\% \text{ of copies blemished.}$$

This means that, following Chartbuster's procedure, 34% or more of the copies in a batch would have to be seriously blemished to bring the chance of erroneously accepting it below 5%.

We can rephrase Chartbuster's quality control procedure as a hypothesis test. They are setting up the hypotheses:

H_0: 3% of the copies are blemished;

H_1: more than 3% of the copies are blemished;

and conducting a one-tailed binomial test with critical region $\{r > 1\}$.

Note that, as usual with a one-tailed hypothesis test, the parameter value for the null hypothesis is quoted as 'proportion blemished = 3%', not as the full null range 'proportion blemished $\leqslant 3\%$'. We do this following the general principle that the null hypothesis is accepted unless there is good evidence that it is false: that is, that none of the values in the full null range is acceptable. Because the most extreme of the null range of parameter values, 'proportion blemished = 3%', will be accepted if any proportion blemished in the null range is, we need quote only this single value. An alternative convention, which we shall not use, is to quote the hypotheses:

H_0: 3% or fewer of the copies are blemished;

H_1: more than 3% of the copies are blemished;

but, none the less, to calculate the distribution of the test statistic under the null hypothesis using 'proportion blemished = 3%'.

The error calculation carried out in (I) above determined the probability of a *type I error*, that is, *rejecting the null hypothesis when it is true*. This probability is given the symbol α and is identical to what you have, so far, called the *significance level* of the test.

We were able to calculate α because we took the null hypothesis to be a *simple hypothesis*. That is, knowing that H_0 is true gives, as explained above, an exact value (of 3%) for the population parameter, p, rather than a range and hence the sampling distribution of the test statistic under H_0 can be calculated.

The error calculation carried out in (II) above determined the probability of a *type II error*, that is, *accepting the null hypothesis when the alternative hypothesis is true*.

Because H_1 is a *composite hypothesis* which states that the population parameter lies in a range of values (here, $0.03 < p \leqslant 1$) we cannot calculate the probability of accepting the null hypothesis merely by knowing that one of the range of alternatives is true. We were able to make this calculation only by picking a specific, simple alternative hypothesis (here $p = 0.1$), and different values of p would have given different probabilities.

Operating characteristic

We have seen that the probability of a type II error is not a single value, but a function of the population parameter, p. The function which gives the probability, for each p, of accepting the null hypothesis is called the *operating characteristic of the test*. If p lies within the region specified by the alternative hypothesis, the probability of a type II error is given by the operating characteristic.

For Chartbuster's test, the operating characteristic (OC) is the probability that a batch is accepted when the true value of the proportion of blemished copies is p.

$$OC(p) = P(\text{at most one copy in the sample is blemished})$$

$$= (1-p)^{12} + \binom{12}{1} p(1-p)^{11} = (1-p)^{11}((1-p) + 12p)$$

$$= (1 + 11p)(1-p)^{11}$$

This function is tabulated below and graphed in figure 3.1

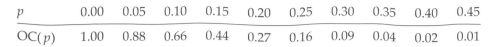

p	0.00	0.05	0.10	0.15	0.20	0.25	0.30	0.35	0.40	0.45
OC(p)	1.00	0.88	0.66	0.44	0.27	0.16	0.09	0.04	0.02	0.01

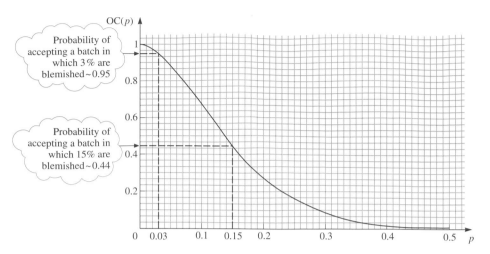

Figure 3.1

The graph shows that if p is above, but close to, the value 0.03 given by the null hypothesis then there is a very high probability that the null hypothesis will be erroneously accepted, that is, that a type II error will be made. This is neither surprising nor particularly worrying for Chartbuster. What might well be a problem for them, however, is that even with 15% of the videos blemished, the quality control will fail to pick this up 44% of the time.

For Discussion

How can the company improve their test?

The effect of changing the significance level of the test

Suppose we change the quality control department's rule so that they accept a batch only if it has no blemished videos in the sample of 12 tested. The value of α, the probability of a type I error, is now:

P(reject null hypothesis if it is true)

$\quad$ = P(reject batch when 3% are blemished)

$\quad$ = P(at least one copy in the sample is blemished)

$\quad$ = 1 − P(zero copies are blemished)

$\quad$ = $1 - (1 - 0.03)^{12}$

$\quad$ = $0.3062 \approx 31\%$

The operating characteristic, which gives the probability of a type II error, is again a function of the proportion, p, of the batch which is blemished.

$$OC(p) = P(\text{accept batch when proportion } p \text{ is blemished})$$
$$= P(\text{no copies in the sample are blemished})$$
$$= (1 - p)^{12}$$

This function is tabulated below and graphed in figure 3.2. The operating characteristic for the original test is shown by a dashed line for comparison.

p	0.00	0.05	0.10	0.15	0.20	0.25	0.30	0.35	0.40	0.45
$OC(p)$	1.00	0.54	0.28	0.14	0.07	0.03	0.01	0.01	0.00	0.00

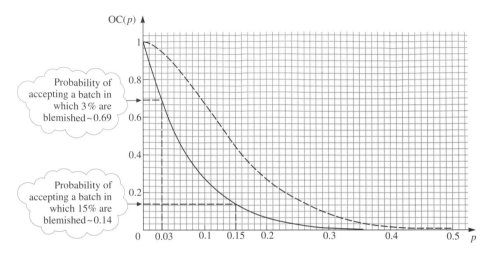

Figure 3.2

This graph shows the test's much reduced probability of accepting batches with high proportions of blemished copies – but this improvement has been bought at a price: the test is rejecting 31% of the perfectly acceptable batches with only 3% blemished copies.

The effect of changing the sample size

Suppose instead that the quality control department takes larger samples, of 27 videos, and rejects the batch if the sample contains three or more blemished copies. The value of α, the probability of a type I error, is now:

$$P(\text{reject null hypothesis if it is true})$$
$$= P(\text{reject batch when 3\% are blemished})$$
$$= P(\text{at least three copies in the sample are blemished})$$
$$= 1 - \left((1 - 0.03)^{27} + \binom{27}{1}(1 - 0.03)^{26}0.03 \right.$$
$$\left. + \binom{27}{2}(1 - 0.03)^{25}(0.03)^2 \right)$$
$$= 0.0462$$

This significance level for the test, 4.62%, is very similar to its original value of

5%. So it is still true that only about 5% of batches with the acceptable proportion, 3%, of blemished copies are being rejected.

The operating characteristic, which gives the probability of a type II error, is, as a function of the proportion, p, of the batch which is blemished:

$$OC(p) = P(\text{accept batch})$$

$$= P(0 \text{ or } 1 \text{ or } 2 \text{ copies in the sample are blemished})$$

$$= (1-p)^{27} + \binom{27}{1}(1-p)^{26}p + \binom{27}{2}(1-p)^{25}p^2$$

$$= (1-p)^{25}(1 + 25p + 325p^2)$$

This function is tabulated below and graphed in figure 3.3. The operating characteristic of the original test is shown by a dashed line for comparison.

p	0.00	0.05	0.10	0.15	0.20	0.25	0.30	0.35	0.40	0.45
$OC(p)$	1.00	0.85	0.48	0.21	0.07	0.02	0.01	0.00	0.00	0.00

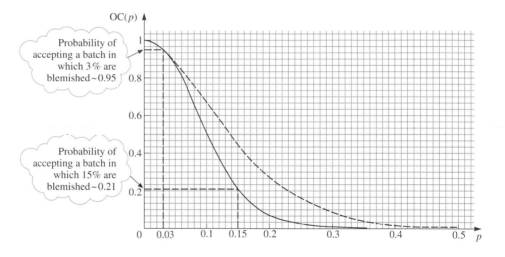

Figure 3.3

The graph shows that this test also greatly reduces the probability of accepting batches with high proportions of blemished copies – but again the improvement only comes at a price: this time, literally, as the cost of paying someone to watch more than twice as many copies in the search for blemishes.

Suppose that two tests, A and B, have the same significance level, but A has a smaller operating characteristic than B for all values of the relevant parameter in the range specified by the alternative hypothesis. In this situation, test A is better than test B in the sense that it is more likely to discriminate accurately between situations where the null hypothesis is and is not true in the population as a whole. However, A may not be a better test to use: it may be more difficult or expensive to carry out.

A related concept used by statisticians is the *power* of a test. This is the function:

$$\text{power} = (1 - \text{operating characteristic})$$

so the power of a test is the probability that the null hypothesis is rejected for a given value of the relevant population parameter. In the situation described in the previous paragraph, test A is *more powerful* than test B.

Normal hypothesis testing

Intelligence tests are designed (by testing on a very large sample) so that scores on the test have a normal distribution with a mean of 100 and a standard deviation of 15 in the population as a whole. Such tests have sometimes been used to try to test whether a particular subset of the population has a higher or lower average intelligence than the population as a whole.

The hypotheses being tested might be:

H_0: the mean intelligence of the subset is 100;

H_1: the mean intelligence of the subset is different from 100;

on the assumption that the intelligences of the subset will have a standard deviation of 15.

Suppose a scientist wishing to test this hypothesis took 50 people and decided to test at the 10% significance level. This means that the probability, α, of a type I error should be 0.1.

We know that if the sample of 50 is chosen randomly from the subset, and H_0 is true then the sample mean has distribution:

$$\bar{X}_{50} \sim N\left(100, \frac{15^2}{50}\right) = N(100, 4.5)$$

so that:

$$\frac{\bar{X}_{50} - 100}{\sqrt{4.5}} \sim N(0, 1)$$

We need to choose a critical value, c, for rejection so that:

$$0.1 = P(\text{reject null hypothesis when it is true})$$

As this is a two-tailed test, we want to determine the two-tailed critical value for a standard normal distribution at the 10% significance level. This is found from normal tables to be:

$$c = \phi^{-1}(0.95) = 1.645$$

The null hypothesis will be rejected if the test statistic is in either tail, that is:

$$\frac{\bar{X}_{50} - 100}{\sqrt{4.5}} > 1.645 \text{ or } \frac{\bar{X}_{50} - 100}{\sqrt{4.5}} < -1.645$$

Rearranging these inequalities gives:

$$\bar{X}_{50} > 100 + 1.645\sqrt{4.5} = 103.49 \text{ or } \bar{X}_{50} < 100 - 1.645\sqrt{4.5} = 96.51$$

Thus, finally, the null hypothesis will be rejected if the sample mean is greater than 103.9 or less than 96.51.

The operating characteristic of this test depends on the true mean intelligence of the subset, μ, and is given by:

$$OC(\mu) = P(\text{accept null hypothesis when true mean} = \mu)$$

That is:

$$OC(\mu) = P(96.51 < \bar{X}_{50} < 103.49)$$

where the distribution of $\bar{X}_{50}$ is $\bar{X}_{50} \sim N(\mu, 4.5)$

So:

$$OC(\mu) = P\left(\frac{96.51 - \mu}{\sqrt{4.5}} < Z < \frac{103.49 - \mu}{\sqrt{4.5}}\right)$$

where z is a standard normal variable

$$= \Phi\left(\frac{103.49 - \mu}{\sqrt{4.5}}\right) - \Phi\left(\frac{96.51 - \mu}{\sqrt{4.5}}\right)$$

For instance:

$$OC(102) = P(\text{accept null hypothesis when true mean intelligence} = 102)$$

$$= \Phi\left(\frac{103.49 - 102}{\sqrt{4.5}}\right) - \Phi\left(\frac{96.51 - 102}{\sqrt{4.5}}\right)$$

$$= \Phi(0.7024) - \Phi(-2.5880)$$

$$= 0.7587 - 0.0048 = 0.7539$$

The values in the following table can be calculated in the same way.

μ	90	92	94	96	98	100	102	104	106	108	110
$OC(\mu)$	0.001	0.017	0.118	0.405	0.754	0.900	0.754	0.405	0.118	0.017	0.001

A graph of the operating characteristic against μ is shown in figure 3.4

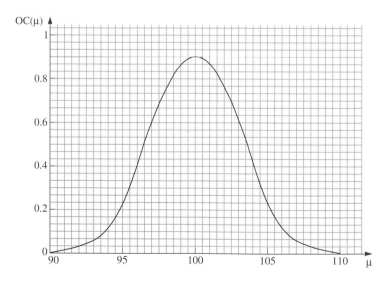

Figure 3.4

It is straightforward (although it involves a considerable amount of work) to repeat the calculation above for the operating characteristic in two other cases (the dashed graph in each case shows the original curve).

The significance level is changed to 1%,
but the sample size remains at 50

μ	90	92	94	96	98	100	102	104	106	108	110
OC(μ)	0.16	0.116	0.400	0.755	0.949	0.990	0.949	0.755	0.400	0.116	0.016

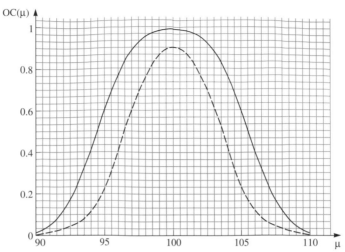

Figure 3.5

The probability of a type I error is now only 0.01, but the operating
characteristic shows that the probability of a type II error is greater at every
possible true value of μ.

The significance level remains at 10%,
but the sample size is raised to 200

μ	90	92	94	96	98	100	102	104	106	108	110
OC(μ)	0.000	0.000	0.000	0.017	0.405	0.900	0.405	0.017	0.000	0.000	0.000

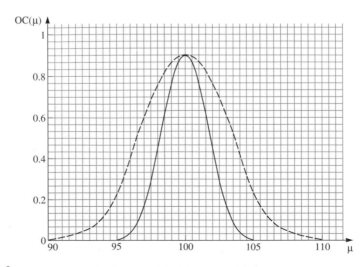

Figure 3.6

The probability of a type I error is unchanged at 0.01, but the operating characteristic shows that the probability of a type II error is less at every possible true value of μ.

Investigation

Suppose that the scientist's alternative hypothesis is that the mean intelligence of his subset is greater, so that he is working with a one-tailed test. Construct the operating characteristics using one of the combinations of significance level and sample size given above, and compare your graph with the one given in the text.

A simple alternative hypothesis

So far, you have met only composite alternative hypotheses – that is, those giving a range of parameter values. However, it is possible for both null and alternative hypotheses to be simple – that is, giving only a single parameter value. For instance, the scientist above may be trying to support, or challenge, the work of another group of researchers who have claimed, on the basis of a substantial sample, that a particular subset has a mean intelligence of 102. His hypotheses would be:

H_0: the mean intelligence of the subset is 100;

H_A: the mean intelligence of the subset is 102;

on the assumption that the intelligence of the subset will have a standard deviation of 15.

As usual, α is the significance level, i.e.

$$\alpha = \text{probability of a type I error}$$
$$= \text{probability of accepting } H_A \text{ when } H_0 \text{ is true}$$
$$= 1 - OC(100)$$

In the case of a simple alternative hypothesis, it is usual also to define:

$$\beta = \text{probability of a type II error}$$
$$= \text{probability of accepting } H_0 \text{ when } H_A \text{ is true}$$
$$= OC(102)$$

Note the symmetry of these definitions: when both null and alternative hypotheses are simple, there is little difference in the status of the two.

Ideally, we would like $\alpha = \beta = 0$, but we already know that this cannot be achieved: in fact choosing a critical value for the test fixes α and β simultaneously so that if we choose a critical value to produce a given α, then a value for β follows automatically.

If we choose the critical value c and a sample size of n, then:

$$\alpha = P(\text{sample mean greater than } c \text{ when population mean is } 100)$$

$$= 1 - \Phi\left(\frac{c - 100}{15/\sqrt{n}}\right)$$

and

$$\beta = P(\text{sample mean less than } c \text{ when population mean is } 102)$$

$$= \Phi\left(\frac{c - 102}{15/\sqrt{n}}\right) = 1 - \Phi\left(\frac{102 - c}{15/\sqrt{n}}\right)$$

The graph in figure 3.7 shows how α and β vary with c, in the case of $n = 400$.

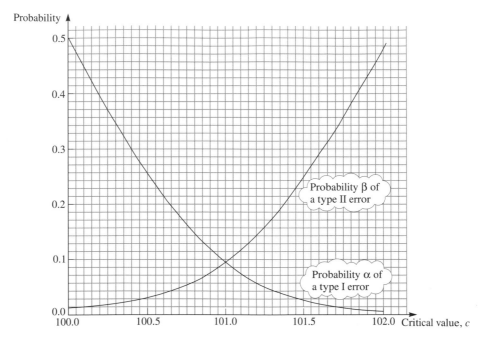

Figure 3.7

The essential point to note is that, with a fixed sample size, reducing α inevitably increases β. We cannot, for instance, with this sample size, have both α and β less than 0.05.

It may seem obvious in this situation that 101 should be chosen as the critical value because it makes errors in either direction equally likely. However, depending on why the work is being done, it may be that errors one way or the other are more important. Any critical value between 100 and 102 could be a sensible choice in the appropriate circumstances.

The graph in figure 3.8 shows the pairs of α, β values which can be achieved by choosing the critical value appropriately for a range of values of n.

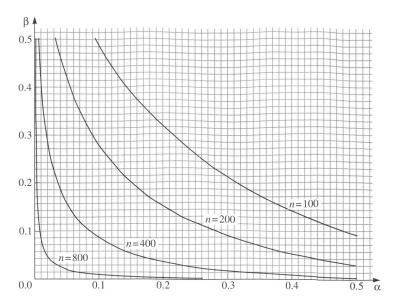

Figure 3.8

A scientist in this situation might well start from what he considers appropriate significance levels and deduce from these the parameters of the experiment he needs to perform. For instance, suppose the scientist wants to ensure that $\alpha = 0.01$ and $\beta = 0.05$. What size of sample should he set and what should the critical value be?

Using the results above, the desired values of α and β mean that:

$$1 - \theta\left(\frac{c - 100}{15/\sqrt{n}}\right) = 0.01$$

and:

$$1 - \theta\left(\frac{102 - c}{15/\sqrt{n}}\right) = 0.05$$

Using the Normal tables, these become:

$$\frac{c - 100}{15/\sqrt{n}} = \Phi^{-1}(0.99) = 2.326$$

and:
$$\frac{102 - c}{15/\sqrt{n}} = \Phi^{-1}(0.95) = 1.645$$

Adding these two equations gives:

$$\frac{2}{15/\sqrt{n}} = 3.971 \text{ or } \sqrt{n} = 29.7825$$

so the sample size required is $n = 887$.

Substitution back into one of the simultaneous equations then gives $c = 101.17$.

For Discussion

You may know that there is considerable controversy over the testing of intelligence: scientists have sometimes asserted that one group in a population has a higher or lower mean intelligence than another and this has aroused very hostile reactions. You should be clear that the objections are not to the statistical reasoning outlined above, but to two additional assumptions which are made: that there is such a thing as innate intellectual ability; and that intelligence tests measure it reliably. Do you think there is such a thing as innate intellectual ability? If you do, what factors other than innate intellectual ability might affect performance in intelligence tests?

Exercise 3A

1. A two-tailed test of the fairness of a coin is being conducted, in which the coin is tossed 20 times and the number of heads noted.

   (i) If the test is to be conducted at the 5% level, use cumulative binomial tables to find the critical region for the test. What is the exact value of α, the probability of a type I error?

   (ii) Use the tables to find the probability of accepting the null hypothesis of no bias if, in fact, the probability of a head is $0.00, 0.05, 0.10, \ldots, 0.90, 0.95, 1.00$, and thus plot the operating characteristic of the test.

2. A one-tailed test is being undertaken to investigate a die which is supposed to show a six too frequently. The die is to be rolled seven times and the null hypothesis of no bias will be rejected if the die shows six more than twice.

   (i) Show that the probability of a type I error for this test is just under 10%.

   (ii) Show that the operating characteristic of this test is given by the expression:
   $$(1-p)^5(1+5p+15p^2)$$
   where p is the probability of the die showing a six, and sketch the graph of this function.

   (iii) For which values of p is the probability of a type II error below 10%?

3. Hugo is buying a tank of tropical fish. There are 16 fish in the tank, and the pet-shop owner claims that half are male and half are female. As sexing this species of fish requires close

examination, Hugo decides to test this hypothesis by removing four fish from the tank at random, without replacement. He will reject the pet-shop owner's claim unless his sample of four contains at least one male and at least one female fish.

   (i) Find the significance level for this test.

   (ii) For each possible number of male fish in the tank (from 0 to 16) determine the probability of a type II error, and thus sketch the operating characteristic of the test.

   (iii) Would the significance level and operating characteristic be very different if Hugo had sampled with replacement?

4. In radio-carbon dating, the number of beta particles emitted per minute by a sample of carbon from a charred bone is given by a Poisson distribution whose mean, λ, depends on the age of the sample.

   A charred bone is found which, because of the deposits with which it is associated, is known to be either 1800 years old, in which case $\lambda = 7.2$, or 2600 years old, in which case $\lambda = 3.8$.

   An archaeologist's strategy for deciding between these hypotheses is to count the number, B, of beta particles emitted by the sample in m minutes, accepting that $\lambda = 7.2$ if $B > c$ and that $\lambda = 3.8$ if $B < c$.

   Define $\alpha = $ P(accepting $\lambda = 3.8$ when $\lambda = 7.2$) and $\beta = $ P(accepting $\lambda = 7.2$ when $\lambda = 3.8$).

   (i) If $m = 1$ and $c = 5.5$, determine the values of α and β.

Exercise 3A continued

(ii) If $m = 8$ and $c = 40$, use a Normal approximation to the Poisson distribution to find α and β.

(iii) Why might an archaeologist choose c so that α and β were not equal?

5. In a test on extra-sensory perception, a supposed clairvoyant is asked to predict the suit of 12 cards selected randomly, with replacement, from a well-shuffled pack. The hypothesis testing strategy is to count the number, C, of cards for which the suit is predicted correctly and then:

if $C > 6$, reject the null hypothesis of no clairvoyance;

if $C < 6$, accept the null hypothesis of no clairvoyance;

if $C = 6$, draw a random number uniformly distributed on $[0, 1]$ from a calculator, accepting the null hypothesis if this is less than r and rejecting if this is greater than r.

(i) Find the value of r which gives this test an exact significance level of 0.05.

(ii) For this value of r, what is the probability of a type II error if the clairvoyant in fact has a probability of 0.5 of correctly predicting the suit of a card?

6. The random variable, X, is distributed uniformly on the range $[0, m]$, where m is claimed to have the value m_0, but is suspected to have a smaller value than this. In order to test the null hypothesis, $m = m_0$, against the alternative, $m < m_0$, a sample of n values of X is drawn and the largest of the n values is recorded as the value of the random variable L. The null hypothesis will be rejected if this largest value is less than some critical value.

(i) Explain why:

$$P(\text{largest of the } n \text{ values is less than } I) = \left(\frac{I}{m}\right)^n$$

(ii) Hence determine:

(a) the critical value of I in terms of α, the significance level of the test, m_0 and n;

(b) the operating characteristic for the test as a function of m.

(iii) If $\alpha = 0.0625$ and $m_0 = 100$, sketch the operating characteristic in the cases $n = 1, 2, 4$.

(iv) Explain why, if we are free to choose n, then, for any simple alternative hypothesis for m, we can have $\beta = 0$, with α as small as we wish. In what sense does this mean that we can actually 'find out' what m is?

7. It is thought that people are likely to perform better on an endurance test, which measures the time for which a weight can be supported with an outstretched arm, if they are in a group than individually. The differences in times (group − individual) are modelled by the random variable D, with distribution $D \sim N(\mu, \sigma^2)$.

Eighty subjects are asked to perform the test individually and in a group and the differences in times are recorded. The results are summarised by the mean difference $\bar{d}$ and the unbiased variance estimate $\hat{\sigma}^2$

(i) State suitable null and alternative hypotheses.

(ii) If α is to equal 0.01, determine the critical value of $\bar{d}$ above which the null hypothesis will be rejected, in terms of $\hat{\sigma}$.

You should assume that a sample size of 80 is sufficiently large that you can take the standard deviation of D to equal $\hat{\sigma}$ and use the Normal rather than the t-distribution for your calculation.

(iii) If $\sigma = 22$ seconds, construct a graph of the operating characteristic of this test.

8. Define the following terms with reference to hypothesis testing:

(i) type I error;

(ii) type II error;

(iii) operating characteristic.

The random variable X is distributed as $N(\mu, 9)$. A test is required of the null hypothesis $H_0: \mu = 20$ against the alternative hypothesis $H_1: \mu \neq 20$, using the customary procedure based on the sample mean $\bar{X}$, with a sample of size 25; thus the test statistic to be used is

$$\frac{(\bar{X} - 20)}{\left(\frac{3}{5}\right)}$$

The probability of a type I error is to be 1%.

(iv) Show that H_0 is to be accepted if
$18.45 < \bar{x} < 21.55$

(v) Show an expression for the operating characteristic of the test

$$P\left(\frac{18.45 - \mu}{0.6} < Z < \frac{21.55 - \mu}{0.6}\right)$$

where $Z \sim N(0, 1)$. Evaluate this expression for $\mu = 17, 18, 19, 20, 21, 22, 23$ and hence draw a sketch of the operating characteristic.

(*You are not required to draw this sketch accurately on graph paper, but you may do so if you wish.*)

9. Independent observations $x_1, x_2, \ldots, x_n$ are taken from the Normally distributed population $N(\mu, \sigma^2)$ where the value of σ^2 is known to be 4. The null hypothesis value of μ is 1 and the only other possible value of μ is 2.

α denotes the probability that the null hypothesis is rejected when, in fact, it is true. β denotes the probability that the null hypothesis is accepted when, in fact, it is false.

(i) Suppose that $n = 25$ and it is decided to reject the null hypothesis if the observed sample mean $\bar{x}$ exceeds 1.4. Determine α and β.

(ii) Suppose $n = 4$ and it is required that $\alpha = 0.05$. Determine the constant k for which observed values of $\bar{x}$ exceeding k lead to rejection of the null hypothesis. Also find β.

(iii) Suppose it is required that $\alpha = \beta = 0.025$. Determine the required sample size n and the constant k for which observed values of $\bar{x}$ exceeding k lead to rejection of the null hypothesis.

10. (i) Define the following terms in connection with hypothesis testing: type I error, type II error, operating characteristic.

(ii) A test is to be made concerning a parameter θ. The null hypothesis is that θ has the particular value θ_0; this is to be tested against the two-sided alternative $\theta \neq \theta_0$.

(a) Draw a quick sketch of the operating characteristic for a *perfect* test that *never* makes an error.

(b) Draw a quick sketch showing the operating characteristics of two hypothesis tests, one of which is 'better' than the other in the sense that it is less likely to accept the null hypothesis whenever it is false. Explain how this is demonstrated by the operating characteristics.

(iii) The random variable X is distributed as $N(\mu, 16)$. A random sample of size 25 is available. The null hypothesis $\mu = 0$ is to be tested against the alternative hypothesis $\mu \neq 0$. The null hypothesis will be accepted if $-1.5 < \bar{x} < 1.5$, where $\bar{x}$ is the value of the sample mean, otherwise it will be rejected. Calculate the probability of a type I error. Calculate the probability of a type II error if, in fact, $\mu = 0.5$; comment on the value of this probability.

KEY POINTS

When analysing a hypothesis test the following notations are used:

- Rejecting the null hypothesis when it is true is called a *type I error*. The probability of a type I error is the significance level of the test.

- Accepting the null hypothesis when it is false is called a *type II error*.

- With a compound alternative hypothesis, the probability of a type II error, viewed as a function of the parameter whose value is being tested, is called the *operating characteristic* of the test.

- The *power* of a test is (1 − the operating characteristic of the test).

4 Probability generating functions

Expect nothing. Live frugally on surprise.

Alice Walker

During the first season of the FA Premier League, 462 football matches were played. The frequency of the number of goals scored in each game by the *away* team, and associated relative frequencies, were recorded as follows:

Number of goals	0	1	2	3	4	5	>5
Frequency	149	179	91	37	3	3	0
Relative frequency	0.322	0.387	0.197	0.080	0.007	0.007	0

Assuming that these relative frequencies reflect the general pattern of scoring in FA Premier League matches, they may be used as *empirical* probabilities of $0, 1, 2, \ldots$ goals being scored by *away* teams per match.

Let X be the discrete random variable representing the number of goals scored per game by away teams, then one way of storing the probabilities is in the *probability generating function* (pgf):

$$\mathrm{G}(t) = 0.322 + 0.387t + 0.197t^2 + 0.080t^3 + 0.007t^4 + 0.007t^5$$

where the coefficients of t^x are the probabilities $\mathrm{P}(X = x)$. The variable t is a *dummy* variable as, in itself, it has no significance. However, it has an important role to play in subsequent analysis, which you will appreciate later on.

By substituting $t = 1$, we get:

$$\mathrm{G}(1) = 0.322 + 0.387 + 0.197 + 0.080 + 0.007 + 0.007 = 1$$

as the sum of the probabilities has to be 1.

Set out in tabular form we have:

t^x	t^0	t^1	t^2	t^3	t^4	t^5
$\mathrm{P}(X = x)$	0.322	0.387	0.197	0.080	0.007	0.007
$t^x \mathrm{P}(X = x)$	0.322	$0.387t$	$0.197t^2$	$0.080t^3$	$0.007t^4$	$0.007t^5$

Thus $G(t) = \sum_x t^x P(X = x) = E(t^x)$, which gives us our general definition for a probability generating function.

The way in which $G(t)$ generates probabilities is best seen from a *theoretical* model. From the shape of the probability distribution for goals scored by away teams, it looks as though a Poisson distribution might produce a good fit.

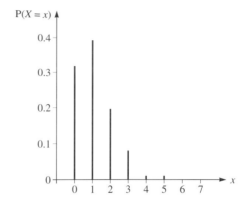

Figure 4.1

Using a suitable chi-square test you can check that, at the 5% level of significance, a Poisson distribution with mean 1.08 (using the sample mean as an unbiased estimate of the population mean) produces a good fit. The *theoretical* probabilities for a Poisson distribution, with mean = 1.08, are given by $P(X = x) = e^{-1.08}\dfrac{1.08^x}{x!}$. Therefore the pgf $G(t)$, given by $E(t^x) = \sum_x t^x P(X = x)$ may be written in a convenient form:

$$G(t) = \sum_{x=0}^{\infty} e^{-1.08}\frac{1.08^x}{x!} t^x$$

$$= e^{-1.08}\left(1 + 1.08t + \frac{1.08^2}{2!}t^2 + \frac{1.08^3}{3!}t^3 + \cdots\right)$$

$$= e^{-1.08}e^{1.08t}$$

$$= e^{1.08(t-1)}$$

NOTE

The pgf for a discrete random variable X, where $X \sim$ Poisson (λ), is given by $G(t) = e^{\lambda(t-1)}$. A formal proof is given on page 62.

For Discussion

Probability generating functions may be used to describe any discrete probability distribution, which may be *finite* or *infinite*. For each of the following distributions, list the values the variable can take and classify the distribution as finite or infinite:

- score on a fair die;

- number of heads when four coins are tossed;

- number of cars passing a road junction per minute;

- number of attempts to get a six by repeatedly throwing a fair die.

Basic properties

The example we have considered illustrates some basic properties of probability generating functions (pgfs) for any discrete random variable X:

Definition:
$$G(t) = E(t^x) = \sum_x t^x P(X = x)$$

$$\Rightarrow \quad G(1) = \sum_x 1^x P(X = x) = \sum_x P(X = x) = 1$$

If X takes non-negative integral values only, then the probability generating function takes the form of a polynomial in t which is often written as:

$$G(t) = \sum_x p_x t^x = p_0 + p_1 t + p_2 t^2 + \cdots + p_n t^n + \cdots$$

where p_x denotes $P(X = x)$, e.g. p_2 denotes $P(X = 2)$. The function $G(t)$ may be either a finite or infinite polynomial, i.e. it may terminate after n terms or continue indefinitely.

EXAMPLE

Uniform distribution
Let X be the discrete random variable that denotes the score when a fair die is thrown. Find the probability generating function (pgf) for X.

Solution:

The probability distribution is given by:

x	1	2	3	4	5	6
$P(X = x)$	$\frac{1}{6}$	$\frac{1}{6}$	$\frac{1}{6}$	$\frac{1}{6}$	$\frac{1}{6}$	$\frac{1}{6}$

The pgf for X is:

$$G(t) = E(t^x) = \frac{1}{6}t + \frac{1}{6}t^2 + \frac{1}{6}t^3 + \frac{1}{6}t^4 + \frac{1}{6}t^5 + \frac{1}{6}t^6$$

$$= \frac{1}{6}t(1 + t + t^2 + t^3 + t^4 + t^5)$$

$$= \frac{1}{6}t \times \frac{1 - t^6}{1 - t} \qquad \text{sum of first 6 terms of a GP with first term 1 and common ratio } t$$

$$= \frac{t(1 - t^6)}{6(1 - t)}$$

EXAMPLE

Binomial distribution
Dan is a keen archer. He has taken part in many competitions. When aiming for the centre of the target, called the gold, he finds that he hits the gold 70% of the

S5

time. Find the pgf for X, the number of gold hits in four consecutive shots at the target.

Solution:

As $X \sim B(4, 0.7)$, probabilities are given by $P(X = x) = {}^4C_x 0.3^{4-x} 0.7^x$, which gives the distribution:

x	0	1	2	3	4
$P(X = x)$	0.3^4	$4 \times 0.3^3 \times 0.7$	$6 \times 0.3^2 \times 0.7^2$	$4 \times 0.3 \times 0.7^3$	0.7^4

The pgf for X is:

$$G(t) = E(t^x) = \sum_{x=0}^{4} p_x t^x = \sum_{x=0}^{4} {}^4C_x \times 0.3^{4-x} \times 0.7^x t^x$$

$$= 0.3^4 + 4 \times 0.3^3 \times 0.7t + 6 \times 0.3^2 \times 0.7^2 t^2 + 4 \times 0.3 \times 0.7^3 t^3 + 0.7^4 t^4$$

$$= (0.3 + 0.7t)^4$$

NOTE

Let $X \sim B(n, p)$, i.e. $P(X = x) = {}^nC_x q^{n-x} p^x$, where $q = 1 - p$. Then the pgf for X is given by $G(t) = (q + pt)^n$. A formal proof is given on page 61.

EXAMPLE

Geometric distribution
A card is selected at random from a normal pack of 52 playing cards. If it is a heart, the experiment ends, otherwise it is replaced, the pack is shuffled and another card is selected. Let X represent the number of cards selected up to and including the first heart. Find the pgf for X.

Solution:

As X follows a geometric distribution, i.e. $X \sim \text{Geometric}(\frac{1}{4})$, probabilities are given by $P(X = x) = (\frac{3}{4})^{x-1} \times \frac{1}{4}$, which gives the distribution:

x	1	2	3	4	5	$\cdots$
$P(X = x)$	$\frac{1}{4}$	$\frac{3}{4} \times \frac{1}{4}$	$(\frac{3}{4})^2 \times \frac{1}{4}$	$(\frac{3}{4})^3 \times \frac{1}{4}$	$(\frac{3}{4})^4 \times \frac{1}{4}$	$\cdots$

The pgf for X is:

$$G(t) = E(t^x) = \sum_{x=1}^{\infty} p_x t^x = \sum_{x=1}^{\infty} (\tfrac{3}{4})^{x-1} (\tfrac{1}{4}) t^x$$

$$= (\tfrac{1}{4})t + (\tfrac{3}{4})(\tfrac{1}{4})t^2 + (\tfrac{3}{4})^2(\tfrac{1}{4})t^3 + (\tfrac{3}{4})^3(\tfrac{1}{4})t^4 + (\tfrac{3}{4})^4(\tfrac{1}{4})t^5 + \cdots$$

$$= (\tfrac{1}{4})t\left[1 + (\tfrac{3}{4}t) + (\tfrac{3}{4}t)^2 + (\tfrac{3}{4}t)^3 + (\tfrac{3}{4}t)^4 + \cdots\right]$$

$$= (\tfrac{1}{4})t\left[\frac{1}{1 - \frac{3}{4}t}\right]$$

sum to infinity of a GP with first term 1 and common ratio $\frac{3}{4}t$

$$= \frac{t}{4 - 3t}$$

NOTE

Let $X \sim \text{Geometric}(p)$, i.e. $P(X = x) = q^{x-1}p$, where $q = 1 - p$. Then the pgf for X is given by $G(t) = \dfrac{pt}{1 - qt}$. A formal proof is given on page 63.

Exercise 4A

1. Let X be the discrete random variable that denotes the sum of the scores when two fair dice are thrown. Construct a table for the probability distribution and so write down the pgf.

2. Let X be the discrete random variable that denotes the absolute difference of the scores when two fair dice are thrown ($x = 0, 1, 2, 3, 4, 5$). Construct a table for the probability distribution and so write down the pgf.

3. A fair coin is spun three times and the number of tails appearing is noted as the discrete random variable X ($x = 0, 1, 2, 3$). Construct a table for the probability distribution and so write down the pgf.

4. A box contains three red balls and two green balls. They are taken out one at a time, *without* replacement. Let X represent the number of withdrawals until a red ball is chosen. Find its pgf.

5. The experiment in Question 4 is repeated, but this time *with* replacement. Find the pgf for the number of withdrawals until a red ball is chosen.

6. A random number generator in a computer game produces values which can be modelled by the discrete random variable X with probability distribution given by: $P(X = r) = kr!$, $r = 1, 2, 3, 4, 5$.

   Determine the value of k and so write down $G(t)$, the pgf for X.

7. A mathematics student is shown three graphs. She is also given three equations, one for each graph. If she matches each graph with its equation at random, construct a table for the probability distribution of X, the number of correctly identified graphs. Deduce the pgf for X.

8. Two students are to be chosen to represent a class containing nine boys and six girls. Assuming that the students are chosen at random, find the pgf for X, the number of girls representing the group.

Expectation and variance

For any discrete probability distribution, the *expectation* (mean) and *variance* may be computed, using the shorthand $P(X = x) = p_x$:

$$\mu = E(X) = \sum_x xp_x$$

$$\sigma^2 = \text{Var}(X) = E(X - \mu)^2 = \sum_x (x - \mu)^2 p_x = \sum_x x^2 p_x - \mu^2 = E(X^2) - \mu^2$$

By successively differentiating $G(t)$, the probability generating function for X, formulae for the expectation and variance can be derived elegantly. It is here that the power of the pgf as an algebraic tool becomes apparent.

Expectation

This may be obtained from the probability generating function $G(t)$ by differentiating with respect to t and evaluating the expression at $t = 1$:

$$G(t) = E[t^X] = \sum_x p_x t^x$$

$$\Rightarrow \quad G'(t) = \sum_x xp_x t^{x-1} = E[Xt^{X-1}]$$

$$\Rightarrow \quad G'(1) = \sum_x xp_x = E[X]$$

Therefore: $\mu = E(X) = G'(1)$

Variance

Differentiating $G'(t)$ and evaluating the expression at $t = 1$:

$$G'(t) = \sum_x x p_x t^{x-1} = E[Xt^{X-1}]$$

$$\Rightarrow \quad G''(t) = \sum_x x(x-1)p_x t^{x-2} = E[X(X-1)t^{X-2}]$$

$$\Rightarrow \quad G''(1) = \sum_x x(x-1)p_x = E[X(X-1)]$$

$$\Rightarrow \quad G''(1) = \sum_x x^2 p_x - \sum_x x p_x = E[X^2] - E[X]$$

$$\Rightarrow \quad E[X^2] = G''(1) + E[X] = G''(1) + G'(1)$$

Therefore:

$$\sigma^2 = G''(1) + G'(1) - (G'(1))^2 \quad \text{or} \quad \sigma^2 = G''(1) + \mu - \mu^2$$

Summary

Whenever a pgf is given for a discrete random variable, the expectation (mean) and variance may be evaluated using the definitions:

$$\mu = E(X) = G'(1) \quad \text{and} \quad \sigma^2 = \text{Var}(X) = G''(1) + G'(1) - (G'(1))^2$$

In the following examples, the first one shows how the polynomial form for a probability generating function $G(t)$ may be differentiated twice in order to derive the expectation and variance. This may seem as complex as the usual calculations for μ and σ^2. However, two further examples demonstrate the power of this method when $G(t)$ can be expressed in shortened form.

EXAMPLE

Let X be the discrete random variable that denotes the absolute difference of scores when two fair dice are thrown. Using a pgf, confirm that $E(X)$ is just under 2 and determine $\text{Var}(X)$.

Solution:

The probability distribution of X was derived in Exercise 4A, Question 2, as:

x	0	1	2	3	4	5
$P(X = x)$	$\frac{3}{18}$	$\frac{5}{18}$	$\frac{4}{18}$	$\frac{3}{18}$	$\frac{2}{18}$	$\frac{1}{18}$

The pgf for X is:

$$G(t) = \frac{3}{18} + \frac{5}{18}t + \frac{4}{18}t^2 + \frac{3}{18}t^3 + \frac{2}{18}t^4 + \frac{1}{18}t^5$$

$$\Rightarrow \quad G'(t) = \frac{5}{18} + \frac{8}{18}t + \frac{9}{18}t^2 + \frac{8}{18}t^3 + \frac{5}{18}t^4$$

$$\Rightarrow \quad G''(t) = \frac{8}{18} + \frac{18}{18}t + \frac{24}{18}t^2 + \frac{20}{18}t^3$$

Therefore:
$$G'(1) = \frac{5}{18} + \frac{8}{18} + \frac{9}{18} + \frac{8}{18} + \frac{5}{18} = \frac{35}{18} = 1\frac{17}{18}$$

and
$$G''(1) = \frac{8}{18} + \frac{18}{18} + \frac{24}{18} + \frac{20}{18} = \frac{70}{18} = 3\frac{8}{9}$$

From this we may deduce:

$$E(X) = G'(1) = 1\tfrac{17}{18}$$

$$\text{Var}(X) = G''(1) + G'(1) - (G'(1))^2$$

$$= 3\tfrac{8}{9} + 1\tfrac{17}{18} - (1\tfrac{17}{18})^2 = 2\tfrac{17}{324} \approx 2.05$$

Confirm that these results may also be derived from first principles, i.e.:

$$\mu = E(X) = \sum_x x p_x \quad \text{and} \quad \sigma^2 = \text{Var}(X) = \sum_x x^2 p_x - \mu^2$$

EXAMPLE

Four unbiased coins are tossed and the number of heads (X) is noted. Show that the pgf for X is given by $G(t) = \tfrac{1}{16}(1+t)^4$. From this calculate the mean and variance of X.

Solution:

As $X \sim B(4, \tfrac{1}{2})$, probabilities are given by:

$$P(X = x) = {}^4C_x(\tfrac{1}{2})^{4-x}(\tfrac{1}{2})^x = {}^4C_x(\tfrac{1}{2})^4 = {}^4C_x\tfrac{1}{16}$$

The pgf for X is:

$$G(t) = E(t^x) = \sum_{x=0}^{4} p_x t^x = \tfrac{1}{16} \sum_{x=0}^{4} {}^4C_x t^x$$

$$= \tfrac{1}{16}(1 + 4t + 6t^2 + 4t^3 + t^4)$$

$$= \tfrac{1}{16}(1+t)^4$$

From the pgf the mean and variance of X are found by differentiation:

$$G'(t) = 4 \times \tfrac{1}{16}(1+t)^3 = \tfrac{1}{4}(1+t)^3 \quad \Rightarrow \quad G'(1) = \tfrac{1}{4} \times 2^3 = 2$$

$$G''(t) = 3 \times \tfrac{1}{4}(1+t)^2 = \tfrac{3}{4}(1+t)^2 \quad \Rightarrow \quad G''(1) = \tfrac{3}{4} \times 2^2 = 3$$

$$\Rightarrow \quad E(X) = G'(1) = 2$$

$$\text{Var}(X) = G''(1) + G'(1) - (G'(1))^2 = 3 + 2 - 2^2 = 1$$

EXAMPLE

A box contains three red balls and two green balls. They are taken out one at a time, with replacement. Let X represent the number of withdrawals until a red ball is chosen. Calculate the mean and variance of X.

Solution:

In this experiment the outcomes follow a geometric distribution. X is Geometric (p), where $p = \tfrac{3}{5}$ and $q = 1 - \tfrac{3}{5} = \tfrac{2}{5}$, and so the pgf is:

$$G(t) = \frac{pt}{1 - qt} = \frac{\tfrac{3}{5}t}{1 - \tfrac{2}{5}t} = \frac{3t}{5 - 2t}$$

Differentiating with respect to t, using the quotient rule:

$$G'(t) = \frac{(5 - 2t) \times 3 - 3t \times (-2)}{(5 - 2t)^2} = \frac{15}{(5 - 2t)^2} \quad \Rightarrow \quad G'(1) = \tfrac{15}{9} = 1\tfrac{2}{3}$$

Differentiating with respect to t, using the chain rule:

$$G''(t) = -2 \times 15 \times (5 - 2t)^{-3} \times (-2) = \frac{60}{(5 - 2t)^3} \quad \Rightarrow \quad G''(1) = \frac{60}{27} = 2\frac{2}{9}$$

$$\Rightarrow \quad E(X) = G'(1) = 1\frac{2}{3}$$

$$\text{Var}(X) = G''(1) + G'(1) - (G'(1))^2 = 2\frac{2}{9} + 1\frac{2}{3} - (1\frac{2}{3})^2 = 1\frac{1}{9}$$

EXAMPLE

A discrete random variable X ($x = 0, 1, 2$) has pgf given by $G(t) = a + bt + ct^2$, where a, b and c are constants. If the mean is $1\frac{1}{4}$ and the variance is $\frac{11}{16}$, find the values of a, b and c.

Solution:

As $P(X = 0) = a$, $P(X = 1) = b$ and $P(X = 2) = c$:

$$G(t) = a + bt + ct^2 \quad \Rightarrow \quad G(1) = a + b + c = 1 \tag{1}$$

As $\mu = 1\frac{1}{4}$ and $E(X) = G'(1)$:

$$G'(t) = b + 2ct \quad \Rightarrow \quad G'(1) = b + 2c = 1\frac{1}{4} \tag{2}$$

As $\sigma^2 = G''(1) + G'(1) - (G'(1))^2$, $\quad G''(1) = \sigma^2 - G'(1) + (G'(1))^2 = 1$:

$$G''(t) = 2c \quad \Rightarrow \quad G''(1) = 2c = 1 \tag{3}$$

From equation (3): $\qquad 2c = 1 \quad \Rightarrow \quad c = \frac{1}{2}$

From equation (2): $\qquad b + 2c - 1\frac{1}{4} \quad \Rightarrow \quad b = 1\frac{1}{4} \quad 2 \times \frac{1}{2} = \frac{1}{4}$

From equation (1): $\qquad a + b + c = 1 \quad \Rightarrow \quad a = 1 - \frac{1}{4} - \frac{1}{2} = \frac{1}{4}$

Therefore: $a = \frac{1}{4}$, $b = \frac{1}{4}$, $c = \frac{1}{2}$

Exercise 4B

1. A random variable has pgf $G(t) = \frac{1}{6} + \frac{1}{3}t + \frac{1}{4}t^3 + \frac{1}{6}t^4 + \frac{1}{12}t^5$. Find its mean and variance.

2. A random variable X has pgf $G(t) = \frac{1}{81}(1 + 2t)^4$. Calculate $E(X)$ and $\text{Var}(X)$.

3. Let X be the discrete random variable that denotes the score when a fair die is thrown. Use its pgf to find $E(X)$ and $\text{Var}(X)$.

4. A fair coin is spun three times and the number of tails appearing is noted as the discrete random variable X ($x = 0, 1, 2, 3$). Use the pgf:

$$G(t) = \frac{1}{8}(1 + 3t + 3t^2 + t^3)$$

to calculate the mean and variance of X.

5. The probability generating function of a discrete random variable, X, is $G(t) = (at + 1 - a)^n$, where a is a constant $(0 \leqslant a \leqslant 1)$ and n is a positive integer. Prove that $E(X) = na$, and find the variance of X.

[Cambridge]

6. An ordinary pack of playing cards is cut four times. Let X represent the number of aces appearing. Find the probability generating function for X and so find the mean and variance of X.

7. The King and Queen of Muldovia want a son and heir to their kingdom. Let X represent the number of children they have until a boy is born.

   (i) Assuming that each pregnancy results in a single child, and that the probability of a boy is 0.5, show that the pgf for X is given by:

   $$G(t) = \frac{t}{2 - t}.$$

   (ii) From this show that both $E(X)$ and $\text{Var}(X) = 2$.

8. A random variable has pgf $G(t) = a + bt + ct^2$. It has mean $\frac{7}{6}$ and variance $\frac{29}{36}$. Find values for a, b and c.

9. Two fair dice are thrown and X represents the larger of the two scores. Find the pgf for X and so find the mean and variance of X.

Investigation

In a competition, the entrant has to match a number of famous landmarks (A, B, C, etc.) with the country in which it is to be found (1, 2, 3, etc.).

Figure 4.2

Let X represent the number of correct matches which the entrant makes. For the purposes of this investigation, assume that the matching of the landmark to its country is chosen at random.

In each case take the correct matching as $A \leftrightarrow 1$, $B \leftrightarrow 2$, $C \leftrightarrow 3$, etc.

(a) For three famous landmarks the possible matchings and values of X are:

A	1	1	2	2	3	3
B	2	3	1	3	1	2
C	3	2	3	1	2	1
X	3	1	1	0	0	1

Find the pgf for X and show that $E(X) = \text{Var}(X) = 1$.

(b) (i) For *four* famous landmarks explain why there are $4! = 24$ possible matchings, only one of which is correct.

(ii) Show that the pgf for X is given by $G(t) = \frac{3}{8} + \frac{1}{3}t + \frac{1}{4}t^2 + \frac{1}{24}t^4$.

(iii) Use the pgf to show that $E(X) = \text{Var}(X) = 1$.

(c) (i) For n $(n > 2)$ famous landmarks there are $n!$ possible matchings.

    (ii) Explain why $P(X = n) = \dfrac{1}{n!}$ and $P(X = n - 1) = 0$.

    (iii) Prove that $P(X = n - 2) = \dfrac{1}{2 \times (n - 2)!}$ and $P(X = n - 3) = \dfrac{1}{3 \times (n - 3)!}$

    (iv) Verify these results for $n = 3$ and $n = 4$.

(d) For *five* famous landmarks, use results from part (c) and the assumption that $E(X) = 1$ to derive the pgf for X.

(e) For *six* famous landmarks, use results from part (c) and the assumptions that $E(X) = 1$ and $\text{Var}(X) = 1$ to derive the pgf for X.

(f) (i) Compare the pgfs in (a), (b), (d) and (e). How are they related to each other?

    (ii) How can you use the pgf for n possible matches to derive the pgf for:

       (a) $n - 1$ possible matches;

       (b) $n + 1$ possible matches?

The sum of independent random variables

At the beginning of the chapter you saw that, with a mean of 1.08 goals per match, the random variable X, the number of goals scored by the *away* team in each game was distributed approximately Poisson (1.08). Let the probability generating function for X be denoted by $G_X(t)$, then $G_X(t) = e^{1.08(t-1)}$.

Let Y represent the number of goals scored by the *home* team, then, from the data collected for the same season for *home* teams:

Number of goals	0	1	2	3	4	5	6	7
Frequency	100	157	110	53	28	10	3	1
Relative frequency	0.216	0.340	0.238	0.115	0.061	0.022	0.006	0.002

the sample mean is 1.57. Again a Poisson distribution is a good fit to model the number of *home* goals; i.e. Y is Poisson (1.57) with pgf $G_Y(t) = e^{1.57(t-1)}$.

The mean number of goals scored per match, $X + Y$, is $1.08 + 1.57 = 2.65$. This can also be found directly from the frequency distribution for total goals scored:

Number of goals	0	1	2	3	4	5	6	7
Frequency	100	157	110	53	28	10	3	1
Relative frequency	0.216	0.340	0.238	0.115	0.061	0.022	0.006	0.002

where the relative frequencies can also be modelled by a Poisson distribution, i.e.:

$$X + Y \text{ is Poisson (2.65) with pgf } G_{X+Y}(t) = e^{2.65(t-1)}.$$

In Chapter 7, on Bivariate Distributions, you can see that there is no significant association between these two variables, i.e. that X and Y might well be *independent*.

Combining results so far we have:

$$G_X(t) \cdot G_Y(t) = e^{1.08(t-1)} e^{1.57(t-1)} = e^{2.65(t-1)} = G_{X+Y}(t)$$

This result suggests that for two *independent* Poisson variables, X and Y, the pgf of the *sum* is the *product* of the individual pgfs. This result is, in fact, true for any two independent random variables, X and Y, which can easily be shown using properties of expectation algebra.

Let X and Y be two *independent* variables, then we have shown that:

$$E[XY] = E[X] \cdot E[Y]$$

and that if $f(X)$ and $g(Y)$ are functions of X and Y respectively:

$$E[f(X)g(Y)] = E[f(X)] \cdot E[g(Y)]$$

In particular, let $f(X) = t^X$ and $g(Y) = t^Y$ then:

$$E[t^X t^Y] = E[t^X] \cdot E[t^Y]$$

Using this equivalence for independent variables:

$$G_{X+Y}(t) = E[t^{X+Y}] = E[t^X t^Y] = E[t^X] \cdot E[t^Y] = G_X(t) \cdot G_Y(t)$$

If X and Y are two **independent** discrete random variables with pgfs
$G_X(t)$ and $G_Y(t)$ then the probability generating function for $X + Y$
is given by:
$$G_{X+Y}(t) = G_X(t) \cdot G_Y(t)$$
i.e. **the pgf of the sum $\equiv$ the product of the pgfs**
This is known as the **Convolution theorem**

EXAMPLE

A discrete random variable X ($x = 0, 1, 2$) has pgf $G_X(t) = \frac{1}{4} + \frac{1}{4}t + \frac{1}{2}t^2$ and another discrete random variable Y ($y = 0, 1$) has pgf $G_Y(t) = \frac{2}{3} + \frac{1}{3}t$. Assume that X and Y are independent.

(i) Find the pgf for $X + Y$, i.e. $G_{X+Y}(t)$.

(ii) Show that $E(X + Y) = E(X) + E(Y)$ and $Var(X + Y) = Var(X) + Var(Y)$.

Solution:

(i) $G_{X+Y}(t) = G_X(t) \cdot G_Y(t) = (\frac{1}{4} + \frac{1}{4}t + \frac{1}{2}t^2)(\frac{2}{3} + \frac{1}{3}t)$

$= \frac{1}{4} \times \frac{2}{3} + (\frac{1}{4} \times \frac{1}{3} + \frac{1}{4} \times \frac{2}{3})t + (\frac{1}{4} \times \frac{1}{3} + \frac{1}{2} \times \frac{2}{3})t^2 + (\frac{1}{2} \times \frac{1}{3})t^3$

$= \frac{1}{6} + \frac{1}{4}t + \frac{5}{12}t^2 + \frac{1}{6}t^3$

(ii) By differentiation:

$$G_X'(t) = \tfrac{1}{4} + t, G_Y'(t) = \tfrac{1}{3} \quad \text{and} \quad G_{X+Y}'(t) = \tfrac{1}{4} + \tfrac{5}{6}t + \tfrac{1}{2}t^2$$

$$\Rightarrow \qquad E(X) = G_X'(1) = \tfrac{1}{4} + 1 = 1\tfrac{1}{4} \quad \text{and} \quad E(Y) = G_Y'(1) = \tfrac{1}{3}$$

$$E(X+Y) = G_{X+Y}'(1) = \tfrac{1}{4} + \tfrac{5}{6} + \tfrac{1}{2} = 1\tfrac{7}{12}$$

$$\Rightarrow \quad E(X) + E(Y) = 1\tfrac{1}{4} + \tfrac{1}{3} = 1\tfrac{7}{12} = E(X+Y)$$

By further differentiation:

$$G_X''(t) = 1, G_Y''(t) = 0 \quad \text{and} \quad G_{X+Y}''(t) = \tfrac{5}{6} + t$$

$$\Rightarrow \qquad \text{Var}\,(X) = G_X''(1) + G_X'(1) - (G_X'(1))^2 = 1 + 1\tfrac{1}{4} - (1\tfrac{1}{4})^2 = \tfrac{11}{16}$$

$$\text{Var}\,(Y) = G_Y''(1) + G_Y'(1) - (G_Y'(1))^2 = 0 + \tfrac{1}{3} - (\tfrac{1}{3})^2 = \tfrac{2}{9}$$

$$\text{Var}\,(X+Y) = G_{X+Y}''(1) + G_{X+Y}'(1) - (G_{X+Y}'(1))^2$$

$$= 1\tfrac{5}{6} + 1\tfrac{7}{12} - (1\tfrac{7}{12})^2 = \tfrac{131}{144}$$

$$\Rightarrow \quad \text{Var}\,(X) + \text{Var}\,(Y) = \tfrac{11}{16} + \tfrac{2}{9} = \tfrac{131}{144} = \text{Var}\,(X+Y)$$

PGF of a linear transformation

A special case of the *convolution theorem* provides us with a useful relationship between probability generating functions for discrete random variables X and Y, where $Y = aX + b$. Let the respective pgfs be $G_X(t)$ and $G_Y(t)$, then:

$$G_Y(t) = E[t^Y] = E[t^{aX+b}] = E[t^{aX}t^b] = E[t^{aX}] \cdot E[t^b]$$

but as b is a constant $E[t^b] = t^b$, and $E[t^{aX}] = E[(t^a)^X]$:

$$\boxed{G_Y(t) = t^b G_X(t^a)}$$

From this definition you can deduce the result for the expectation of $G_Y(t)$. Differentiating with respect to t, using the product rule:

$$G_Y'(t) = t^b at^{a-1} G_X'(t^a) + bt^{b-1} G_X(t^a)$$

$$\Rightarrow \quad G_Y'(1) = 1^b a 1^{a-1} G_X'(1^a) + b1^{b-1} G_X(1^a) \longleftarrow \left(G_X(1) = 1 \right)$$

$$\Rightarrow \quad G_Y'(1) = a G_X'(1) + b$$

$$\text{i.e. } E[Y] = a E[X] + b$$

By further differentiation it is possible to deduce the equivalent result for the variance of $G_Y(t)$, viz. $\text{Var}\,[Y] = a^2 \text{Var}\,[X]$. These are formal proofs, using pgfs, of results which you will have met when studying discrete random variables.

EXAMPLE

In a multiple choice test each question has five choices, only one of which is correct. Assuming that I guess the answer to each question, what linear transformation of X, the number of correct answers, could be applied so that the mean score is zero?

Deduce the corresponding pgf.

Solution:

For each question, let p represent the probability that I get a question correct. Assuming I guess, $p = 0.2$. For a test with n questions, $E(X) = np = 0.2n$. Let $Y = aX + b$ then $E(Y) = aE(X) + b \Rightarrow 0 = a \times 0.2n + b$ This is satisfied by, say, $a = 5$ and $b = -n$, i.e. $Y = 5X - n$. Since $G_X(t) = (0.8 + 0.2t)^n$, $G_Y(t) = t^{-n}(0.8 + 0.2t^5)^n$.

Extension to three or more random variables

The result, that the pgf of the sum of two independent random variables is the product of the pgfs, can be extended to three or more variables, e.g.:

> If X, Y and Z are three independent discrete random variables with pgfs
> $G_X(t)$, $G_Y(t)$ and $G_Z(t)$ then the probability generating function for
> $X + Y + Z$ is given by:
> $$G_{X+Y+Z}(t) = G_X(t) \cdot G_Y(t) \cdot G_Z(t)$$
> If n independent discrete random variables all have the same pgf, $G(t)$, then
> the probability generating function for their sum $= [G(t)]^n$

EXAMPLE

Find the probability generating function for the total number of sixes when five fair dice are thrown. Deduce the mean and variance.

Solution:

When *one* die is thrown, a six occurs with probability $\frac{1}{6}$, therefore the pgf for the number of sixes is $G(t) = \frac{5}{6} + \frac{1}{6}t$. Therefore, when *five* dice are thrown, the pgf for X, the total number of sixes, is given by $G_X(t) = [G(t)]^5 = (\frac{5}{6} + \frac{1}{6}t)^5$.

Applying the results derived earlier:

$$G_X'(t) = 5 \times (\tfrac{5}{6} + \tfrac{1}{6}t)^4 \times \tfrac{1}{6} = \tfrac{5}{6}(\tfrac{5}{6} + \tfrac{1}{6}t)^4$$

$$G_X''(t) = 4 \times \tfrac{5}{6}(\tfrac{5}{6} + \tfrac{1}{6}t)^3 \times \tfrac{1}{6} = \tfrac{5}{9}(\tfrac{5}{6} + \tfrac{1}{6}t)^3$$

$$\Rightarrow \quad E(X) = G'(1) = \tfrac{5}{6}(\tfrac{5}{6} + \tfrac{1}{6})^4 = \tfrac{5}{6} \qquad (\text{as } \tfrac{5}{6} + \tfrac{1}{6} = 1)$$

$$\text{and} \quad \text{Var}(X) = G''(1) + G'(1) - (G'(1))^2$$

$$= \tfrac{5}{9}(\tfrac{5}{6} + \tfrac{1}{6})^3 + \tfrac{5}{6} - (\tfrac{5}{6})^2 = \tfrac{5}{9} + \tfrac{5}{6} - \tfrac{25}{36} = \tfrac{25}{36}$$

NOTE

As $X \sim B(5, \frac{1}{6})$, the results that $E(X) = 5 \times \frac{1}{6}$ and $\text{Var}(X) = 5 \times \frac{1}{6} \times \frac{5}{6}$ have been verified.

The proof for the mean and variance of $X \sim B(n, p)$ is given on page 62.

EXAMPLE

Gina likes having a go at the coconut shy whenever she goes to the fair. From experience, she knows that the probability of her knocking over a coconut at any throw is $\frac{1}{3}$.

(i) Find the pgf $G(t)$ of the number of throws until she hits her first coconut.

(ii) Show that the pgf of the number of throws until she hits her second coconut is $[G(t)]^2$.

(iii) Explain why the pgf of the number of throws until she hits her kth coconut is $[G(t)]^k$.

Solution:

(i) Let X represent the number of throws up to and including Gina's *first* hit, then the random variable X forms a geometric distribution with:

$$P(X = r) = (\tfrac{2}{3})^{r-1}\tfrac{1}{3}.$$

The pgf for X is:

$$G_X(t) = (\tfrac{1}{3})t + (\tfrac{2}{3})(\tfrac{1}{3})t^2 + (\tfrac{2}{3})^2(\tfrac{1}{3})t^3 + (\tfrac{2}{3})^3(\tfrac{1}{3})t^4 + (\tfrac{2}{3})^4(\tfrac{1}{3})t^5 + \cdots$$

$$= (\tfrac{1}{3})t[1 + (\tfrac{2}{3}t) + (\tfrac{2}{3}t)^2 + (\tfrac{2}{3}t)^3 + (\tfrac{2}{3}t)^4 + \cdots]$$

$$= (\tfrac{1}{3})t\left[\frac{1}{1 - \tfrac{2}{3}t}\right]$$

$$= \frac{t}{3 - 2t}$$

(ii) Let Y represent the number of throws up to and including Gina's *second* hit. This is called a *negative binomial distribution*, given by the formula:

$$P(Y = r) = {}^{r-1}C_1(\tfrac{2}{3})^{r-2}(\tfrac{1}{3})^2 = (r-1)(\tfrac{2}{3})^{r-2}(\tfrac{1}{3})^2.$$

The pgf for Y is

$$G_Y(t) = (\tfrac{1}{3})^2t^2 + 2(\tfrac{2}{3})(\tfrac{1}{3})^2t^3 + 3(\tfrac{2}{3})^2(\tfrac{1}{3})^2t^4 + 4(\tfrac{2}{3})^3(\tfrac{1}{3})^2t^5 + \cdots$$

$$= (\tfrac{1}{3}t)^2[1 + 2(\tfrac{2}{3}t) + 3(\tfrac{2}{3}t)^2 + 4(\tfrac{2}{3}t)^3 + \cdots]$$

$$= (\tfrac{1}{3}t)^2\left[\frac{1}{(1 - \tfrac{2}{3}t)^2}\right]$$

$$= \left[\frac{t}{3 - 2t}\right]^2 = [G_X(t)]^2$$

(iii) The number of throws required until the kth success is equivalent to the sum of k geometric distributions, so the pgf for this sum is the product of the pgfs, i.e. $[G(t)]^k$.

Exercise 4C

1. (i) A fair die is thrown repeatedly until a six occurs. Show that the pgf for the number of throws required is given by:

$$G(t) = \frac{t}{6 - 5t}$$

(ii) Obtain the pgf for the number of throws required to obtain two sixes (not necessarily consecutively).

(iii) Calculate the expected value and variance of the number of throws required to obtain two sixes.

2. The probability distributions of two independent random variables, X and Y, are:

x	1	2
$P(X = x)$	0.6	0.4

y	1	2	3
$P(Y = y)$	0.2	0.5	0.3

(i) Write down the pgfs for X and Y. Hence show that the pgf for $X + Y$ is given by $G(t) = t^2(0.12 + 0.38t + 0.38t^2 + 0.12t^3)$.

(ii) Show that $E(X + Y) = E(X) + E(Y)$ and Var $(X + Y) =$ Var $(X) +$ Var (Y).

3. The discrete random variable X has pgf $G_X(t)$.

(i) Given that $Y = X + c$, where c is a constant, prove that its pgf $G_Y(t)$ is given by $G_Y(t) = t^c G_X(t)$.

(ii) Show that $E(X + c) = E(X) + c$ and Var $(X + c) =$ Var (X).

4. In a traffic census, on a two-way stretch of road, the number of vehicles per minute, X, travelling past a checkpoint in one direction is modelled by a Poisson distribution with parameter 3.4, and the number of vehicles per minute, Y, travelling in the other direction is modelled by a Poisson distribution with parameter 4.8, i.e. $X \sim$ Poisson (3.4) and $Y \sim$ Poisson (4.8).

(i) Find the pgfs for both X and Y.

(ii) Show that $E(X) =$ Var $(X) = 3.4$

(iii) Find the pgf for $X + Y$, the total number of vehicles passing the checkpoint per minute, assuming X and Y are independent.

(iv) Demonstrate in two ways that $E(X + Y) =$ Var $(X + Y) = 8.2$

5. In a machine game of chance, when a lever is pulled one of the numbers 1, 2, 3 appears in a window. The lever is pulled five times and the total score is recorded. The probabilities associated with the numbers 1, 2, 3 are $\frac{1}{6}, \frac{1}{3}, \frac{1}{2}$, respectively.

(i) Write down the pgf for the numbers appearing in the window and so deduce the pgf for the possible total scores.

(ii) Calculate the expected value and variance of the total score.

6. A game consists of rolling two dice, one six-sided and the other four-sided, and adding the scores together. Both dice are fair, the first is numbered 1 to 6 and the second is numbered 1 to 4.

Show that the pgf of Z, where Z is the sum of the scores on the two dice, is:

$$G(t) = \frac{t^2}{24} \times \frac{(1 - t^6)(1 - t^4)}{(1 - t)^2}.$$

PGFs for some standard discrete probability distributions

There are several standard discrete probability distributions which are useful for modelling statistical data. Three of these, the binomial, the Poisson and the geometric distributions, you have met and used before. In this final section you will see how the pgf is derived for each of these discrete distributions and how it is used to provide neat proofs for the expectation, $E(X)$, and variance, Var (X).

The binomial distribution

Let Y be the discrete random variable with probability distribution:

y	0	1
$P(Y = y)$	q	p

The pgf for Y is therefore $G(t) = q + pt$ and $G(1) = q + p = 1$.

Now let the discrete random variable X be defined by $X = Y_1 + Y_2 + \cdots + Y_n$, where each Y_i has pgf $G(t) = q + pt$, then X has pgf $G_X(t)$, given by:

$$G_X(t) = [G(t)]^n = (q + pt)^n.$$

If '1' represents 'success' and '0' represents 'failure', then X represents the number of 'successes' in n independent trials, for which the probability of 'success' is p and the probability of failure is q.

Therefore $X \sim B(n, p)$ with pgf $G_X(t) = (q + pt)^n$.

Having established the pgf, the mean and variance may be proved.

Differentiating with respect to t:

$$G_X'(t) = n(q + pt)^{n-1} \times p = np(q + pt)^{n-1}$$

$$\Rightarrow \quad G_X'(1) = np(q + p)^{n-1} = np$$

$$\text{and} \quad G_X''(t) = (n - 1)np(q + pt)^{n-2} \times p = n(n - 1)p^2(q + pt)^{n-2}$$

$$\Rightarrow \quad G_X''(1) = n(n - 1)p^2(q + p)^{n-2} = n(n - 1)p^2$$

Therefore:

$$E(X) = G_X'(1) = np$$

$$\text{Var}(X) = G_X''(1) + G_X'(1) - (G_X'(1))^2 = n(n - 1)p^2 + np - (np)^2$$

$$= n^2p^2 - np^2 + np - n^2p^2$$

$$= np(1 - p) = npq$$

i.e. $E(X) = np$ and $\text{Var}(X) = npq$

The Poisson distribution

Let X be a Poisson random variable with parameter λ, i.e. $X \sim \text{Poisson}(\lambda)$, then the pgf for X is:

$$G_X(t) = e^{-\lambda} + e^{-\lambda} \times \lambda t + e^{-\lambda} \times \frac{\lambda^2}{2!}t^2 + \cdots + e^{-\lambda} \times \frac{\lambda^r}{r!}t^r + \cdots$$

$$= e^{-\lambda}\left(1 + \lambda t + \frac{(\lambda t)^2}{2!} + \cdots + \frac{(\lambda t)^r}{r!} + \cdots\right) = e^{-\lambda} \times e^{\lambda t} = e^{\lambda(t-1)}$$

Having established the pgf, the mean and variance may be proved.

Differentiating with respect to t:

$$G_X'(t) = \lambda e^{\lambda(t-1)} \quad \Rightarrow \quad G_X'(1) = \lambda e^0 = \lambda$$

$$G_X''(t) = \lambda^2 e^{\lambda(t-1)} \quad \Rightarrow \quad G_X''(1) = \lambda^2 e^0 = \lambda^2$$

Therefore:

$$E(X) = G_X'(1) = \lambda$$

$$\text{Var}(X) = G_X''(1) + G_X'(1) - (G_X'(1))^2 = \lambda^2 + \lambda - (\lambda)^2 = \lambda$$

i.e. $E(X) = \text{Var}(X) = \lambda$

Poisson approximation to the binomial

We know that if $X \sim \text{Binomial}(n, p)$, and n is large, p is small and np is finite (e.g. $n = 150$, $p = 0.02$, $np = 3$), then a good approximation to the distribution of

X is $X \sim \text{Poisson}(\lambda)$, where $\lambda = np$. We now use pgfs to show that the Poisson distribution is the limit of the binomial distribution as $n \to \infty$, $p \to 0$ and np remains finite.

For the binomial distribution $G(t) = (q + pt)^n$, where $q = 1 - p$

$$\Rightarrow \quad G(t) = (1 - p + pt)^n = (1 + p(t - 1))^n$$

But $\lambda = np \Rightarrow p = \dfrac{\lambda}{n}$

$$\Rightarrow \quad G(t) = \left(1 + \frac{\lambda(t - 1)}{n}\right)^n$$

Using the result that $e^x = \lim\left(1 + \dfrac{x}{n}\right)^n$ as $n \to \infty$, the limit of $G(t)$ as $n \to \infty$ is given by:

$$G(t) = \lim\left(1 + \frac{\lambda(t - 1)}{n}\right)^n \text{ as } n \to \infty = e^{\lambda(t-1)}$$

The geometric distribution

If a sequence of independent trials is conducted, for each of which the probability of success is p and that of failure q (where $q = 1 - p$), and the random variable X is the number of the trial on which the first success occurs, then X has a geometric distribution with $P(X = r) = pq^{r-1}$, $r \geqslant 1$.

The corresponding pf is given by:

$$G(t) = pt + pqt^2 + pq^2t^3 + \cdots + pq^{r-1}t^r + \cdots$$

$$= pt\left[1 + qt + (qt)^2 + \cdots + (qt)^{r-1} + \cdots\right]$$

$$= pt\left(\frac{1}{1 - qt}\right) = \frac{pt}{1 - qt}$$

Differentiating with respect to t, using the quotient rule:

$$G'(t) = \frac{(1 - qt) \times p - pt \times (-q)}{(1 - qt)^2} = \frac{p}{(1 - qt)^2} \quad \Rightarrow \quad G'(1) = \frac{p}{(1 - q)^2} = \frac{1}{p}$$

Differentiating with respect to t, using the chain rule:

$$G''(t) = -2p(1 - qt)^{-3} \times (-q) = \frac{2pq}{(1 - qt)^3} \quad \Rightarrow \quad G''(1) = \frac{2pq}{(1 - q)^3} = \frac{2q}{p^2}$$

$$\Rightarrow \quad E(X) = G'(1) = \frac{1}{p}$$

$$\text{Var}(X) = G''(1) + G'(1) - (G'(1))^2$$

$$= \frac{2q}{p^2} + \frac{1}{p} - \left(\frac{1}{p}\right)^2 = \frac{2q + p - 1}{p^2} = \frac{q}{p^2}$$

i.e. $E(X) = \dfrac{1}{p}$ and $\text{Var}(X) = \dfrac{q}{p^2}$

Exercise 4D

1. (i) The random variable X can take values $1, 2, 3, \ldots$ and its pgf is $G(t)$. Show that the probability that X is even is given by $\frac{1}{2}[1 + G(-1)]$.

   (ii) For each of the following probability distributions, state the pgf and, from this, find the probability that the outcome is even:

   (a) the total score when two ordinary dice are thrown;

   (b) the number of attempts it takes Kerry to pass her driving test, given that the probability of passing at any attempt is $\frac{2}{3}$.

2. Two people, A and B, fire alternately at a target, the winner of the game being the first to hit the target. The probability that A hits the target with any particular shots is $\frac{1}{3}$ and the probability that B hits the target with any particular shot is $\frac{1}{4}$.

   Given that A fires first, find:

   (i) the probability that B wins the game with his first shot;

   (ii) the probability that A wins the game with his second shot;

   (iii) the probability that A wins the game.

   (iv) If R is the total number of shots fired by A and B, show that the probability generating function of R is given by:

   $$G(t) = \frac{2t + t^2}{3(2 - t^2)}$$

   Find $E(R)$.

   [Cambridge]

3. (i) The variable X has a Poisson distribution with mean λ. Write down the value of $P(X = r)$ and the pgf for X in the form $G_X(t) = \cdots$

   (ii) The variable Y can take only the values $1, 2, 3, \ldots$ and is such that $P(Y = r) = kP(X = r)$, where k is a constant and $r > 0$. Find the value of k.

   (iii) Show that the pgf of Y is given by

   $$G_Y(t) = \frac{e^{\lambda t} - 1}{e^{\lambda} - 1}.$$

   (iv) Calculate $E(Y)$ and show that $\mathrm{Var}\,(Y) = \mu(\lambda + 1 - \mu)$, where $\mu = E(Y)$.

   [Cambridge]

4. Two duellists take alternate shots at each other until one of them scores a 'hit' on the other. If the probability that the first duellist scores a 'hit' is $\frac{1}{5}$ and the probability that the second scores a 'hit' is $\frac{1}{3}$, find the expected number of shots *before* a hit.

5. Independent trials, on each of which the probability of a 'success' is p $(0 < p < 1)$, are being carried out. The random variable, X, counts the number of trials up to and including that on which the first 'success' is obtained.

   (i) Write down an expression for $P(X = x)$ for $x = 1, 2, \ldots$ and show that the probability generating function of X is:

   $$G(t) = \frac{pt}{1 - qt}$$

   where $q = 1 - p$.

   (ii) Use $G(t)$ to find the mean and variance of X.

   (iii) The random variable Y counts the number of trials up to and including that on which the kth 'success' is obtained. Write down, in terms of p, q and t, an expression for the probability generating function of Y.

   [MEI]

6. The independent random variables X and Y have Poisson distributions with parameters θ_1 and θ_2 respectively.

   (i) Write down an expression for $P(X = x)$ and an expression for $P(Y = y)$ and, from this, derive an expression for $P(X + Y = z)$, where x, y, z are non-negative integers. Simplify the expression for $P(X + Y = z)$ as far as possible.

   (ii) Obtain the probability generating function (pgf) of the random variable X; deduce the pgf of Y and hence obtain the pgf of $X + Y$.

   (iii) Use this pgf to find:

   (a) $P(X + Y = z)$, where z is a non-negative integer;

(b) the mean of $X + Y$;

(c) the variance of $X + Y$.

[**MEI**]

7. The variable R has probability generating function given by $G(t) = ke^{t^2+t}$, where k is a constant. Find k and obtain:

(i) $P(R = 0)$, $P(R = 1)$, $P(R = 2)$, $P(R = 3)$ and $P(R = 4)$;

(ii) the mean of R;

(iii) the variance of R;

(iv) the smallest value r_0 of R for which $P(R > r_0) < 0.4$.

[**Cambridge**]

8. In a simple model for forecasting the weather at a seaside resort, each day's weather is classified as either dull or fine. The probability that the weather on any one day will be the same as that on the preceding day has a constant value, p, independently of the weather on earlier days. The probability that the first day of the holiday season will be fine is θ.

Let P_n denote the probability that the nth day of the holiday season will be fine, so that $P_1 = \theta$.

(i) Show that, for $n \geqslant 2$,
$$P_n = (2p - 1)P_{n-1} + (1 - p) \qquad (*)$$

(ii) Let $H(t)$ denote the generating function for the probabilities P_n, i.e.

$$H(t) = \sum_{n=1}^{\infty} P_n t^n, \text{ for an appropriate range}$$

of values of t. By multiplying each side of $(*)$ by t^n and summing from $n = 2$ to $n = \infty$, show that:

$$H(t) - \theta t = (2p - 1)tH(t) + (1 - p)\frac{t^2}{1 - t}$$

and therefore that $H(t) =$
$\theta t + t^2(1 - p - \theta)[1 - t]^{-1}[1 - (2p - 1)t]^{-1}$

(iii) From this, or otherwise, obtain an expression for P_n [**MEI**]

9. Every packet of a well-known brand of cornflakes contains a plastic spaceman, drawn at random from a set of N different spacemen. I am trying to collect a complete set. Suppose that, at the stage when I have managed to collect $j - 1$ different spacemen, the variable X_j $(j = 1, 2, \ldots, N)$ denotes the number of

additional packets I have to buy until I get my jth new spaceman.

(i) Show that the probability that $X_j = k$ (for $k = 1, 2, 3, \ldots$) may be expressed in the form $q_j^{k-1}p_j$, for some suitable p_j, q_j which should be specified.

(ii) Find the generator for these probabilities and use it to find $E(X_j)$.

(iii) Also show that the variance $\mathrm{Var}\,(X_j) = N(j - 1)/(N - j + 1)^2$.

(iv) Let X be the total number of packets I have to buy, starting from scratch, in order to collect the full set of spacemen. Use the relation:

$$X = X_1 + X_2 + \cdots + X_N$$

to show that

$$E(X) = N\left(1 + \frac{1}{2} + \frac{1}{3} + \cdots + \frac{1}{N}\right)$$

and find an expression of a similar kind for $\mathrm{Var}\,(X)$.

[**O&C, SMP**]

10. Three balls, **a**, **b**, **c** are placed at random in three boxes **A**, **B**, **C** (with one ball in each box). The random variable X is defined by: $X = 1$ if ball **a** is in box **A**, $X = 0$ otherwise.

(i) Find the probability generator for X.

The variable Y is defined in the table:

	Box			Value
	A	**B**	**C**	of Y
Contents	a	b	c	1
	c	a	b	0
	b	c	a	0
	a	c	b	0
	b	a	c	1
	c	b	a	1

(ii) Deduce the probability generator of Y.

(iii) The variable S is defined by $S = X + Y + 1$. Given that X, Y are independent, show that S has generator $\frac{1}{6}(t^3 + 3t^2 + 2t)$ and deduce the mean and variance of S.

[**O&C, SMP**]

K E Y   P O I N T S

- For a discrete probability distribution, the *probability generating function (pgf)* is defined by:

$$G(t) = E(t^X) = \sum_x t^x p_x, \quad \text{where} \quad p_x = P(X = x)$$

- Sum of probabilities $= 1 \Rightarrow G(1) = 1$

- *Expectation:* $E(X) = G'(1) = \mu$

- *Variance:* $\operatorname{Var}(X) = G''(1) + G'(1) - (G'(1))^2 = G''(1) + \mu - \mu^2$

- Special probability generating functions:

Probability distribution	$P(X = r)$	pgf $G_X(t)$	Expectation $E(X)$	Variance $\operatorname{Var}(X)$
Binomial	$^nC_r q^{n-r} p^r$	$(q + pt)^n$	np	npq
Poisson	$e^{-\lambda} \dfrac{\lambda^r}{r!}$	$e^{\lambda(t-1)}$	λ	λ
Geometric	$q^{r-1} p$	$\dfrac{pt}{1 - qt}$	$\dfrac{1}{p}$	$\dfrac{q}{p^2}$

- For two *independent* random variables X and Y: $G_{X+Y}(t) = G_X(t)G_Y(t)$

5 Moment generating functions

The human mind has first to construct forms, independently, before we can find them in things.

Albert Einstein

In Chapter 4, on probability generating functions, you saw how useful the concept of auxiliary functions of this kind can be. One illustration of their usefulness is in obtaining means and variances, e.g. it is very much easier to obtain the mean and variance of a binomial distribution using its probability generating function than by using standard algebraic summation techniques.

However, this is only a small part of the value of probability generating functions. Their real worth is in giving an alternative approach to specifying *all* our knowledge about discrete random variables. In most of the examples and exercises in Chapter 4, you worked 'forwards' in the sense that you were given a probability distribution and asked to find its probability generating function. However, this process can also be carried out 'backwards' – if you are given a probability generating function, you can, so to speak, 'undo it' and obtain the complete set of probabilities for the underlying random variable. In other words, *all the information about a discrete random variable* is contained in its probability generating function. In the work you have done so far, it has rarely, if ever, been necessary for you to use probability generating functions in this way; it has been more natural, and usually easier, to work with the individual probabilities or the probability function. In more advanced work, however, this is very often not so – it can be much easier to use the probability generating function to obtain results. Indeed, the ease with which the mean and variance of the binomial (or Poisson) distribution can be obtained is, perhaps, a first step in this direction.

There is, however, an obvious drawback in this use of probability generating functions. They only make sense for discrete random variables. This is, of course, because continuous random variables do not have individual probabilities to generate. So all the advantages of the generating functions approach would be restricted to discrete random variables if probability generating functions were the only functions that could be used in this sort of work. Fortunately, however, this is not the case. There is another generating function, called the *moment generating function*, which can sensibly be applied for both discrete and continuous random variables. As its name suggests, it generates quantities called *moments*. It is now necessary to break off the thread of the development of this work in order to introduce the concept of moments.

Moments

Moments are merely expected values of particular functions of a random variable. In a sense, they generalise the very familiar ideas of mean and variance. (If you are studying advanced mechanics, you will also be able to see analogies with the concepts of centre of mass and moment of inertia.)

Given any random variable, X, the mean is simply the expected value of X itself. Using the customary notation of the Greek letter μ, the definition of the mean is

$$\mu = E[X] = \sum_x x \cdot P(X = x)$$
for a discrete random variable, X, where the summation is over all the values that x can take;

$$= \int x f(x) \, dx$$
for a continuous random variable, X, where $f(x)$ is the pdf.

Similarly, the variance σ^2 is defined as $E[(X - \mu)^2]$. This expected value has a similar definition as a sum for a discrete random variable or an integral for a continuous one. In most expressions of this type from now on, only the integral giving the continuous definition will be displayed; you will need to understand that for discrete random variables an analogous expression involving a summation is required. Thus the variance is given by:

$$\sigma^2 = \int (x - \mu)^2 f(x) \, dx.$$

Notice that both the mean and the variance are defined as the expected value of a *power* of a deviation of X from a specified *point*. The point is 0 (zero) in the case of the mean, and the mean μ itself in the case of the variance. The power is 1 in the case of the mean and 2 in the case of the variance. We can now generalise this idea by considering the expected value of any power of the deviation of X from any point as follows:

$$E[(X - a)^r].$$

This quantity is called the r*th moment of the distribution of X about the point a* (the words 'the distribution of' and 'the point' are sometimes omitted). Usually the power, r, is limited to positive integers. The point, a, in the definition can be any point but is usually taken to be either 0 (giving what are called 'moments about zero' or 'moments about the origin') or the mean μ (giving what are called 'moments about the mean', or sometimes 'central moments' on the (somewhat misleading!) basis that the mean can be considered as the 'centre' of the distribution).

NOTE

Sometimes it is also convenient to include the case r = 0, *giving what is sometimes called the 'zeroth moment' or the 'moment of zero order'. This is* always *equal to 1, no matter what the point,* a, *in the definition is. This is because any quantity raised to power zero is 1; thus* $E[(X - a)^0] = E[1]$ *which is, of course, equal to 1.*

If you consider the mean and the variance in terms of this generalised definition, you can see that the mean is the first moment about zero and the variance is the second moment about the mean. Thus moments about zero can be thought of, in a sense, as a sort of generalisation of the idea of the mean; and, similarly, moments about the mean are a sort of generalisation of the idea of variance.

A special notation is often used for moments about zero and about the mean. The rth moment about zero is denoted by μ'_r (read this as '$\mu\, r$ dash') and the rth moment about the mean as μ_r (without the dash; read it as '$\mu\, r$'). So, in this general moments notation, the mean would be written as μ'_1 and the variance as μ_2.

You already know, of course, that the mean and variance give important summaries of a distribution – its 'location' and 'spread', respectively. Some higher moments also have helpful geometrical interpretations concerning the shape of the distribution.

Thus the third moment gives a measure of *skewness*. For a distribution that is symmetrical, $\mu_3 = 0$. Unfortunately this is not true in reverse – asymmetric distributions can be constructed which have $\mu_3 = 0$ (a very simple case is shown in the exercise on page 71). Usually, however, distributions that are 'skewed to the left' have $\mu_3 > 0$ and are therefore called 'positively skew', while distributions that are 'skewed to the right' have $\mu_3 < 0$ and are called 'negatively skew'. (Simple examples of this are also shown in the exercises.) You may have worked out skewness measures for data, perhaps as part of coursework exercises at an early stage in your study of statistics. What is being done here is to find the corresponding measures for the whole distribution.

Proceeding onwards, the fourth moment gives a measure of how flat-topped or otherwise the 'peak' that typically occurs in the centre of a distribution is. This is sometimes referred to as a measure of the *kurtosis* of a distribution, 'kurtosis' being a Greek word that means 'flatness'. Further geometrical interpretations can be found for yet higher moments, although they quickly become rather obscure.

You can obtain moments for any distribution by working out the sum or integral that gives the expected value. Sometimes this is easy and sometimes, of course, it can be very difficult! Sometimes it turns out that the moments are given by a fairly simple formula, an example of which follows.

EXAMPLE

Exponential distribution
Find a formula for the rth moment about the origin for the exponential distribution and from this find the mean and variance of this distribution.

Solution:

The exponential distribution (sometimes called the negative exponential distribution) with parameter λ (where $\lambda > 0$) has probability density function:

$$\mathrm{f}(x) = \lambda \mathrm{e}^{-\lambda x} \quad \text{for } x \geqslant 0$$

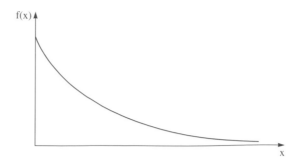

Figure 5.1

This distribution provides a useful model for many situations such as waiting times in queues. The rth moment about the origin is:

$$\mu'_r = E[X^r] = \int_0^\infty x^r \cdot \lambda e^{-\lambda x}\, dx$$

$$= \lambda \int_0^\infty x^r e^{-\lambda x}\, dx.$$

You can readily find this integral by repeated integration by parts and you will get:

$$\mu'_r = \frac{r!}{\lambda^r}$$

This is valid for any positive integer r (and also for the trivial case $r = 0$).

You can now quickly write down the mean and variance using this general formula. The mean is simply μ'_1 which is $1/\lambda$. To obtain the variance, use the familiar expression $\text{Var}(X) = E[X^2] - \{E[X]\}^2$ which, in general moments notation, becomes:

$$\text{Var}(X) = \mu'_2 - \{\mu'_1\}^2$$

$$= \frac{2!}{\lambda^2} - \left(\frac{1}{\lambda}\right)^2 = \frac{1}{\lambda^2}$$

You have seen in this subsection that moments give a sort of generalisation of the ideas of mean and variance and can have useful geometrical interpretations. This, however, is not the real point of introducing and studying the general idea of moments. Their real power is that they give *an alternative way of specifying all the information about a distribution*. In the example above, about the negative exponential distribution, and in the exercises, you start with a distribution whose probabilities or probability density function are known, from which you find some moments. However, this process can also be done *in reverse*. If you know all the moments of a distribution, you can 'undo' them and discover the probabilities or probability density function for the distribution. It will not be obvious to you how to do this (and sometimes it is very difficult!) but the point is that it *can* be done. It may also not be obvious to you *why* you should want to do this! Certainly there has been no need to do it in any of the work you have studied so far. In more advanced statistical theory, however, it is actually very often useful and more convenient to work with moments of distributions rather than directly with the underlying probabilities; the fact that this *can be done* makes moments very important in statistics.

You will remember that in the introduction to this chapter much the same thing was said about probability generating functions. As you move on to study moment generating functions, you will see the ideas come together – the moment generating function will give you another way of specifying all the information about a distribution, and it will do this in a way that is often very convenient to use in advanced work.

You should note, however, that there is a problem when working with moments. Sometimes, in obtaining a moment by working out a sum or integral, the answer comes to ∞ or to $-\infty$, or, even worse, does not converge to a sensible answer (even to $\pm\infty$) at all. In such cases, all that can be said is that the moment concerned does not exist. Fortunately, this does not happen with most of the everyday distributions that are useful models and which are met in usual statistical practice. Nevertheless, it can happen, and this introduces considerable complications in the full advanced theory connected with moments. These complications are a long way beyond the scope of this book and you need not be concerned about them, but you should know that they exist.

Exercise 5A

1. The discrete random variable, X, takes values -2, 1 or 3 with probabilities:

$$P(X = -2) = 2/5$$

$$P(X = 1) = 1/2$$

$$P(X = 3) = 1/10$$

Find the value of μ_3 for this distribution.
[**HINT:** *Notice that the mean of the distribution is 0, so μ_3 is simply $E[X^3]$.*]
[**NOTE:** *You should find $\mu_3 = 0$ – yet this is clearly an* **asymmetric** *distribution.*]

2. Prove the results:

(i) $\mu_2 = \mu_2' - \{\mu_1'\}^2$

(ii) $\mu_3 = \mu_3' - 3\mu_1'\mu_2' + 2\{\mu_1'\}^3$

[**NOTE:** *Notice that the first of these results expresses the familiar formula*
$\mathrm{Var}\,(X) = E[X^2] - \{E[X]\}^2$ *in general moments notation, and shows how the second moment about the mean can be worked out from moments about the origin. Similarly, the second result expresses the third moment about the mean in terms of moments about the origin.*

Similar results can be found for fourth and higher moments. These results are often useful when trying to work out moments about the mean.]

3. The continuous random variable, X, has probability density function:

$$f(x) = \begin{cases} 3x^2 & 0 < x < 1 \\ 0 & \text{elsewhere} \end{cases}$$

(i)   Sketch the graph of $f(x)$ and notice that it is 'skewed to the right'.

(ii) Using the results of Question 2, or otherwise, find μ_3.

4. Repeat Question 3 for the random variable with probability density function:

$$f(x) = \begin{cases} 3(1 - x)^2 & 0 < x < 1 \\ 0 & \text{elsewhere} \end{cases}$$

noticing that this graph is 'skewed to the left'.

Activity

Investigate the third moment about the mean, μ_3, for some continuous distributions. Work out the value of μ_3 for some symmetric distributions, confirming that it is always zero. (You will probably find the second result in Exercise 5A, Question 2 helpful. The simplest case to work with is the uniform or rectangular distribution, but you should try some others as well.) Now work it out for some asymmetric distributions (you could start with the exponential distribution – remember that a general formula for its moments about the origin was found in the worked example earlier in this chapter); you will nearly always find it to be non-zero (as happened in Exercise 5A, Questions 3 and 4).

Now try to create some continuous distributions that are asymmetric and yet have $\mu_3 = 0$. You will probably find it best to make sure the mean is zero, and then try probability density functions which are a different shape for negative x than for positive x. Distributions that you create in this way are likely to be somewhat artificial and not particularly useful models, but you should begin to get a good appreciation of shape.

Moment generating functions

The moment generating function for a discrete or a continuous random variable, X, is defined in the following way. (You will see a little later on how this function generates the moments.) First, recall again that for the probability generating function, the definition is given by $E[t^X]$. For the moment generating function, often abbreviated to mgf and often denoted by $M_X(\theta)$, the definition is:

$$M_X(\theta) = E[e^{\theta X}] = \sum_x e^{\theta x} \cdot P(X = x)$$ for a discrete random variable, X, where the summation is over all the values, x, that it can take;

$$= \int e^{\theta x} f(x)\, dx$$ for a continuous random variable, X, where $f(x)$ is the pdf.

The θ in this definition is merely a 'dummy variable', just like the t in the definition of the probability generating function. You can, of course, use any letter you like for this; t, θ and z are commonly used.

You will next see several worked examples of obtaining moment generating functions using this definition. In the first few examples, you will see cases where the mgf is easy to obtain; but gradually it will become more difficult and you will see examples where it cannot be obtained at all because the sum or integral in the definition does not come out to a sensible finite answer. This is, in fact, another aspect of the problem referred to at the end of the subsection on moments, that moments sometimes do not exist. In the same way, moment generating functions sometimes do not exist. As with moments themselves, this (fortunately!) does not happen for distributions that commonly turn up in statistical work. However, it can happen and this complicates the general theory of generating functions. Nevertheless, moment generating functions are *extremely* useful in statistics.

Just to give you a look ahead to yet more advanced work, well beyond the scope of this book, there is another auxiliary function, called the 'characteristic function', which is similar to the moment generating function but which is defined using a complex variable instead of the real variable θ. By going to this higher level of mathematical sophistication, it turns out that you get a function which always exists and so can be used in a completely general way in statistical theory.

After you have looked at the examples, you will learn about the general properties of moment generating functions, including how they can be used to generate the moments. You will also see some of the many other uses of moment generating functions.

One of the uses that you will see is in proving results about sums of random variables. To help you to follow the thread of the development of mgf work, one very important result about sums will gradually be built up for you as you come to various stages of the work. This is the result that, roughly speaking, 'Normal distributions add up'. Strictly speaking, the result is that if:

$$X_1 \sim N(\mu_1, \sigma_1^2),$$

$$X_2 \sim N(\mu_2, \sigma_2^2),$$

$$\dots,$$

$$X_n \sim N(\mu_n, \sigma_n^2)$$

and all these random variables are independent, then:

$$X_1 + X_2 + \cdots + X_n \sim N(\mu_1 + \mu_2 + \cdots + \mu_n, \sigma_1^2 + \sigma_2^2 + \cdots + \sigma_n^2).$$

You will already have used this result a large number of times and are probably quite familiar with proving that the mean and variance of the sum are as stated. However, you will not have proved that the distribution of the sum is Normal. You will see how to do this using moment generating functions. It would be very much more difficult to do it otherwise!

Questions 1 and 2 in Exercise 5B at the end of this chapter ask you to prove similar results for binomial and Poisson distributions.

EXAMPLE

Binomial distribution $B(n, p)$
Find the mgf for the $B(n, p)$ distribution.

Solution:

Here the probability is:

$$P(X = x) = \binom{n}{x} p^x q^{n-x}$$

You may have learnt this using r rather than x as is used here

$$\text{for } x = 0, 1, 2, \dots, n$$

so the mgf is:

$$M_X(\theta) = E[e^{\theta X}] = \sum_{x=0}^{n} e^{\theta x} \binom{n}{x} p^x q^{n-x}$$

Notice $e^{\theta x} p^x = (p e^\theta)^x$

$$= \sum_{x=0}^{n} \binom{n}{x} (p e^\theta)^x q^{n-x}$$

You ought to recognise this as a binomial expansion but, in case you don't, you can write out a few terms of it as follows (this shows the terms for $x = 0, 1, 2$ and n):

$$q^n + \binom{n}{1}(pe^\theta)q^{n-1} + \binom{n}{2}(pe^\theta)^2 q^{n-2} + \cdots + (pe^\theta)^n$$

You can now see this to be the binomial expansion of:

$$(q + pe^\theta)^n$$

and so this is the moment generating function for $B(n, p)$.

Before proceeding to the next example, recall the probability generating function for $B(n, p)$. Using θ as the dummy variable, this is $(q + p\theta)^n$. You should now notice that the moment generating function is *exactly the same functional form* as the probability generating function except that e^θ has replaced θ. You will see this happen again in the next example.

Another point you should notice is that there is no problem at all here of the mgf not existing. It is a simple finite sum of finite terms and is therefore bound to come out to a finite answer.

EXAMPLE

Poisson distribution Poisson (m)
Find the mgf for the Poisson (m) distribution.

Solution:

In this example, the letter m is used as the Poisson parameter to avoid any possible confusion with the θ that is the dummy variable of the mgf. The probability function is:

$$P(X = x) = \frac{e^{-m}m^x}{x!} \quad \text{for } x = 0, 1, 2, \ldots$$

so the mgf is:

$$M_X(\theta) = E[e^{\theta X}] = \sum_{x=0}^{\infty} e^{\theta x}\frac{e^{-m}m^x}{x!}$$

$$= e^{-m}\sum_{x=0}^{\infty} \frac{(me^\theta)^x}{x!}$$

As in the previous example, you ought to recognise the form of the summation here, but, again, if you don't recognise it, write out a few terms to see what is happening:

$$M_X(\theta) = e^{-m}\left\{1 + me^\theta + \frac{(me^\theta)^2}{2!} + \frac{(me^\theta)^3}{3!} + \cdots\right\}$$

$$= e^{-m}e^{me^\theta}$$

This, then, is the moment generating function for Poisson (m).

As with the $B(n, p)$ example, recall now the probability generating function for Poisson (m). Using θ as the dummy variable, this is $e^{-m}e^{m\theta}$. Notice again that the moment generating function is *exactly the same functional form* as the probability generating function except that e^θ has replaced θ.

Another point to notice is that there is no problem of the mgf not existing. Although in this case it is an infinite sum, it comes out to a finite answer.

5

Standard Normal distribution $N(0,1)$
Find the mgf for the $N(0,1)$ distribution.

Solution:

The probability density function here is:

$$f(x) = \frac{1}{\sqrt{2\pi}} e^{-x^2/2}$$

and the moment generating function is:

$$M_X(\theta) = E[e^{\theta X}] = \frac{1}{\sqrt{2\pi}} \int_{-\infty}^{\infty} e^{\theta x - x^2/2}\, dx.$$

This integral can be found by completing the square in the exponent:

$$\theta x - \frac{x^2}{2} = \frac{\theta^2}{2} - \tfrac{1}{2}(x - \theta)^2$$

and so

$$M_X(\theta) = \frac{1}{\sqrt{2\pi}} e^{\theta^2/2} \int_{-\infty}^{\infty} e^{-(x-\theta)^2/2}\, dx$$

This integral may appear daunting but, in fact, it is trivial once you spot the fact that you don't really need to work it out at all! For, taking the $1/\sqrt{(2\pi)}$ with the integrand, you will see that you have created the probability density function of $N(\theta, 1)$ which *simply* integrates to 1. So the moment generating function of $N(0,1)$ is:

$$e^{\theta^2/2}$$

This is a result you should try to remember.

This is the first intermediate result that you will need in proving the result about 'Normal distributions adding up'. Recall that it is the mgf for $N(0,1)$. You will see later how to obtain the mgf for the general Normal distribution $N(\mu, \sigma^2)$ from this mgf.

As $N(0,1)$ is a continuous random variable, there is no probability generating function here with which to compare the moment generating function. However, you can see again the point about there being no problem of non-existence. You had to evaluate an integral, both of whose limits were infinite – but it came out to a simple finite answer.

Exponential distribution
Find the moment generating function for the exponential distribution.

Solution:

The probability density function here is:

$$f(x) = \lambda e^{-\lambda x} \quad \text{for } x \geqslant 0, \text{ where } \lambda \text{ is a parameter } (\lambda > 0)$$

and the moment generating function is:

$$M_X(\theta) = E[e^{\theta X}] = \int_0^\infty e^{\theta x} \cdot \lambda e^{-\lambda x}\, dx$$

$$= \lambda \int_0^\infty e^{-(\lambda-\theta)x}\, dx$$

$$= \lambda \left[\frac{e^{-(\lambda-\theta)x}}{-(\lambda-\theta)} \right]_{x=0}^{x=\infty}$$

$$= [0] - \left[\lambda \frac{1}{\theta - \lambda} \right]$$

$$= \frac{\lambda}{\lambda - \theta} = \left(1 - \frac{\theta}{\lambda} \right)^{-1}$$

You might have noticed some problems in working out this integral. Remember that θ is simply a real variable which, at first sight, may take any value. On the other hand, λ is a (positive) parameter whose value is fixed for any particular exponential distribution. You should be able to see immediately that you cannot allow θ to equal λ, for this would give rise to division by zero.

Rather more subtly, you also cannot allow θ to be greater than λ. This is because, in evaluating the upper limit of the integral, you have to take $x = \infty$ in the expression $e^{-(\lambda-\theta)x}$. If $\lambda - \theta$ is itself negative, you will get $e^{+\infty}$ which is, of course, infinite; so you cannot allow θ to be greater than λ. Provided $\lambda - \theta$ is positive, there is no difficulty – you simply get $e^{-\infty}$ which is zero, as is shown in the derivation above.

This means that the exponential distribution is a case where the moment generating function can only sensibly be defined for a *limited range* of values of the dummy real variable θ – you have to limit it to $\theta < \lambda$. Recalling that λ is a positive parameter, you can see that this means that θ is restricted to only some positive values, although it can be allowed to take any negative value. This is in contrast with the binomial, Poisson and Normal distributions in the first three examples, where θ can take any value at all.

In the next two examples, you will meet cases where the required restrictions on θ get progressively worse.

You need not worry if you do not understand the technical details in the next two examples. They are included merely to show cases of 'things going wrong'. If you want to, you could ignore these next examples and pick up the thread of the work again on page 77.

EXAMPLE

This is a rather artificial example. It is unlikely to be a good model for any practical situation, but it gives you a good illustration of 'something going wrong'. Consider the discrete random variable, X, which takes values $1, 2, 3, \ldots$ and for which the probability function is:

$$P(X = x) = \frac{6}{\pi^2 x^2}$$

for $x = 1, 2, 3, \ldots$. Although this is artificial, you can show that it is a well-defined random variable – all the probabilities are positive and less than one, and the sum of them all comes to one. However, the moment generating function would be:

$$E[e^{\theta X}] = \sum_{x=1}^{\infty} \frac{6e^{\theta x}}{\pi^2 x^2}$$

You should be able to see that if θ is positive then, as x increases, the numerator terms are going to get larger and larger more quickly (*much* more quickly!) than the denominator terms, so that the sum cannot possibly converge to any finite answer. On the other hand, if θ is negative then the numerator terms are all negative powers of e, which become smaller and smaller (i.e. tend to zero) as x increases, so the sum will converge to a finite answer. There remains the special case $\theta = 0$. This is trivial for, in this case, the numerator is simply 6 (because $e^0 = 1$), so the sum is simply the same as the sum of the individual probabilities and is therefore equal to one.

This example provides a case where the moment generating function could not be defined for any positive values of θ, although it would be all right for all negative values (and for zero).

The next example is one stage even worse – you will see that the moment generating function in it cannot be defined for any non-zero values of θ.

EXAMPLE

Cauchy distribution
The continuous random variable, X, is said to have a Cauchy distribution if its probability density function is:

$$f(x) = \frac{1}{\pi(1 + x^2)}$$

for all values of x (i.e. for $-\infty < x < \infty$). It is trivial to show that this is a well-defined random variable – the density function is positive everywhere and the integral of it over the full range of x is 1. You might wish to spend a few minutes sketching the graph of the density function – notice that it is very similar to the Normal distribution in its general shape, but slightly 'flatter in the middle' and 'thicker in the tails'.

However, the moment generating function would be:

$$E[e^{\theta x}] = \int_{-\infty}^{\infty} \frac{e^{\theta x}}{\pi(1 + x^2)} \, dx$$

Without going into details, you should be able to see that this integral must give an infinite answer, at the upper limit if θ is positive or at the lower limit if θ is negative. The only value of θ for which the integral gives a finite answer is $\theta = 0$, for in this case it reduces trivially to the integral of the density function itself, which, of course, is one.

It is usual to regard the moment generating function as existing only if the sum or integral defining it converges to a finite answer for, *at least*, all values of θ in some finite interval *around* the origin – that is, *at least for some positive AND for some negative* values of θ. Thus the binomial, Poisson and Normal distributions immediately qualify, for with these the answer is finite for all positive and all negative values of θ. The exponential distribution also qualifies, for the answer is finite for some positive and all negative values of θ. The artificial distribution in the example on page 76 does not qualify, for there are *no* positive values of θ that give a finite answer. Nor does the Cauchy distribution do so, for there are no non-zero values of θ at all that give a finite answer.

As was stated before the examples, this problem of non-existence does limit the theoretical usefulness of moment generating functions but, nevertheless, they are very useful because for the routine 'everyday' distributions the problem of non-existence does not arise.

You saw that, even in the 'awkward' examples, the moment generating function came out to a simple finite answer (1) in the special case $\theta = 0$. This is, in fact, trivial to prove in general. By definition, the moment generating function is $E[e^{\theta X}]$ which, in the case $\theta = 0$, reduces to $E[e^0]$ which is, immediately, $E[1] = 1$.

Properties of moment generating functions

Relationship with probability generating functions

In the first two examples (the binomial and Poisson distributions), you saw that the functional form of the moment generating function was exactly the same as that of the probability generating function except that the dummy variable, θ, in the pgf was replaced by e^θ in the mgf. This is true in general and can very easily be seen from the basic definitions.

The general result is as follows: if a discrete random variable has pgf $G(\theta)$, then its mgf is $G(e^\theta)$. This follows because the mgf is $E[e^{\theta X}]$ by definition, and the pgf is $E[\theta^X]$ by definition – so you can see straight away in the definitions that all that has happened is that θ in the pgf has become e^θ in the mgf.

'Linear transformation' result

You can easily obtain the moment generating function of a random variable that is a linear transformation of another random variable whose mgf is known. Suppose a random variable, X, has mgf, $M(\theta)$, which is known, and a random variable, Y, is given by $Y = a + bX$ where a and b are known constants. Then the mgf of Y is, by definition:

$$E[e^{\theta Y}] = E[e^{\theta(aX+b)}]$$

$$= E[e^{b\theta} \cdot e^{a\theta X}] \quad \text{(remember now that } \theta \text{ is not a random variable;}$$
$$\text{the expectation is with respect to } X)$$

$$= e^{b\theta}E[e^{(a\theta)X}] \quad \text{(now notice that } E[e^{(a\theta)X}] \text{ is simply the mgf of } X$$
$$\text{with } \theta \text{ replaced by } a\theta)$$

$$= e^{b\theta}M(a\theta)$$

This result is often useful. Two examples of how to apply it follow. The first is somewhat artificial but gives a simple illustration of the technique; the second is more important, showing how the mgf of the general Normal distribution can be obtained from the mgf of $N(0,1)$ which you saw on page 75.

EXAMPLE

Suppose X is the binomial random variable $B(n, p)$ and $Y = 7X - 4$. Find the mgf for Y.

Solution:

You saw in the example on page 75 that the mgf, $M(\theta)$, for the random variable $X \sim B(n, p)$ is $(q + pe^{\theta})^n$. Now you have $Y = 7X - 4$ which is a linear transformation of $X : Y = aX + b$ with $a = 7$ and $b = -4$. So you can immediately write down the answer that the mgf of Y is:

$$e^{-4\theta}(q + pe^{7\theta})^n$$

EXAMPLE

Find the mgf for the general Normal random variable $Y \sim N(\mu, \sigma^2)$.

Solution:

In the example on page 75, you saw that the mgf for the standard Normal random variable $X \sim N(0, 1)$ is:

$$e^{\theta^2/2}$$

You now have that Y is a linear transformation of $X : Y = \sigma X + \mu$. So you can write down the answer that the mgf of Y is:

$$e^{\mu\theta}e^{(\sigma\theta)^2/2} = e^{\mu\theta + (\sigma^2\theta^2/2)}$$

You can, incidentally, obtain this by explicit integration using the probability density function of $N(\mu, \sigma^2)$ but, as you have already obtained the mgf of $N(0, 1)$, it is much easier to use the linear transformation result as shown here.

The result in this example is the next stage in proving the result about 'Normal distributions adding up'. You now have the mgf for the general Normal distribution $N(\mu, \sigma^2)$. You can apply this for each of the Normal random variables $X_1, X_2, \ldots, X_n$ in the result by putting the appropriate subscript $1, 2, \ldots n$ on each of μ and σ^2.

You may remember that there is a similar 'linear transformation' result for probability generating functions. This is also true for the next result – most aspects of probability and moment generating functions are very similar.

Convolution theorem

This is a *very important* result. It is also very simple, both to state and to prove. It simply says that the moment generating function for a *sum* of *independent* random variables is the *product* of their separate moment generating functions.

To prove the result, consider the case of two independent random variables, X and Y, both of whose moment generating functions are known, and let Z be their sum, $Z = X + Y$. Then the mgf of Z is, by definition:

$$E[e^{\theta Z}] = E[e^{\theta(X+Y)}] = E[e^{\theta X} \cdot e^{\theta Y}]$$

You now need to use the theorem that the expected value of a product involving independent random variables is the product of the separate expected values. (This theorem is proved in the theory of bivariate distributions). Using the theorem, you get:

$$E[e^{\theta X} \cdot e^{\theta Y}] = E[e^{\theta X}] \cdot E[e^{\theta Y}]$$

which, immediately, is the product of the two separate moment generating functions. Obviously, this proof can be extended to a sum of any number of independent random variables.

The convolution theorem often provides the easiest way of handling problems involving sums of (independent) random variables.

Continuing with the result about 'Normal distributions adding up', you can now write down the mgf for the sum of the independent Normal random variables – it is simply the product of their individual moment generating functions. So it is:

$$e^{\mu_1\theta+(\sigma_1^2\theta^2/2)} \cdot e^{\mu_2\theta+(\sigma_2^2\theta^2/2)} \cdot \ldots \cdot e^{\mu_n\theta+(\sigma_n^2\theta^2/2)}$$

$$= e^{(\mu_1+\mu_2+\cdots+\mu_n)\theta} + \frac{(\sigma_1^2 + \sigma_2^2 + \cdots + \sigma_n^2)\theta^2}{2}$$

To complete the result, you now need to know how to show that the distribution underlying this new mgf is $N(\mu_1 + \mu_2 + \cdots + \mu_n, \sigma_1^2 + \sigma_2^2 + \cdots + \sigma_n^2)$. You will see how to do this a little later on.

Generation of moments

There are two ways in which you can obtain moments from a moment generating function.

First, consider expanding the mgf in a power series. Letting $M(\theta)$ denote a general mgf, for a random variable X, we get:

$$M(\theta) = E[e^{\theta X}]$$

$$= \left[1 + \theta X + \frac{\theta^2 X^2}{2!} + \frac{\theta^3 X^3}{3!} + \cdots \right] \qquad \text{(now take expected values term by term)}$$

$$= 1 + \theta E[X] + \frac{\theta^2}{2!} E[X^2] + \frac{\theta^3}{3!} E[X^3] + \cdots \qquad \text{(which we now write in general moments notation)}$$

$$= 1 + \theta \mu_1' + \frac{\theta^2}{2!} \mu_2' + \frac{\theta^3}{3!} \mu_3' + \cdots$$

So the rth moment about the origin, μ_r', appears as the coefficient of $\theta^r/r!$ in this expansion.

Normal distribution $N(0, 1)$

Use the power series expansion method to obtain the moments of the $N(0, 1)$ distribution.

Solution:

For $N(0, 1)$ you have:

$$M(\theta) = e^{\theta^2/2}$$

$$= 1 + (\theta^2/2) + \left(\frac{(\theta^2/2)^2}{2!}\right) + \left(\frac{(\theta^2/2)^3}{3!}\right) + \cdots$$

$$= 1 + 0 \cdot \theta + \frac{\theta^2}{2!} \cdot 1 + 0 \cdot \theta^3 + \frac{\theta^4}{4!} \cdot 3 + 0 \cdot \theta^5 + \frac{\theta^6}{6!} \cdot 15 + \cdots$$

So, picking out the coefficients, you can see that:

$$\mu_1' = 0 \quad \mu_2' = 1 \quad \mu_3' = 0 \quad \mu_4' = 3 \quad \mu_5' = 0 \qquad \text{and so on.}$$

One feature of the $N(0, 1)$ distribution that you can see straight away from this expansion is that all the odd-order moments are zero.

The second method is to differentiate the moment generating function with respect to θ and then set $\theta = 0$. To see how and why this works, look at the power series on page 80 and differentiate it term by term. Letting $M'(\theta)$ denote differentiation of the mgf with respect to θ, you get:

$$M'(\theta) = \mu_1' + \theta\mu_2' + \frac{\theta^2}{2!}\mu_3' + \cdots$$

and now setting $\theta = 0$ gives:

$$M'(0) = \mu_1'$$

Differentiating a second time:

$$M''(\theta) = \mu_2' + \theta\mu_3' + \cdots$$

and so:

$$M''(0) = \mu_2'$$

Continuing in this way, you can obtain μ_r' as $M^{(r)}(0)$, i.e. the rth derivative of the mgf with respect to θ evaluated at $\theta = 0$.

Normal distribution $N(0, 1)$

Use the differentiation method to obtain the moments of the $N(0, 1)$ distribution.

Solution:

From:

$$M(\theta) = e^{\theta^2/2}$$

you get:

$$M'(\theta) = e^{\theta^2/2} \cdot \theta$$

and so:

$$\mu_1' = M'(0) = 0.$$

Differentiating a second time:

$$M''(\theta) = e^{\theta^2/2} \cdot 1 + \theta \cdot e^{\theta^2/2} \cdot \theta$$

and so:

$$\mu_2' = M''(0) = 1 + 0 = 1$$

You can continue this process to find higher moments.

From this you can see that moment generating functions do indeed generate moments. (Moments about the origin are the ones that appear immediately from the mgf, but moments about other points can be found by a little algebraic manipulation.) This is useful in itself, for the mgf is often the easiest way to find means and variances. However, it also opens the door to the real point of moment generating functions, to their central importance in much of statistical theory. You will remember that, at the end of the subsection on moments, it was pointed out that moments do, in fact, specify all the information about a distribution. You can now see that the moment generating function specifies the moments. So it must necessarily follow that *the moment generating function specifies all the information about a distribution.*

In the examples, you were always given the underlying distribution, either by specifying the probability function if it was a discrete distribution, or by specifying the probability density function if it was continuous. You worked 'forwards' from there to find the moment generating function. However, this process can also be done 'backwards'. You can start from a moment generating function and 'undo' it to find the probability function or probability density function of the underlying distribution. This is a unique one-to-one process. Any given distribution has only one mgf; and any given mgf has only one distribution underlying it.

You will remember that this ability to work 'backwards' has already been pointed out for probability generating functions. The advantage of using moment generating functions is that they can be applied to continuous as well as discrete random variables.

The techniques for 'undoing' (the proper technical word is 'inverting') a moment generating function are quite advanced and certainly beyond the scope of this book. However, in many applications of this work, you do not actually need explicitly to 'undo' a moment generating function to find the underlying distribution. You might well be able to recognise the mgf as being one you have met before, i.e. the mgf of a distribution with which you are familiar. Then, because the relationship between a distribution and its mgf is unique, you can at once conclude that the underlying distribution must be this one.

You can now complete the proof of the result that 'Normal distributions add up'.

First, recall that the mgf of the general Normal distribution $N(\mu, \sigma^2)$ is $e^{\mu\theta + (\sigma^2\theta^2/2)}$. Think of this as being:

$$e^{(\text{something})\theta + ((\text{something else})\theta^2/2)}$$

where the 'something' is the mean and the 'something else' is the variance.

Now recall that you have found the mgf of the sum to be:

$$e^{(\mu_1 + \mu_2 + \cdots + \mu_n)\theta} + \frac{(\sigma_1^2 + \sigma_2^2 + \cdots + \sigma_n^2)\theta^2}{2}$$

and notice that this is exactly of the form:

$$e^{(\text{something})\theta + ((\text{something else})\theta^2/2)}$$

which implies that you can deduce straight away that the underlying distribution must be Normal and that its mean is $\mu_1 + \mu_2 + \cdots + \mu_n$ and its variance is $\sigma_1^2 + \sigma_2^2 + \cdots + \sigma_n^2$.

Many results about sequences or sums of random variables are proved in this way, and so is the Central Limit Theorem. To give you a flavour of how the work goes, you might like to consider the result that the B(n, p) distribution is well approximated by the Normal distribution with parameters np and npq if n is large. You will have used this result many times in your earlier work in statistics. You will know that the approximation works best if p is fairly near $\frac{1}{2}$, but it eventually becomes good, if n is large enough, whatever the value of p. It is really a result about a sequence of B(n, p) random variables, investigating what happens to this sequence as n increases. The method of proving the result is to consider the moment generating function of B(n, p) and investigate what happens to this function as n increases. The technical mathematical details of doing this are not straightforward, but it turns out that, as n increases, the function approaches the mathematical form of the mgf of the Normal distribution. Because of the uniqueness of moment generating functions, it therefore follows that the distribution itself approaches the Normal form as n increases.

Generating functions are very important in handling results of this kind, which would be extremely difficult to deal with in any other way. The further you go in more advanced statistical work, the more useful you are likely to find the generating function approach.

Exercise 5B

1. State the moment generating function for the B(n, p) distribution.

   Independent random variables $X_1, X_2, \ldots, X_k$ have binomial distributions as follows:

   $$X_1 \sim B(n_1, p), X_2 \sim B(n_2, p), \ldots, X_k \sim B(n_k, p)$$

   (i) Use the convolution theorem to find the moment generating function of the random variable:

   $$Y = X_1 + X_2 + \cdots + X_k$$

   (ii) By considering the functional form of this moment generating function, deduce that the distribution of Y is B$(n_1 + n_2 + \cdots + n_k, p)$.

   [**NOTE:** *Notice that this would not work if p was not the same for each of the original binomial distributions.*]

2. State the moment generating function for the Poisson (m) distribution.

   Independent random variables $X_1, X_2, \ldots, X_n$ have Poisson distributions as follows:

   $$X_1 \sim \text{Poisson}(m_1),$$

   $$X_2 \sim \text{Poisson}(m_2), \ldots,$$

   $$X_n \sim \text{Poisson}(m_n).$$

   (i) Use the convolution theorem to find the moment generating function of the

Exercise 5B continued

random variable:

$$Y = X_1 + X_2 + \cdots + X_n$$

(ii) Deduce the distribution of Y.

3. Obtain the mean and variance of the $B(n, p)$ distribution from its mgf.

4. **HINT:** In this question, you may use the result that $\int_0^\infty u^m e^{-u} \, du = m!$ for any non-negative integer m.

The random variable, X, has probability density function:

$$f(x) = \begin{cases} \lambda^{k+1} x^k e^{-\lambda x}/k! & x > 0 \\ 0 & \text{elsewhere} \end{cases}$$

where $\lambda > 0$ and k is a non-negative integer.

(i) Show that the moment generating function of X is $\{\lambda/(\lambda - t)\}^{k+1}$, explaining why this is valid for $t < \lambda$.

(ii) The random variable, Y, is the sum of n independent random variables each distributed as X. Find the moment generating function of Y and hence find the mean and variance of Y.

(iii) Write down the probability density function of Y.

[MEI, June 1996]

5. (i) The moment generating function (mgf) of the random variable, X, is denoted by $M_X(t)$. Prove that the mgf of the random variable, $Y = aX + b$, where a and b are constants, is $e^{bt} M_X(at)$.

(ii) Derive the mgf of the $N(0, 1)$ random variable.

(iii) Using the results of (i) and (ii), derive the mgf of the $N(\mu, \sigma^2)$ random variable.

(iv) X_1 and X_2 are independent Normal random variables with the same mean μ and the same variance σ^2. Use moment generating functions to show that $X_1 + X_2$ and $X_1 - X_2$ are both Normal random variables and to obtain their means and variances.

[MEI, June 1995]

6. (i) Show that $h(t)$, the generating function for moments about the mean μ of a probability distribution, is given by:

$$h(t) = e^{-\mu t} g(t)$$

where $g(t)$ is the generating function for moments about the origin.

(ii) Hence, or otherwise, show that the generating function for moments about the mean μ of a Poisson distribution is:

$$\exp\left(\mu e^t - \mu - \mu t\right)$$

(iii) Find μ_2, μ_3 and μ_4, respectively the second, third and fourth moments about the mean.

(iv) Find also the value of:

$$(\mu_4/\mu_2^2) - (\mu_3^2/\mu_2^3)$$

[O&C, June 1990]

7. The probability density function of the random variable, X, having the χ_n^2 distribution is:

$$f(x) = K x^{(n-2)/2} e^{-(x/2)} \quad x \geqslant 0$$

where K is a constant (dependent on n), for any positive integer n.

(i) By making the substitution $x(\frac{1}{2} - \theta) = \frac{1}{2} u$ and reconsidering the form of $f(x)$, or otherwise, obtain the moment generating function $M(\theta)$ of X.

(ii) Using arguments based on moment generating functions:

(a) Show that the sum of n independent random variables each having the χ_1^2 distribution is the random variable having the χ_n^2 distribution.

(b) Prove the additive property of χ^2 distributions, namely that the sum of a random variable having the χ_m^2 distribution and an independent random variable having the χ_n^2 distribution is a random variable having the χ_{m+n}^2 distribution.

[MEI, June 1994]

8. The number of breakdowns per hour of a small firm's photocopier has a Poisson distribution with mean 0.001. Breakdowns are independent of each other. Whenever the machine breaks down, it is repaired immediately and put back into use.

(i) If X hours is the time which elapses between the photocopier being repaired and the next breakdown, you may assume that:

$$P(X > x) = e^{-0.001x}$$

Find the distribution function and the probability density function of X.

(ii) Prove that $G(t)$, the moment generating function of X, is given by:

$$G(t) = 1/(1 - 1000t) \quad (t < 0.001)$$

(iii) Use this function to show that the mean time between failures is 1000 hours.

(iv) The repair company offers the firm a choice of two payment arrangements to guarantee the immediate repair service. They are:

Option 1: an immediate payment of £P to cover call-out charges for the next 9 months.

Option 2: an immediate payment of £P to cover call-out charges for the next ten breakdowns.

By considering the expected time to the tenth consecutive breakdown, use the moment generating function to decide which option you would advise the firm to choose.

[O&C, June 1993]

9. (i) The random variable, V, has the exponential distribution with parameter λ, i.e. its probability density function is:

$$f(\nu) = \begin{cases} \lambda e^{-\lambda \nu} & \nu \geqslant 0 \\ 0 & \nu < 0 \end{cases}$$

where $\lambda > 0$. Show that the moment generating function of V is:

$$M(\theta) = \frac{\lambda}{\lambda - \theta} \text{ for } \theta < \lambda$$

(ii) Independent random variables, X and Y, have exponential distributions with parameters α and β respectively ($\alpha \neq \beta$; α and β both greater than zero). Write down the moment generating function of $X + Y$.

(iii) By finding the moment generating function of the random variable, Z, whose probability density function is:

$$\begin{cases} \dfrac{\alpha\beta}{\beta - \alpha}(e^{-\alpha z} - e^{-\beta z}) & z \geqslant 0 \\ 0 & z < 0 \end{cases}$$

show that $X + Y$ has the same distribution as Z.

(iv) Using the moment generating function, or otherwise, find the mean of Z.

[MEI, June 1992]

10. (i) The time between arrivals of cars at a checkpoint is a random variable, X, with probability density function:

$$f(x) = \begin{cases} \lambda e^{-\lambda x} & x > 0 \\ 0 & \text{elsewhere} \end{cases}$$

where $\lambda > 0$. Obtain the moment generating function of X and hence find the mean and variance of X.

(ii) The checkpoint is set up at time $x = 0$ and the first car arrives at time X_1. The time between the arrival of car $i - 1$ and the arrival of car i is X_i, $i = 2, 3, \ldots$. The X_i may be taken to be independent identically distributed random variables each with the same probability density function $f(x)$ as defined in (i). Interpret the random variable $S_n = X_1 + X_2 + \cdots + X_n$ and write down its moment generating function.

(iii) Verify that the function:

$$g(y) = \begin{cases} \dfrac{\lambda^n y^{n-1} e^{-\lambda y}}{(n-1)!} & y > 0 \\ 0 & \text{elsewhere} \end{cases}$$

is a probability density function for some random variable Y. Obtain the moment generating function of Y.

HINT: You may use the result that, if

$$I_m = \int_0^\infty y^m e^{-\lambda y}\, dy, \text{ then } I_m = (m/\lambda)I_{m-1}$$

for any positive integer m.

(iv) State the probability density function of S_n. Justify your answer.

[MEI, June 1993]

KEY POINTS

- For a probability distribution, the **moment generating function** (mgf) is defined by:

$$M(\theta) = E(e^{\theta X}) = \sum_x e^{\theta x} P(X = x) \text{ for \textbf{discrete} random variables;}$$

$$= \int_x e^{\theta x} f(x)\, dx \text{ for \textbf{continuous} random variables.}$$

- The kth moment about zero $= \mu'_k = E(X^k)$.

- The kth moment about the mean $= \mu_k = E[(X - \mu)^k]$

- $M(\theta) = E(e^{\theta X}) = 1 + \dfrac{\theta}{1!} E(X) + \dfrac{\theta^2}{2!} E(X^2) + \dfrac{\theta^3}{3!} E(X^3) + \dfrac{\theta^4}{4!} E(X^4) + \cdots$

- *Expectation:* $E(X) = M'(0)$ *or* the coefficient of θ in expansion of $M(\theta)$;

$$E(X^2) = M''(0) \text{ \textit{or} the coefficient of } \dfrac{\theta^2}{2!} \text{ in expansion of } M(\theta);$$

$$E(X^3) = M'''(0) \text{ \textit{or} the coefficient of } \dfrac{\theta^3}{3!} \text{ in expansion of } M(\theta).$$

- *Variance:* $\text{Var}(X) = E(X - \mu)^2$

$$= E(X^2) - \mu^2 = M''(0) - [M'(0)]^2$$

- *Linear transformation:* $Y = a + bX$

$$M_Y(\theta) = e^{b\theta} M_X(a\theta)$$

- *Convolution theorem:* $Z = X + Y$

$$M_Z(\theta) = M_X(\theta) M_Y(\theta)$$

6
Maximum Likelihood estimators

Unless we have complete information, we need thinking in order to make the best use of the information we have.

Edward de Bono

When a beta particle passes through a plastic sheet, the probability that it is absorbed depends only on the thickness of the sheet. When 20 beta particles are passed through two identical plastic sheets, seven are absorbed by the first sheet and nine by the second. How should the probability, p, that a particle is absorbed by a single sheet, be estimated?

Assuming that the passage of each particle is independent of the others, four possible estimates are as follows.

1. When 20 particles were passed through the first sheet, seven were absorbed; so the probability should be estimated as $\hat{p} = \frac{7}{20} = 0.35$

2. When the 13 remaining particles were passed through the second sheet, nine were absorbed; so the probability should be estimated as $\hat{p} = \frac{9}{13} = 0.6923$

3. The probability that a particle is absorbed by the second sheet is $(1 - p)p$, and we found nine out of 20 absorbed by the second sheet, so we could try to choose:

$$(1 - \hat{p})\hat{p} = \frac{9}{20}$$

but this has no real solutions.

4. The probability that a particle is not absorbed at all is $(1 - p)^2$, and we found four out of 20 not absorbed at all, so we could choose:

$$(1 - \hat{p})^2 = \frac{4}{20} \quad \Rightarrow \quad \hat{p} = 1 - \frac{1}{\sqrt{5}} = 0.5528$$

Some of these estimators have nice properties. For instance (1) is unbiased: but this merely means that *if we repeated the experiment many times*, the average estimate made by this method should approach the true value – and here we have substantial evidence (nine out of 13 remaining particles absorbed by the second sheet) that *in this case* the method has given too low a value for p.

How can we take all the information we have into account in settling on a good estimate for p?

Likelihood

The *likelihood* of the set of observations in a sample is simply the probability that this particular sample occurs. In a context where a parameter is unknown, the likelihood will be a function of this unknown parameter.

Here, for example, the probability that, of 20 particles, seven will be stopped by the first sheet, nine by the second and four will pass through will depend on p, so we can calculate the likelihood, $L(p)$, as follows. Any particular sample of this type, whatever the order in which those particles stopped by the first sheet, the second sheet or neither sheet are observed, has probability (as the fates of the particles are independent)

$$P(\text{stopped by first sheet})^7 \times P(\text{stopped by second sheet})^9 \times P(\text{not stopped})^4$$

How many samples of this sort are there? In other words, in how many different orders can the particles stopped by the first sheet, the second sheet or neither sheet be observed? Equivalently, how many ways are there of arranging seven Fs (stopped by first sheet), nine Ss (stopped by second sheet) and four Ns (not stopped) in a row? Twenty letters can be arranged in 20! ways, but this overcounts the distinct arrangements by factors of 7! (the Fs rearranged among themselves), 9! (the Ss) and 4! (the Ns), so that, in fact, there are $\dfrac{20!}{7!9!4!}$ such samples.

Thus:

$$L(p) = \frac{20!}{7!9!4!} \times P(\text{stopped by first sheet})^7 \times P(\text{stopped by second sheet})^9$$
$$\times P(\text{not stopped})^4$$

but, in terms of the unknown parameter, p:

$$P(\text{stopped by first sheet}) = p$$

$$P(\text{stopped by second sheet}) = (1-p)p$$

$$P(\text{not stopped}) = (1-p)^2$$

so, finally:

$$L(p) = \frac{20!}{7!9!4!} \times [p]^7 \times [(1-p)p]^9 \times [(1-p)^2]^4$$
$$= 55\,426\,800 \times p^{16} \times (1-p)^{17}$$

The three estimates we obtained above and the likelihoods of the sample results if each was correct, are:

$$(1)\ \hat{p} = 0.35 \qquad L(\hat{p}) = 0.001\,855$$
$$(2)\ \hat{p} = 0.6923 \qquad L(\hat{p}) = 0.000\,307$$
$$(4)\ \hat{p} = 0.5528 \qquad L(\hat{p}) = 0.004\,824$$

We can see that, for instance, if p were equal to estimate (2), the sample we obtained would have a rather small probability of occurring, whereas if p were equal to estimate (4), the probability of the sample we actually obtained would be much higher – about 16 times as great. This makes estimate (4) seem intuitively more sensible than estimate (2).

We can follow this argument further: if we think that estimate (4) is better than estimate (2) because it makes the probability of the sample actually obtained greater, then an even better estimate of p would be the value which makes the probability of the sample actually obtained as great as possible. That is, we should choose $\hat{p}$ to make $L(\hat{p})$ a maximum.

A graph of $L(p)$ against p is shown in figure 6.1.

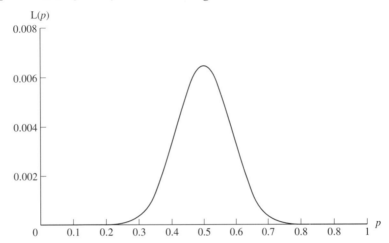

Figure 6.1

The value of p which makes $L(p)$ a maximum is just under 0.5. We can determine the exact value by differentiation:

$$L(p) = 55\,426\,800 \times p^{16} \times (1-p)^{17}$$

so:

$$\frac{dL}{dp} = 55\,426\,800 \times [16p^{15} \times (1-p)^{17} + p^{16} \times -17(1-p)^{16}]$$

$$= 55\,426\,800 \times p^{15} \times (1-p)^{16} \times [16(1-p) - 17p]$$

$$= 55\,426\,800 \times p^{15} \times (1-p)^{16} \times (16 - 33p)$$

The maximum occurs when this expression is equal to zero, i.e. when $p = \frac{16}{33} = 0.485$, as we can see from figure 6.1 that the other two turning points, $p = 0$ and $p = 1$, are minima of L. Note that, having found this estimate by maximising the likelihood, we can see that it makes sense. The fraction is just

$$\frac{\text{total number of particles stopped by a sheet}}{\text{total number of particles approaching a sheet}}$$

This method for deriving an estimate for a parameter from a set of data is called the *maximum likelihood method*.

Activity

You can use the same method to produce a complete estimator for this problem. Suppose that, in an experiment, a particles were stopped by the first sheet, b by the second sheet and c were not stopped. $N = a + b + c$ is the total number of particles fired at the sheets.

(i)   Show that:

$$L(p) = K \times p^{a+b} \times (1-p)^{b+2c}$$

where K stands for the combinatorial constant $\dfrac{(a+b+c)!}{a!\,b!\,c!}$

(ii) Find $\dfrac{\mathrm{d}L}{\mathrm{d}p}$ and from this show that the maximum likelihood estimator for p is:

$$\hat{p} = \frac{a+b}{a + 2b + 2c}$$

(iii) The general form of estimator (1) – using only the data from the first sheet – is:

$$\hat{p} = \frac{a}{a+b+c}$$

and the general form of estimator (2) – using only the data from the second sheet – is:

$$\hat{p} = \frac{b}{b+c}$$

In fact, the maximum likelihood estimator lies between these two. Prove this.

Summary

The *maximum likelihood criterion for estimation* suggests that if we are trying to estimate a parameter, t, then, given any set of data, we should choose as our estimate the value of t which makes the likelihood of the actual data as great as possible.

Logarithmic differentiation

When finding the maximum likelihood estimate above, we differentiated the expression $L(p)$. This was relatively straightforward in the example we had, but this is not always the case and the technique of logarithmic differentiation is often useful in maximum likelihood problems. This relies on the observation that as the expression $L(p)$ is a probability, it is always positive and so we can find its natural logarithm $\ln[L(p)]$. Because the graph of the logarithm function has a positive gradient, the largest value of $\ln[L(p)]$ will occur when $L(p)$ itself is largest, so that we can replace the problem of finding the value of p which maximises $L(p)$, with the problem of finding the value of p which maximises $\ln[L(p)]$. The advantage of the method is that this is often much easier!

Formally, we have:

$$\frac{d}{dp} \ln [L(p)] = \frac{1}{L(p)} \frac{dL}{dp}$$

which is equal to zero whenever $\dfrac{dL}{dp}$ is.

EXAMPLE

Find the maximum value of $L(p) = \dfrac{(a+b+c)!}{a!\,b!\,c!} \times p^{a+b} \times (1-p)^{b+2c}$

Solution:

$$\ln [L(p)] = \ln \frac{(a+b+c)!}{a!\,b!\,c!} + \ln (p^{a+b}) + \ln ((1-p)^{b+2c})$$

(because $\ln (A \times B) = \ln A + \ln B$)

$$= \ln \frac{(a+b+c)!}{a!\,b!\,c!} = (a+b)\ln(p) + (b+2c)\ln(1-p)$$

(because $\ln (A^n) = n \ln (A)$)

so:

$$\frac{d}{dp} \ln [L(p)] = \frac{a+b}{p} - \frac{b+2c}{1-p}$$

which must be set equal to zero to determine the value of p giving a maximum:

$$\frac{a+b}{p} - \frac{b+2c}{1-p} = 0 \quad \Rightarrow \quad (a+b)(1-p) - (b+2c)p = 0$$

$$\Rightarrow \quad (a+b) = (a+2b+2c)p \quad \Rightarrow \quad p = \frac{(a+b)}{(a+2b+2c)}$$

as we had before, but with rather less work.

EXAMPLE

In an investigation of arctic lichen cover, a botanist records, for each of 24 randomly located square metres of tundra, whether it contains no, one or more than one lichen colony.

His results are:

no colonies	11 square metres
one colony	6 square metres
more than one colony	7 square metres

Assuming that the number of colonies of lichen in each square metre of tundra follows a Poisson distribution, find an equation satisfied by the maximum likelihood estimate $\hat{\lambda}$ of λ, the mean number of colonies per square metre, and show that your equation is approximately satisfied by $\hat{\lambda} = 0.94$.

Solution:

The assumption of a Poisson distribution with mean λ implies that for each square metre:

$$P(\text{no colonies}) = e^{-\lambda}$$

$$P(\text{one colony}) = \lambda e^{-\lambda}$$

$$P(\text{more than one colony}) = 1 - [P(\text{no colonies}) + P(\text{one colony})] = 1 - (1+\lambda)e^{-\lambda}$$

so that the likelihood of these observations is:

$$L(p) = \frac{24!}{11!6!7!}[e^{-\lambda}]^{11}[\lambda e^{-\lambda}]^{6}[1-(1+\lambda)e^{-\lambda}]^{7}$$

$$= \frac{24!}{11!6!7!}e^{-11\lambda} \cdot \lambda^{6} \cdot e^{-6\lambda} \cdot [1-(1+\lambda)e^{-\lambda}]^{7}$$

$$= \frac{24!}{11!6!7!}e^{-17\lambda} \cdot \lambda^{6} \cdot [1-(1+\lambda)e^{-\lambda}]^{7}$$

We can use the technique of logarithmic differentiation here:

$$\ln[L(p)] = \ln\left[\frac{24!}{11!6!7!}\right] - 17\lambda + 6\ln\lambda + 7\ln[1-(1+\lambda)e^{-\lambda}]$$

so:

$$\frac{d}{d\lambda}\ln[L(\lambda)] = -17 + \frac{6}{\lambda} + \frac{7}{1-(1+\lambda)e^{-\lambda}} \cdot \lambda e^{-\lambda}$$

The maximum likelihood estimator, $\hat\lambda$, therefore satisfies the equation:

$$-17 + \frac{6}{\hat\lambda} + \frac{7}{1-(1+\hat\lambda)e^{-\hat\lambda}} \cdot \hat\lambda e^{-\hat\lambda} = 0$$

$$(6 - 17\hat\lambda)(1-(1+\hat\lambda)e^{-\hat\lambda}) + 7\hat\lambda^{2}e^{-\hat\lambda} = 0$$

$$(24\hat\lambda^{2} + 11\hat\lambda - 6)e^{-\hat\lambda} + (6 - 17\hat\lambda) = 0$$

The value $\hat\lambda = 0.94$ given is an approximate solution to this equation, correct to two significant figures, because the value of the left-hand side when $\hat\lambda = 0.935$ is 0.024, which is positive, and when $\hat\lambda = 0.945$ is -0.026, which is negative.

As we have not sketched the likelihood function in this case, we need to check that 0.94 gives a maximum of L – we can do this by showing $\frac{d^{2}L}{d\lambda^{2}} < 0$, and there is a useful logarithmic technique for this. Note that:

$$\frac{d^{2}}{d\lambda^{2}}\ln[L(\lambda)] = \frac{d}{d\lambda}\left\{\frac{1}{L(\lambda)}\frac{dL}{d\lambda}\right\}$$

$$= \frac{1}{L(\lambda)}\frac{d^{2}L}{d\lambda^{2}} - \frac{1}{[L(\lambda)]^{2}}\left\{\frac{dL}{d\lambda}\right\}^{2}$$

We are interested in the sign of $\frac{d^{2}L}{d\lambda^{2}}$ at the value, $\hat\lambda$, of λ where $\frac{dL}{d\lambda} = 0$: at $\hat\lambda$, therefore second term in the expression for $\frac{d^{2}L}{d\lambda^{2}}$ is zero and can be omitted

$$\frac{d^{2}}{d\lambda^{2}}\ln[L(\lambda)] = \frac{1}{L(\lambda)}\frac{d^{2}L}{d\lambda^{2}}$$

As $L(\lambda)$ is a probability and so positive, the sign of $\frac{d^{2}L}{d\lambda^{2}}$ is the same as the sign of $\frac{d^{2}}{d\lambda^{2}}\ln[L(\lambda)]$, so the criterion for a maximum of the likelihood is that the second derivative of $\ln L$ is negative at a turning point of $\ln L$.

In this example:

$$\frac{d^2}{d\lambda^2} \ln[L(\lambda)] = \frac{d}{d\lambda}\left\{-17 + \frac{6}{\lambda} + \frac{7}{1-(1+\lambda)e^{-\lambda}} \cdot \lambda e^{-\lambda}\right\}$$

$$= -\frac{6}{\lambda^2} + \frac{7e^{-\lambda}\{(1-\lambda) - e^{-\lambda}\}}{[1-(1+\lambda)e^{-\lambda}]^2}$$

$$= -25.7$$

at $\lambda = 0.94$, which confirms that that value gives the maximum likelihood.

Properties of maximum likelihood estimators

You should be clear that the maximum likelihood method is *one* way of deciding how to estimate a parameter – but *not necessarily* the best way. In general, there is no guarantee that a maximum likelihood estimator will be efficient, unbiased, have a small mean square error or, indeed, possess any nice properties, but, in practice, these estimators are often among the most satisfactory that can be obtained, particularly in large samples. The following example, however, illustrates a case where the maximum likelihood method produces an intuitively unsatisfactory estimator.

EXAMPLE

A tub contains a complete set of one each of N different model farm animals where N is unknown. A small boy pulls animals from the tub until he removes the cow, which occurs on his fifth draw. Estimate N using the method of maximum likelihood.

Solution:

The probability that the cow is drawn on the fifth draw is zero if there are fewer than five animals and $\frac{1}{N}$ if there are five or more animals. A graph of the likelihood function is shown in figure 6.2.

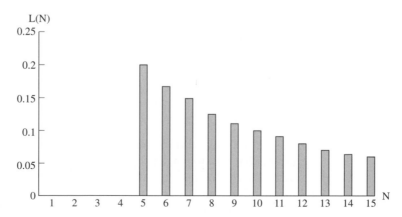

Figure 6.2

and the maximum likelihood occurs when $N = 5$. This is the estimate we require, but it should strike you that there is something rather odd about the estimator $\hat{N} = $ 'the number of the draw on which the cow is drawn'. For example, it is certainly not unbiased because, for a given value of N, the possible draws on which the cow may be drawn are the first, second, ..., Nth and these are all equally likely so that the expected draw for the cow, and therefore $E[\hat{N}]$, is $\dfrac{N+1}{2}$.

In general, where the range of possible sample values depends on the parameter being estimated, the maximum likelihood method can give rather unexpected results!

This example shows that the maximum likelihood estimator cannot always be found by differentiating, either because the parameter may be restricted to take a discrete rather than a continuous range of values – here, N must be a positive integer – or because there may be a limited range of permissible parameter values and the maximum likelihood may occur at one end of this range rather than within the permitted interval – here, N must be greater than or equal to 5 and the maximum likelihood, in fact, occurs at the lowest point of this permitted range.

Continuous distributions

The times between successive arrivals of customers in a shop are often taken to have an exponential distribution; that is, the probability density of the random variable T which measures the time between successive arrivals is:

$$f(t) = \lambda e^{-\lambda t}$$

with parameter λ.

The times, in seconds, between four successive arrivals in one shop were:

$$t_1 = 27; \quad t_2 = 19; \quad t_3 = 16; \quad t_4 = 38.$$

Assuming the inter-arrival times are exponentially distributed, how could we estimate the value of λ?

If we try to use the maximum likelihood method here, we meet an immediate problem – with a continuously distributed random variable, the probability of any particular sample value is zero! All is not lost, however. In the examples we considered above, it was not, in fact, important that the likelihood was *equal* to the probability of the sample values obtained: we only needed a likelihood which was *proportional* to the probability of the sample values obtained. If we multiply or divide the likelihood function by any constant of proportionality independent of the parameter, there will always be a maximum at the same value of λ and so the same maximum likelihood estimator will be produced.

For a continuous random variable, the probability densities at two possible values of that variable are proportional to the relative probabilities of those values. Therefore, the relative probabilities of two samples are proportional to the probability densities of the samples, which, in turn, are equal to the products of the densities for each member of the sample, provided these are drawn independently.

This motivates the following definition.

DEFINITION

If a random variable X *has a continuous distribution, described by the probability density function* f(x) *and we draw an independent random sample of size* n *from this distribution, then the likelihood of the set of sample values* $x_1, x_2, \ldots, x_n$ *of* X *is* $L = f(x_1) \cdot f(x_2) \cdot \cdots \cdot f(x_n)$.

If the distribution of X *has an unknown parameter, then* L *will be a function of this parameter.*

In this example, therefore, we have L depending on λ, and equal to:

$$L(\lambda) = \lambda e^{-27\lambda} \cdot \lambda e^{-19\lambda} \cdot \lambda e^{-16\lambda} \cdot \lambda e^{-38\lambda} = \lambda^4 e^{-\lambda(27+19+16+38)} = \lambda^4 e^{-100\lambda}$$

The maximum value of $L(\lambda)$ occurs at the value of λ for which $\dfrac{dL}{d\lambda} = 0$:

$$\frac{dL}{d\lambda} = 4\lambda^3 e^{-100\lambda} - 100\lambda^4 e^{-100\lambda} = \lambda^3 e^{-100\lambda}(4 - 100\lambda) = 0 \quad \Rightarrow \quad \lambda = 0.04 \text{ or } \lambda = 0$$

and

$$\frac{d^2L}{d\lambda^2} = (12\lambda^2 - 400\lambda^3)e^{-100\lambda} - 100(4\lambda^3 - 100\lambda^4)e^{-100\lambda}$$

$$= \lambda^2 e^{-100\lambda}(12 - 800\lambda + 10\,000\lambda^2)$$

$$= (0.04)^2 e^{-4}(12 - 32 + 16) = -0.0064e^{-4} < 0 \text{ at } \lambda = 0.04$$

so the maximum likelihood estimator of λ is $\hat{\lambda} = 0.04$ (as $\lambda = 0$ gives $L = 0$ which must be a minimum of L as likelihoods are always positive).

EXAMPLE

X has a Normal distribution with mean μ and variance σ^2. A sample drawn from X gives the n values $\{x_1, x_2, \ldots, x_n\}$. Estimate the values of μ and σ^2.

Solution:

The likelihood of the sample values is:

$$L(\mu, \sigma^2) = f(x_1)f(x_2) \cdots f(x_n)$$

where $f(x)$ is the density function for the Normal distribution with mean μ and variance σ^2:

$$f(x) = \frac{1}{\sqrt{2\pi}\sigma} e^{-((x-\mu)^2/2\sigma^2)}$$

so that:

$$L(\mu, \sigma^2) = \frac{1}{\sqrt{2\pi}\sigma} e^{-((x_1-\mu)^2/2\sigma^2)} \cdot \frac{1}{\sqrt{2\pi}\sigma} e^{-((x_2-\mu)^2/2\sigma^2)} \cdot \cdots \cdot \frac{1}{\sqrt{2\pi}\sigma} e^{-((x_n-\mu)^2/2\sigma^2)}$$

$$= \left(\frac{1}{\sqrt{2\pi}\sigma}\right)^n e^{-((x_1-\mu)^2 + (x_2-\mu)^2 + \cdots + (x_n-\mu)^2/2\sigma^2)}$$

$$= \left(\frac{1}{\sqrt{2\pi}\sigma}\right)^n e^{-(\Sigma_{i=1}^{n}(x_i-\mu)^2/2\sigma^2)}$$

which gives:

$$\ln[L(\mu, \sigma^2)] = n\ln\left(\frac{1}{\sqrt{2\pi}}\right) - n\ln\sigma - \frac{\sum_{i=1}^{n}(x_i - \mu)^2}{2\sigma^2}$$

In this case, L depends on both μ and σ^2 but the strategy is the same: we will choose as estimates of μ and σ^2 those values which maximise the likelihood.

Whatever the value of σ^2:

$$\frac{\partial}{\partial\mu}\ln[L(\mu, \sigma^2)] = \frac{\sum_{i=1}^{n}2(x_i - \mu)}{2\sigma^2} = 0$$

$$\Rightarrow \quad \sum_{i=1}^{n}(x_i - \hat{\mu}) = 0$$

$$\Rightarrow \quad \sum_{i=1}^{n}x_i - n\hat{\mu} = 0$$

$$\Rightarrow \quad \hat{\mu} = \frac{\sum_{i=1}^{n}x_i}{n}$$

i.e. the maximum value of L will be produced by this value of $\hat{\mu}$, regardless of how we choose our estimate of σ^2. Also:

$$\frac{\partial}{\partial\sigma}\ln[L(\mu, \sigma^2)] = -\frac{n}{\sigma} + \frac{\sum_{i=1}^{n}(x_i - \mu)^2}{\sigma^3} = 0$$

$$\Rightarrow \quad -n\hat{\sigma}^2 + \sum_{i=1}^{n}(x_i - \mu)^2 = 0$$

$$\Rightarrow \quad \hat{\sigma}^2 = \frac{\sum_{i=1}^{n}(x_i - \mu)^2}{n}$$

i.e. for any given estimate of μ, the likelihood will be maximised by choosing this expression as our estimate of σ^2.

The combination of these two results tells us that the estimators of μ and σ^2 which maximise the likelihood of the sample values are:

$$\hat{\mu} = \frac{\sum_{i=1}^{n}x_i}{n}$$

$$\hat{\sigma}^2 = \frac{\sum_{i=1}^{n}(x_i - \hat{\mu})^2}{n}$$

You should note here that the maximum likelihood method does not give the unbiased estimator for the population variance, with denominator $(n-1)$, that you would normally use. This is a useful reminder that 'maximum likelihood' does not equal 'best in every sense'.

Exercise 6A

1. The number of cars passing a point on a road travelling east has mean λ per minute. The number of cars passing the same point travelling west also has mean λ per minute. An observer counts a cars travelling east in a 5-minute period; b cars travelling west in a further 3-minute period; and c cars passing in either direction in a final 6-minute period.

   (i) Find an expression in terms of a, b and c for the likelihood of these observations, and determine a maximum likelihood estimate of λ.

   (ii) Explain why this estimate is intuitively reasonable.

2. Genetic theory predicts that a characteristic determined by a single gene will occur in the population in three genotypes, called dd, dr and rr, in the proportions:

dd	p^2
dr	$2p(1-p)$
rr	$(1-p)^2$

   where p is an unknown parameter.

   In an experiment, the number of each type of genotype found is:

dd	a
dr	b
rr	c

   where $n = a + b + c$ is the sample size.

   Find the maximum likelihood estimator of p.

   If you are also studying Chapter 10, on regression, you will find there the least squares estimate of p, and you can compare the results of the two methods.

3. In a plant survey, the number of orchids found in each of 12 fifty-metre squares of downland is counted. It is thought that the numbers can be modelled by the distribution:

   P(r orchids found in a square)

   $$= \binom{r+2}{2} \cdot (1-p)^3 p^r$$

   $(r = 0, 1, 2, \dots)$

Given the data:

r	0	1	2	3	>3
frequency	4	5	2	1	0

determine a maximum likelihood estimate for p.

4. Batches of apples are classified on the basis of a sample of size 4. If none of the sample is bruised, the batch is classified 'perfect', if one is bruised the batch is classified 'excellent' and if two or more are bruised then the batch is classified 'good'.

   (i) Use a binomial model, with p being the probability that an apple is not bruised, to derive an expression for the likelihood of the observations:

   a perfect batches
   b excellent batches
   c good batches
   in $(a + b + c)$ batches.

   (ii) Find a cubic equation satisfied by the maximum likelihood estimate of p, and show that if $a = 231$, $b = 156$, $c = 113$, then the maximum likelihood estimate of p is $\frac{4}{5}$.

5. Two types of motherboard which contain a series of integrated circuits are being made. When the boards are constructed, the probability that each integrated circuit is fitted correctly is p, and a board functions correctly only if all the integrated circuits are fitted correctly.

   Boards of type 1 contain four integrated circuits and boards of type 2 contain eight integrated circuits.

   (i) Find an expression for the likelihood of the observations:

   a motherboards of type 1 out of m manufactured function correctly;
   b motherboards of type 2 out of n manufactured function correctly;

   and find an equation satisfied by the maximum likelihood estimate $\hat{p}$ of p.

   (ii) Show that this equation reduces to a quadratic in $\hat{p}$, and from this find $\hat{p}$ if $a = 17$, $m = 28$, $b = 18$, $n = 20$.

Exercise 6A continued

6. The number of enquiries received by a travel firm about a particular destination is recorded in the weeks after a television series set in that area is begun. The number of enquiries in the week after the nth episode of the series is broadcast is thought to follow a Poisson distribution with mean either:

(a) $120 + \mu n$ or (b) $120\lambda^n$

the distributions for the separate weeks being independent.

(i) If the numbers of enquiries in the weeks after the first, second and third episodes of the series are a, b and c respectively, find equations satisfied by the maximum likelihood estimates of:

μ, assuming model (a) is correct;

and λ, assuming model (b) is correct.

(ii) Find each of these estimates if $a = 160$, $b = 210$ and $c = 270$.

7. Given that an unknown number β of the n balls in a box are blue, and that in a sample of size s, taken without replacement, B of the balls are blue, investigate the process of finding a maximum likelihood estimate of β.

$\left(\text{Hint: consider the ratio } \dfrac{L(n + 1)}{L(n)}. \right)$

8. The time for which a light bulb lasts is a random variable with density function:

$$f(x) = \frac{1}{2\beta\sqrt{x}} e^{-(\sqrt{x}/\beta)}$$

for some unknown parameter β.

Light bulbs are tested by passing current through n bulbs, waiting for time τ and recording the number, r, of bulbs which have failed at this time, and the times $t_1, t_2, \ldots, t_r$ at which these failed.

Write down an expression for the likelihood of these results, and from this find an expression for the maximum likelihood estimator of β.

9. Figure 6.3 shows a cross-section of a radiating wire, W, an unknown distance, δ, from the flat plate of a scintillation counter. The emissions from wire W are distributed uniformly in angular direction, Θ, and, when they strike the

plate, the coordinate, X, of the point of reception is recorded by the counter.

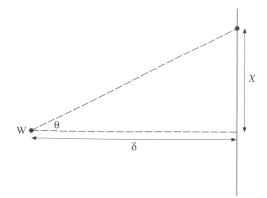

Figure 6.3

(i) Find the density function of X.

(ii) Find an equation obeyed by the maximum likelihood estimate of δ based on n independent observations of X.

(iii) Repeat parts (i) and (ii) when the scintillation counter plate extends only as far as $x = \pm H$, so that the distribution of Θ is uniform on $\left[-\arctan\left(\dfrac{H}{\delta}\right), \arctan\left(\dfrac{H}{\delta}\right) \right]$ only.

(iv) If, instead, δ is known, but W is misplaced at a distance, ξ, above the horizontal line, $x = 0$, find an equation satisfied by the maximum likelihood estimate of ξ based on n independent observations of X.

10. The time, T, of failure of a component has density function:

$$f(t) = \begin{cases} \alpha e^{-\alpha(t-\beta)} & (t > \beta) \\ 0 & (\text{otherwise}) \end{cases}$$

so that failure does not occur until unknown time β.

Seven components fail at times 31, 34, 35, 37, 40, 46, 58.

(i) If α is known, find the maximum likelihood estimate of β.

(ii) Assuming that β has the value you determined in (i), find the maximum likelihood estimate of α.

11. The distribution of a randomly determined ratio, which can take the values in $[0, 1]$ only, is modelled by the density function:

$$f(x) = \kappa(\kappa + 1)x^{\kappa-1}(1 - x) \quad (0 \leqslant x \leqslant 1)$$

where κ is unknown.

(i) Derive a quadratic equation for the maximum likelihood estimator based on the measured ratios $x_1, x_2, \ldots, x_n$ in a sample of size n.

(ii) Write down the solution to this equation in terms of $s = -\ln(g)$, where g is the geometric mean $(x_1 x_2 \cdots x_n)^{1/n}$ of the sample.

(iii) Find the value of this estimate when the measured ratios are:

0.19, 0.47, 0.68, 0.81, 0.87, 0.92, 0.94, 0.98.

12. Assume that the bivariate observations (x_i, Y_i) $(i = 1, 2, \ldots, n)$ are made, where each x_i is a non-random, exact value, and that the corresponding Y_i is an independent observation of a Normal random variable with mean $\alpha + \beta x_i$ and variance σ^2.

Derive equations for the maximum likelihood estimates of α and β.

If you are also studying Chapter 10, on regression, you should recognise the *normal equations* defined in that chapter, which give the least squares estimates of α and β.

KEY POINTS
- The *likelihood* of a set of observations of a discrete random variable is the probability of that set of observations arising, given the distribution of the random variable. If the distribution contains an unknown parameter, the likelihood will be a function of that parameter.

- The likelihood of a set of observations $x_1, x_2, \ldots, x_n$ of a continuous random variable is the product of the values of its probability density function at each observation:

$$L = f(x_1)f(x_2) \cdots f(x_n)$$

- Given a set of observations of a random variable, X, the *maximum likelihood estimation* strategy is to choose as an estimate for parameter τ of the distribution of X that value which makes the likelihood of the observations as great as possible.

7

Bivariate distributions

The increase in male unemployment between 1971 and 1972 can be fully explained by the almost continuous fall in male employment in this period.

Department of Employment

During the first season of the FA Premier League, 462 football matches were played. The frequencies of the number of goals scored by home teams and away teams in each game were recorded as follows:

		Number of goals by away teams						
		0	1	2	3	4	5	Total
	0	38	37	21	4	0	0	100
	1	52	66	28	11	1	0	158
	2	33	43	19	10	2	2	109
Number of goals	3	18	19	8	7	0	1	53
by home teams	4	5	10	9	4	0	0	28
	5	3	3	3	1	0	0	10
	6	1	0	2	0	0	0	3
	7	0	1	0	0	0	0	1
Total		150	179	90	37	3	3	462

Assuming that the relative frequencies for this season reflect the general pattern of scoring in FA Premier League matches, they may be used as empirical probabilities. Let X be the discrete random variable representing the number of goals scored per game by home teams and let Y represent the number of goals scored per game by away teams, then we have the *bivariate probability distribution*:

		Values of Y						
		0	1	2	3	4	5	$P(X = x)$
Values of X	0	0.082	0.080	0.045	0.009	0	0	0.216
	1	0.113	0.143	0.061	0.024	0.002	0	0.342
	2	0.071	0.093	0.041	0.022	0.004	0.004	0.236
	3	0.039	0.041	0.017	0.015	0	0.002	0.115
	4	0.011	0.022	0.019	0.009	0	0	0.061
	5	0.006	0.006	0.006	0.002	0	0	0.022
	6	0.002	0	0.004	0	0	0	0.006
	7	0	0.002	0	0	0	0	0.002
$P(Y = y)$		0.325	0.388	0.195	0.080	0.006	0.006	1

The probabilities in the body of the table are *joint probabilities*, e.g., the probability of a 1–1 draw is given by $P(X = 1, Y = 1) = 0.143$. The row and column totals are known as *marginal probabilities*, representing $P(X = x)$ and $P(Y = y)$ respectively. For example, $P(X = 2) = 0.236$ and $P(Y = 1) = 0.388$.

Notice that the grand total of 462 in the frequency table is equivalent to the probability of 1 in the probability table.

The marginal probabilities may be used to find expectations and variances in the usual way. Using the row and column totals from the probability table:

$$E(X) = \Sigma x P(X = x) = 0 \times 0.216 + 1 \times 0.340 + 2 \times 0.238 + 3 \times 0.115$$

$$+ 4 \times 0.061 + 5 \times 0.022 + 6 \times 0.006 + 7 \times 0.002$$

$$= 1.565$$

$$\text{Var}(X) = E(X^2) - [E(X)]^2 = \Sigma x^2 P(X = x) - [E(X)]^2$$

$$= 0^2 \times 0.216 + 1^2 \times 0.340 + 2^2 \times 0.238 + 3^2 \times 0.115$$

$$+ 5^2 \times 0.022 + 6^2 \times 0.006 + 7^2 \times 0.002 - 1.565^2$$

$$= 1.718$$

Similarly: $E(Y) = 1.076$ and $\text{Var}(Y) = 0.996$

As well as being derived from empirical probabilities, bivariate distributions may be defined in various ways. One way is to specify a bivariate distribution in terms of a table of probabilities; another is to derive bivariate probabilities from a practical situation by consideration of theoretical probabilities of combined events; and a third is to define a bivariate distribution by specifying a formula for joint probabilities. The examples which follow illustrate each method in turn.

EXAMPLE X and Y are discrete random variables whose joint distribution is shown in the table:

		Values of Y		
		1	3	5
Values of X	1	0.20	0.25	0
	4	0.10	0.15	0.05
	9	0.25	0	0

(i) Find the marginal distributions of X and Y.

(ii) Find:

(a) $P(X > Y)$;

(b) $P(XY < 10)$.

(iii) Calculate $E(X)$ and $Var(X)$.

Solution:

(i) The marginal probabilities for X and Y are found by summing the rows and the columns of the table:

		Values of Y			
		1	4	9	$P(X = x)$
	1	0.20	0.25	0	0.45
Values of X	3	0.10	0.15	0.05	0.30
	5	0.25	0	0	0.25
$P(Y = y)$		0.55	0.40	0.05	1

(ii) (a) $P(X > Y) = 0.10 + 0.15 + 0.25 = 0.5$

(b) $P(XY < 10) = 0.20 + 0.25 + 0.10 + 0.25 = 0.8$

(iii) $E(X) - \Sigma x P(X - x) - 1 \times 0.45 + 3 \times 0.30 + 5 \times 0.25 - 2.65$

$Var(X) = E(X^2) - [E(X)]^2 = \Sigma x^2 P(X = x) - [E(X)]^2$
$= 1^2 \times 0.45 + 3^2 \times 0.30 + 5^2 \times 0.25 - 2.65^2 - 2.3775$

EXAMPLE Two unbiased dice have their faces labelled as follows: red die: 1, 1, 2, 2, 3, 3; green die: 1, 2, 2, 3, 3, 3. Each die is thrown and the scores, X and Y respectively, noted.

(i) Construct a table of marginal and joint probabilities for X and Y.

(ii) Illustrate the distribution by a suitable diagram.

(iii) Write down the probability distribution for $X + Y$.

(iv) Show that $E(X + Y) = E(X) + E(Y)$ and $Var(X + Y) = Var(X) + Var(Y)$.

Solution:

(i) As events X and Y are independent, the joint probabilities for X and Y are found by finding the products of the marginal probabilities:

		Scores on green die			
		1	2	3	$P(X = x)$
	1	$\frac{1}{18}$	$\frac{1}{9}$	$\frac{1}{6}$	$\frac{1}{3}$
Scores on red die	2	$\frac{1}{18}$	$\frac{1}{9}$	$\frac{1}{6}$	$\frac{1}{3}$
	3	$\frac{1}{18}$	$\frac{1}{9}$	$\frac{1}{6}$	$\frac{1}{3}$
$P(Y = y)$		$\frac{1}{6}$	$\frac{1}{3}$	$\frac{1}{2}$	1

(ii)

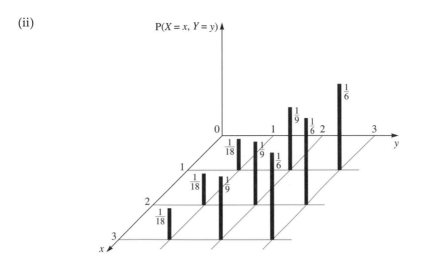

Figure 7.1

(iii) Values for $X + Y$ range from 2 to 6 inclusive with probabilities given by:

$x + y$	2	3	4	5	6
$P(X + Y = x + y)$	$\frac{1}{18}$	$\frac{1}{6}$	$\frac{1}{3}$	$\frac{5}{18}$	$\frac{1}{6}$

(iv) Using the marginal probabilities for X and Y:

$$E(X) = \Sigma x P(X = x) = 1 \times \tfrac{1}{3} + 2 \times \tfrac{1}{3} + 3 \times \tfrac{1}{3} = 2$$

$$\text{Var}(X) = E(X^2) - [E(X)]^2 = 1^2 \times \tfrac{1}{3} + 2^2 \times \tfrac{1}{3} + 3^2 \times \tfrac{1}{3} - 2^2 = \tfrac{2}{3}$$

$$E(Y) = \Sigma y P(Y = y) = 1 \times \tfrac{1}{6} + 2 \times \tfrac{1}{3} + 3 \times \tfrac{1}{2} = 2\tfrac{1}{3}$$

$$\text{Var}(Y) = E(Y^2) - [E(Y)]^2 = 1^2 \times \tfrac{1}{6} + 2^2 \times \tfrac{1}{3} + 3^2 \times \tfrac{1}{2} - 2\tfrac{1}{3}^2 = \tfrac{5}{9}$$

From the distribution for $X + Y$, tabulated above:

$$E(X + Y) = \Sigma(x + y)P(X + Y = x + y)$$

$$= 2 \times \tfrac{1}{18} + 3 \times \tfrac{1}{6} + 4 \times \tfrac{1}{3} + 5 \times \tfrac{5}{18} + 6 \times \tfrac{1}{6} = 4\tfrac{1}{3} = E(X) + E(Y)$$

$$\text{Var}(X + Y) = E([X + Y]^2) - [E(X + Y)]^2$$

$$= 4 \times \tfrac{1}{18} + 9 \times \tfrac{1}{6} + 16 \times \tfrac{1}{3} + 25 \times \tfrac{5}{18} + 36 \times \tfrac{1}{6} - 4\tfrac{1}{3}^2$$

$$= 1\tfrac{2}{9} = \text{Var}(X) + \text{Var}(Y)$$

EXAMPLE

X and Y are discrete random variables whose joint distribution is defined by:

$$P(X = x, Y = y) = k(x + y); \qquad x = 1, 2, 3, 4; \quad y = -1, 0, 1$$

(i) Construct a table of joint and marginal probabilities.

(ii) Construct a probability distribution for $Z = 2X + 3Y$ and find $E(Z)$ and $\text{Var}(Z)$.

(iii) Show that:

$$E(2X + 3Y) = 2E(X) + 3E(Y), \quad \text{whereas } \text{Var}(2X + 3Y) > 2\,\text{Var}(X) + 3\,\text{Var}(Y).$$

Solution:

(i) First form a table of joint probabilities in terms of constant k:

		Values of Y		
		−1	0	1
Values of X	1	0	k	$2k$
	2	k	$2k$	$3k$
	3	$2k$	$3k$	$4k$
	4	$3k$	$4k$	$5k$

Using the fact that $\Sigma P(X = x, Y = y) = 1$, gives:

$$(1 + 2 + 1 + 2 + 3 + 2 + 3 + 4 + 3 + 4 + 5)k = 1 \quad \Rightarrow \quad 30k = 1 \quad \Rightarrow \quad k = \tfrac{1}{30}$$

Now a table of joint and marginal probabilities may be constructed:

		Values of Y			$P(X = x)$
		−1	0	1	
Values of X	1	0	$\frac{1}{30}$	$\frac{1}{15}$	$\frac{1}{10}$
	2	$\frac{1}{30}$	$\frac{1}{15}$	$\frac{1}{15}$	$\frac{1}{5}$
	3	$\frac{1}{15}$	$\frac{1}{10}$	$\frac{2}{15}$	$\frac{3}{10}$
	4	$\frac{1}{10}$	$\frac{2}{15}$	$\frac{1}{6}$	$\frac{2}{5}$
$P(Y = y)$		$\frac{1}{5}$	$\frac{1}{3}$	$\frac{7}{15}$	1

(ii) Let $Z = 2X + 3Y$, then Z has probability distribution:

z	1	2	3	4	5	6	7	8	9	10	11
$P(Z = z)$	$\frac{1}{30}$	$\frac{1}{30}$	$\frac{1}{15}$	$\frac{1}{15}$	$\frac{1}{6}$	$\frac{1}{10}$	$\frac{1}{10}$	$\frac{2}{15}$	$\frac{2}{15}$	0	$\frac{1}{6}$

$$E(Z) = 1 \times \tfrac{1}{30} + 2 \times \tfrac{1}{30} + 3 \times \tfrac{1}{15} + \cdots + 9 \times \tfrac{2}{15} + 10 \times 0 + 11 \times \tfrac{1}{6} = 6\tfrac{4}{5}$$

$$\mathrm{Var}\,(Z) = 1 \times \tfrac{1}{30} + 4 \times \tfrac{1}{30} + 9 \times \tfrac{1}{15} + \cdots + 81 \times \tfrac{2}{15} + 100 \times 0 + 121 \times \tfrac{1}{6} - 6\tfrac{4}{5}^2 = 7\tfrac{19}{25}$$

(iii) Using the marginal probabilities for X and Y:

$$E(X) = 1 \times \tfrac{1}{10} + 2 \times \tfrac{1}{5} + 3 \times \tfrac{3}{10} + 4 \times \tfrac{2}{5} = 3$$

$$\mathrm{Var}\,(X) = 1^2 \times \tfrac{1}{10} + 2^2 \times \tfrac{1}{5} + 3^2 \times \tfrac{3}{10} + 4^2 \times \tfrac{2}{5} - 3^2 = 1$$

$$E(Y) = -1 \times \tfrac{1}{5} + 0 \times \tfrac{1}{3} + 1 \times \tfrac{7}{15} = \tfrac{4}{15}$$

$$\mathrm{Var}\,(Y) = (-1)^2 \times \tfrac{1}{5} + 0^2 \times \tfrac{1}{3} + 1^2 \times \tfrac{7}{15} - (\tfrac{4}{15})^2 = \tfrac{134}{225}$$

From the distribution for $Z = 2X + 3Y$, tabulated above:

$$2E(X) + 3E(Y) = 2 \times 3 + 3 \times \tfrac{4}{15} = 6\tfrac{4}{5} = E(Z) = E(2X + 3Y)$$

whereas:

$$2\,\mathrm{Var}\,(X) + 3\,\mathrm{Var}\,(Y) = 2 \times 1 + 3 \times \tfrac{134}{225} = 3\tfrac{59}{75}$$

$$< 7\tfrac{19}{25} = \mathrm{Var}\,(Z) = \mathrm{Var}\,(2X + 3Y)$$

The examples illustrate properties of combining expectations and variances for bivariate distributions. For any two discrete random variables, X and Y, and constants a and b :

$$\mathrm{E}(aX + bY) \equiv a\mathrm{E}(X) + b\mathrm{E}(Y)$$
$$\mathrm{Var}(aX + bY) \geqslant a\,\mathrm{Var}(X) + b\,\mathrm{Var}(Y)$$

The circumstances under which the equality holds for the variance formula will be investigated in the next section. However, the equivalence of the expectations holds for any two discrete random variables, the general proof of which is given below.

Theorem

For two discrete random variables X and Y: $\mathrm{E}(aX + bY) = a\mathrm{E}(X) + b\mathrm{E}(Y)$

Proof:

$$
\begin{aligned}
\mathrm{E}(aX + bY) &= \sum_x \sum_y (ax + by)\mathrm{P}(X = x, Y = y) \\
&= \sum_x \sum_y [ax\mathrm{P}(X = x, Y = y) + by\mathrm{P}(X = x, Y = y)] \\
&= a \sum_x x \sum_y \mathrm{P}(X = x, Y = y) + b \sum_y y \sum_x \mathrm{P}(X = x, Y = y) \\
&= a \sum_x x\mathrm{P}(X = x) + b \sum_y y\mathrm{P}(Y = y) \\
&= a\mathrm{E}(X) + b\mathrm{E}(Y)
\end{aligned}
$$

Investigation

Choose a class at your school or college. Investigate the absence pattern for girls and boys for a period of 50 (or 100) consecutive days. Record your results in a table which contains the number of days on which various combinations of numbers of girls and boys were absent.

		Number of boys absent					
		0	1	2	3	$\cdots$	Total
Number of girls absent	0 1 2 3 $\cdots$						
	Total						50

Let X represent the number of boys absent on any particular day. Let Y represent the number of girls absent on any particular day.

Investigation continued

- Construct a bivariate probability distribution based on your frequency distribution.
- Add a row and column for respective marginal probabilities.
- Find $E(X)$, $Var(X)$, $E(Y)$, $Var(Y)$.
- Form a probability distribution for $X + Y$.
- Verify that $E(X + Y) = E(X) + E(Y)$.
- Does $Var(X + Y) \approx Var(X) + Var(Y)$?
- Form a probability distribution for XY.
- Does $E(XY) \approx E(X) \times E(Y)$?

Keep the results of your investigation. As the chapter unfolds, use them to:

- test for *independence*;
- find the *correlation coefficient* between boys' and girls' absences.

Exercise 7A

1. The bivariate probability distribution of two discrete random variables, X and Y, is displayed in the following table:

		Values of Y		
		0	1	2
	0	0.1	0.1	0.1
Values of X	1	0.1	0.2	0.2
	2	0	0.1	0.1

(i) Illustrate this joint distribution using a vertical line diagram.

(ii) Find the marginal probabilities for X and Y.

(iii) Find (a) $P(X + Y = 2)$, (b) $P(X + Y \geqslant 2)$, (c) $P(X > Y)$.

(iv) Find $E(X)$ and $E(Y)$.

(v) Deduce (a) $E(X + Y)$, (b) $E(3X + 4Y)$, (c) $E(5X - Y)$.

2. A bag contains four balls, marked 1, 2, 3 and 4. One is selected at random and then another at random from those that remain. Let X represent the number on the first ball and Y the number on the second ball.

(i) Show that the bivariate probability distribution may be defined by the function:

$$P(X = x, Y = y) = \tfrac{1}{12};$$

$$x = 1, 2, 3, 4; \quad y = 1, 2, 3, 4; \quad x \neq y$$

Write out a table of probabilities for the joint distribution.

(ii) Find the marginal probabilities for X and Y.

(iii) Write out the probability distribution for $X + Y$.

(iv) Verify that $E(X + Y) = E(X) + E(Y)$.

3. A bivariate probability distribution is defined by:

$$P(X = x, Y = y) = kxy;$$

for $x = 1, 2, 3$ and $y = 1, 2, 3, 4$.

(i) Show that $k = \tfrac{1}{60}$.

(ii) Find $E(X)$ and $E(Y)$, and find $Var(X)$ and $Var(Y)$.

(iii) Construct a probability distribution for $X + Y$.

(iv) Verify that $E(X + Y) = E(X) + E(Y)$, and $Var(X + Y) = Var(X) + Var(Y)$.

(v) Construct a probability distribution for XY.

(vi) Verify that $E(XY) = E(X)E(Y)$.

4. Two refills for a ballpoint pen are selected at random from a box that contains three blue refills, two red refills and three green refills. Let X represent the number of blue refills and Y the number of red refills selected.

(i) Construct a bivariate probability distribution for X and Y by completing the following table:

	Values of Y		
	0	1	2
Values of X 0	$\frac{3}{28}$		
1			0
2		0	0

(ii) Find the marginal probabilities for X and Y.

(iii) Calculate the probability that neither of the two refills is a green one.

(iv) Find $E(X)$ and $E(Y)$ and from this deduce $E(X + Y)$, explaining what this represents.

5. Two fair dice are thrown and the scores noted. Let X represent the smaller of the two scores and Y the absolute difference between the two scores.

(i) Construct separate probability distributions for the random variables X and Y.

(ii) Construct a bivariate probability distribution for X and Y.

(iii) Calculate:

(a) $P(X = Y)$;

(b) $P(X < Y)$.

(iv) Find the marginal probabilities for X and Y and show that they correspond to the distributions found in (i).

(v) Find $E(X)$ and $E(Y)$ and deduce $E(X - Y)$.

6. A bivariate probability distribution for X and Y is given by the following table:

	Values of Y		
	1	2	3
1	0.04	a	0.17
Values of X 2	b	0	0.24
3	0.07	0.13	c

It is known that $E(X) = 1.94$ and $E(Y) = 2.15$.

(i) Find the marginal probabilities for X and Y in terms of a, b and c.

(ii) Find values for a, b and c.

7. Three fair coins are tossed and those landing heads uppermost are eliminated. The remainder are tossed for a second time. Random variables X and Y are chosen to represent the number of heads appearing uppermost before and after the elimination process. (Y is taken to be 0 if there is no second toss.)

(i) Complete the table of the bivariate distribution for X and Y:

	Values of Y			
	0	1	2	3
0	$\frac{1}{64}$			$\frac{1}{64}$
Values of X 1				0
2			0	0
3	$\frac{1}{8}$	0	0	0

(ii) Represent the distribution by a vertical line diagram.

(iii) Derive the marginal distributions for X and Y.

(iv) Find the mean and variance of X; find the mean and variance of Y.

(v) Deduce the values of $E(X + Y)$ and $E(X - Y)$.

8. Three fair dice are thrown. Random variables L and S represent the largest and the smallest of the three scores respectively.

(i) Complete the table of the bivariate distribution for L and S:

	Values of S					
	1	2	3	4	5	6
1	$\frac{1}{216}$	0	0	0	0	0
2			0	0	0	0
Values 3				0	0	0
of L 4					0	0
5						0
6	$\frac{30}{216}$					$\frac{1}{216}$

(ii) Illustrate this distribution by a suitable diagram.

(iii) Derive the marginal distributions for L and S.

(iv) Find the mean and variance of L; find the mean and variance of S.

(v) Deduce the values of $E(L + S)$ and $E(L - S)$.

Conditional probability

When considering a bivariate distribution, an important consideration is that of dependence. To what extent do the probabilities for X depend on Y, and vice versa? If X and Y are independent then there is no association between them. You will have already seen how to test for independence between two variables for empirical data using the chi-squared test for contingency tables. A chi-squared test on the frequency of the number of goals scored by home teams and away teams, during the first season of the Premier League, results in the acceptance of the null hypothesis that there is no association between the number of home team goals and away team goals. Here, however, we are dealing with bivariate probability distributions and so need to employ the idea of conditional probability which you met earlier in *Statistics 1*.

Tables of *conditional probabilities* of the form $P(X = x | Y = y)$ and $P(Y = y | X = x)$ may be compiled and comparison made with the unconditional probabilities $P(X = x)$ and $P(Y = y)$ to test for dependency.

To find $P(X = x | Y = y)$, we use the definition of conditional probability:

$$P(X = x | Y = y) = \frac{P(X = x, Y = y)}{P(Y = y)}$$

e.g. $P(X = 3 | Y = 1) = \dfrac{P(X = 3, Y = 1)}{P(Y = 1)} = \dfrac{0.041}{0.388} = 0.106$

Similarly: $P(Y = y | X = x) = \dfrac{P(Y = y, X = x)}{P(X = x)}$

e.g. $P(Y = 0 | X = 2) = \dfrac{P(X = 2, Y = 0)}{P(X = 2)} = \dfrac{0.071}{0.236} = 0.301$

A table of conditional probabilities, the conditional distribution of X for each value of Y, is given below. (You will be asked to construct the conditional distribution of Y for each value of X as part of Exercise 7B.)

		Values of Y						$P(X = x)$
		0	1	2	3	4	5	
	0	0.253	0.207	0.233	0.108	0	0	0.216
	1	0.347	0.369	0.156	0.297	0.333	0	0.342
	2	0.220	0.240	0.211	0.270	0.667	0.667	0.236
Values of X	3	0.120	0.106	0.089	0.189	0	0.333	0.115
	4	0.033	0.056	0.100	0.108	0	0	0.061
	5	0.020	0.017	0.033	0.027	0	0	0.022
	6	0.007	0	0.022	0	0	0	0.006
	7	0	0.006	0	0	0	0	0.002
	Totals	1.000	1.000	1.000	1.000	1.000	1.000	1.000

Compare each column of conditional probabilities with the column of marginal probabilities and with each other. There is enough similarity to suggest that the two variables X and Y are close to being independent, i.e. $P(X = x | Y = y) = P(X = x)$ and $P(Y = y | X = x) = P(Y = y)$.

Remember that this is an *empirical model*, based on a *population* of just 462 results. We now consider the concept of independence for a bivariate probability distribution.

Independence

For any discrete bivariate distribution, the two random variables X and Y are **independent** if the choice of X has no influence on the choice of Y and vice versa.

Using the definition of independence from *Statistics 1*:

Two events A and B are independent if and only if

$$P(A \cap B) = P(A) \times P(B)$$

From this definition we derive the equivalent definition for two random variables, X and Y:

Two *random variables*, X and Y, are independent if and only if

$$P(X = x, Y = y) = P(X = x) \times P(Y = y) \text{ for all values of } x \text{ and } y.$$

As a consequence, two variables X and Y are *not* independent if:

$P(X = x, Y = y) \neq P(X = x) \times P(Y = y)$ for any one pair of values of x and y.

Consider the bivariate distribution given by $P(X = x, Y = y) = \frac{1}{60}xy$ for $x = 1, 2, 3$ and $y = 1, 2, 3, 4$, which you met in Exercise 7A.

The table of joint and marginal probabilities for this distribution is:

		Values of Y				
		1	2	3	4	$P(X = x)$
	1	$\frac{1}{60}$	$\frac{1}{30}$	$\frac{1}{20}$	$\frac{1}{15}$	$\frac{1}{6}$
Values of X	2	$\frac{1}{30}$	$\frac{1}{15}$	$\frac{1}{10}$	$\frac{2}{15}$	$\frac{1}{3}$
	3	$\frac{1}{20}$	$\frac{1}{10}$	$\frac{3}{20}$	$\frac{1}{5}$	$\frac{1}{2}$
	$P(Y = y)$	$\frac{1}{10}$	$\frac{1}{5}$	$\frac{3}{10}$	$\frac{2}{5}$	1

For each value of X and Y you can see that $P(X = x, Y = y) = P(X = x) \times P(Y = y)$

e.g.: $P(X = 2, Y = 3) = \frac{1}{10} = \frac{1}{3} \times \frac{3}{10} = P(X = 2) \times P(Y = 3)$

This should not be surprising as by inspecting the marginal probability distributions we have:

$$P(X = x) = \tfrac{1}{6}x; \quad x = 1, 2, 3; \qquad P(Y = y) = \tfrac{1}{10}y; \quad y = 1, 2, 3, 4$$

$$\text{and } P(X = x, Y = y) = \tfrac{1}{60}xy = \tfrac{1}{6}x \times \tfrac{1}{10}y = P(X = x) \times P(Y = y)$$

When working through Exercise 7A, Question 3, you will have found:

$$E(X) = 2\tfrac{1}{3} \text{ and } E(Y) = 3; \qquad \text{Var}(X) = \tfrac{5}{9} \text{ and Var}(Y) = 1.$$

The probability distribution for $X + Y$ is:

$x + y$	2	3	4	5	6	7
$P(X + Y = x + y)$	$\frac{1}{60}$	$\frac{1}{15}$	$\frac{1}{6}$	$\frac{4}{15}$	$\frac{17}{60}$	$\frac{1}{5}$

$$E(X + Y) = \Sigma(x + y)P(X + Y = x + y) = 5\tfrac{1}{3} = 2\tfrac{1}{3} + 1 = E(X) + E(Y)$$

$$\text{Var}(X + Y) = E[(X + Y)^2] - [E(X + Y)]^2$$

$$= 30 - 5\tfrac{1}{3}^2 = 1\tfrac{5}{9} = \tfrac{5}{9} + 1 = \text{Var}(X) + \text{Var}(Y)$$

The probability distribution for XY is:

xy	1	2	3	4	5	6	7	8	9	10	11	12
$P(XY = xy)$	$\frac{1}{60}$	$\frac{1}{15}$	$\frac{1}{10}$	$\frac{2}{15}$	0	$\frac{1}{5}$	0	$\frac{2}{15}$	$\frac{3}{20}$	0	0	$\frac{1}{5}$

$$E(XY) = \Sigma(xy)P(XY = xy) = 7 = 2\tfrac{1}{3} \times 3 = E(X)E(Y).$$

The result that $E(X + Y) = E(X) + E(Y)$ is true for any discrete random variables X and Y.

But in this example, X and Y are *independent*, which leads to the results:

$$\textbf{Var}(X + Y) = \textbf{Var}(X) + \textbf{Var}(Y) \quad \text{and} \quad \textbf{E}(XY) = \textbf{E}(X)\textbf{E}(Y)$$

The idea that $\text{Var}(X + Y) = \text{Var}(X) + \text{Var}(Y)$ for independent events will be discussed later, but we now state and prove the result that for independent events 'the expectation of the product is the product of the expectations'.

Theorem

For two discrete random variables X and Y:

$$X \text{ and } Y \text{ are independent} \quad \Rightarrow \quad E(XY) = E(X)E(Y)$$

Proof:

$$E(XY) = \sum_x \sum_y xyP(X = x, Y = y)$$

$$= \sum_x \sum_y xyP(X = x)P(Y = y) \qquad \text{as } X \text{ and } Y \text{ are independent}$$

$$= \sum_x \sum_y xP(X = x)yP(Y = y)$$

$$= \sum_x xP(X = x) \sum_y yP(Y = y)$$

$$= E(X)E(Y)$$

The property that $E(XY) = E(X)E(Y)$ is a *necessary but not sufficient* condition for independence of X and Y,

i.e. $\qquad$ **X and Y are independent** $\quad \Rightarrow \quad$ **$E(XY) = E(X)E(Y)$;**

but $\qquad$ **$E(XY) = E(X)E(Y)$** $\quad \not\Rightarrow \quad$ **X and Y are independent.**

For X and Y to be *dependent* variables, it is only necessary to provide one counter-example, i.e. to show that $P(X = x, Y = y) \neq P(X = x) \times P(Y = y)$ for any one pair of values of X and Y.

Consider the bivariate distribution, together with marginal probabilities, defined by:

		Values of Y			
		1	2	3	$P(X = x)$
	2	0.2	0	0.2	0.4
Values of X	4	0	0.2	0	0.2
	6	0.2	0	0.2	0.4
	$P(Y = y)$	0.4	0.2	0.4	1

From the marginal distributions:

$$E(X) = \Sigma x P(X = x) = 2 \times 0.4 + 4 \times 0.2 + 6 \times 0.4 = 4$$

$$E(Y) = \Sigma y P(Y = y) = 1 \times 0.4 + 2 \times 0.2 + 3 \times 0.4 = 2$$

Let $Z = XY$, then Z has probability distribution:

z	2	4	6	8	12	18
$P(Z = z)$	0.2	0	0.4	0.2	0	0.2

Therefore:

$$E(Z) = \Sigma z P(Z = z)$$

$$= 2 \times 0.2 + 4 \times 0 + 6 \times 0.4 + 8 \times 0.2 + 12 \times 0 + 18 \times 0.2 = 8$$

Evidently $E(XY) = 8 = 4 \times 2 = E(X)E(Y)$, but X and Y are *not* independent as $P(X = x, Y = y) \neq P(X = x) \times P(Y = y)$ for *any* pair of values X and Y.

The idea of conditional probabilities for bivariate distributions can be extended to conditional expectation. The following examples illustrate this and other ideas.

EXAMPLE

The bivariate distribution for two random variables, X and Y, is shown in the table:

		Values of Y		
		1	2	3
	0	0	$\frac{1}{12}$	$\frac{1}{4}$
Values of X	1	$\frac{1}{8}$	$\frac{1}{4}$	0
	2	$\frac{1}{4}$	0	$\frac{1}{24}$

(i) Find the marginal probabilities for X and Y and obtain $E(X)$.

(ii) Find the conditional distribution of X for each value of Y.

(iii) Obtain $E(X|Y = 1)$, $E(X|Y = 2)$ and $E(X|Y = 3)$. Further, verify that:

$$E(X) = \sum_{\text{all } y} E(X|Y = y) \times P(Y = y)$$

Solution:

(i) The marginal distributions of X and Y are formed by the row and column totals:

		Values of Y		$P(X=x)$
		1	2	3	
Values of X	0	0	$\frac{1}{12}$	$\frac{1}{4}$	$\frac{1}{3}$
	1	$\frac{1}{8}$	$\frac{1}{4}$	0	$\frac{3}{8}$
	2	$\frac{1}{4}$	0	$\frac{1}{24}$	$\frac{7}{24}$
$P(Y=y)$		$\frac{3}{8}$	$\frac{1}{3}$	$\frac{7}{24}$	1

$$E(X) = \Sigma x P(X=x) = 0 \times \tfrac{1}{3} + 1 \times \tfrac{3}{8} + 2 \times \tfrac{7}{24} = \tfrac{23}{24}$$

(ii) Conditional distribution of X for each value of Y:

		Values of Y		
		1	2	3
Values of X	0	0	$\frac{1}{4}$	$\frac{6}{7}$
	1	$\frac{1}{3}$	$\frac{3}{4}$	0
	2	$\frac{2}{3}$	0	$\frac{1}{7}$
Total		1	1	1

e.g.
$$P(X=2\,|\,Y=1) = \frac{P(X=2, Y=1)}{P(Y=1)} = \frac{\frac{1}{4}}{\frac{3}{8}} = \frac{2}{3}$$

(iii)
$$E(X\,|\,Y=1) = \Sigma x P(X=x\,|\,Y=1) = 0 \times 0 + 1 \times \tfrac{1}{3} + 2 \times \tfrac{2}{3} = \tfrac{5}{3}$$
$$E(X\,|\,Y=2) = \Sigma x P(X=x\,|\,Y=2) = 0 \times \tfrac{1}{4} + 1 \times \tfrac{3}{4} + 2 \times 0 = \tfrac{3}{4}$$
$$E(X\,|\,Y=3) = \Sigma x P(X=x\,|\,Y=3) = 0 \times \tfrac{6}{7} + 1 \times 0 + 2 \times \tfrac{1}{7} = \tfrac{2}{7}$$

$$\sum_{\text{all } y} E(X\,|\,Y=y) \times P(Y=y)$$

$$= E(X\,|\,Y=1) \times P(Y=1) + E(X\,|\,Y-2) \times P(Y=2)$$
$$+ E(X\,|\,Y=3) \times P(Y=3)$$
$$= \tfrac{5}{3} \times \tfrac{3}{8} + \tfrac{3}{4} \times \tfrac{1}{3} + \tfrac{2}{7} \times \tfrac{7}{24} = \tfrac{5}{8} + \tfrac{1}{4} + \tfrac{1}{12} = \tfrac{23}{24} = E(X)$$

EXAMPLE

A bivariate probability distribution, for variables X and Y, is defined by:
$$P(X=x, Y=y) = k|x-y| \text{ for } x = 1,3,5 \text{ and } y = 1,2,3$$

(i) Show that $k = \frac{1}{15}$.

(ii) Find the marginal probabilities for X and Y.

(iii) Are X and Y independent? Give a reason for your answer.

Solution:

(i) Using the definition, the joint probability distribution for X and Y in terms of k is:

		Values of Y		
		1	2	3
Values of X	1	0	k	$2k$
	3	$2k$	k	0
	5	$4k$	$3k$	$2k$

As $k(0+1+2+2+1+0+4+3+2) = 15k = 1$, $k = \frac{1}{15}$.

(ii) The marginal distributions of X and Y are formed by the row and column totals:

		Values of Y			
		1	2	3	$P(X = x)$
Values of X	1	0	$\frac{1}{15}$	$\frac{2}{15}$	$\frac{1}{5}$
	3	$\frac{2}{15}$	$\frac{1}{15}$	0	$\frac{1}{5}$
	5	$\frac{4}{15}$	$\frac{1}{5}$	$\frac{2}{15}$	$\frac{3}{5}$
$P(Y = y)$		$\frac{2}{5}$	$\frac{1}{3}$	$\frac{4}{15}$	1

(iii) Although: $P(X = 3, Y = 2) = \frac{1}{15} = \frac{1}{5} \times \frac{1}{3} = P(X = 3) \times P(Y = 2)$,

$P(X = 1, Y = 1) = 0 \neq \frac{1}{5} \times \frac{2}{5} = P(X = 1) \times P(Y = 2)$;

just one counter-example is sufficient to show that X and Y are *not* independent.

EXAMPLE

An ordinary pack of playing cards is shuffled and a card is chosen at random. The random variable X has value 3 if an ace is chosen, 2 if a picture card is chosen and 1 otherwise.

A second pack of cards has all its queens removed. The remaining cards are then shuffled and a card is chosen at random. The random variable Y has value 3 if an ace is chosen, 2 if a picture card is chosen and 1 otherwise.

(i)   Explain why X and Y are independent.

(ii) Construct a bivariate probability distribution for X and Y.

(iii) Verify that $E(XY) = E(X) \times E(Y)$.

Solution:

(i)   As the value of X depends entirely on the outcome of the first draw and the value of Y depends on the outcome of the second draw, from a different pack of cards, either outcome has no influence on the other, so X and Y must be independent.

(ii) First tabulate probability distributions for X and Y separately:

X	1	2	3
$P(X = x)$	$\frac{9}{13}$	$\frac{3}{13}$	$\frac{1}{13}$

Y	1	2	3
$P(Y = y)$	$\frac{3}{4}$	$\frac{1}{6}$	$\frac{1}{12}$

As X and Y are independent, $P(X = x, Y = y) = P(X = x) \times P(Y = y)$ for all values of X and Y. We may multiply the marginal probabilities given to find the joint probabilities:

		Values of Y			
		1	2	3	$P(X = x)$
Values of X	1	$\frac{27}{52}$	$\frac{3}{26}$	$\frac{3}{52}$	$\frac{9}{13}$
	2	$\frac{9}{52}$	$\frac{1}{26}$	$\frac{1}{52}$	$\frac{3}{13}$
	3	$\frac{3}{52}$	$\frac{1}{78}$	$\frac{1}{156}$	$\frac{1}{13}$
$P(Y = y)$		$\frac{3}{4}$	$\frac{1}{6}$	$\frac{1}{12}$	1

(iii) From the original distribution for X and Y:

$$E(X) = 1 \times \tfrac{9}{13} + 2 \times \tfrac{3}{13} + 3 \times \tfrac{1}{13} = \tfrac{18}{13} = 1\tfrac{5}{13}$$

$$E(Y) = 1 \times \tfrac{3}{4} + 2 \times \tfrac{1}{6} + 3 \times \tfrac{1}{12} = \tfrac{4}{3} = 1\tfrac{1}{3}$$

Let $Z = XY$, then Z has the probability distribution:

z	1	2	3	4	5	6	7	8	9
$P(Z = z)$	$\tfrac{27}{52}$	$\tfrac{15}{52}$	$\tfrac{3}{26}$	$\tfrac{1}{26}$	0	$\tfrac{5}{156}$	0	0	$\tfrac{1}{156}$

Therefore $E(Z) = 1 \times \tfrac{27}{52} + 2 \times \tfrac{15}{52} + 3 \times \tfrac{3}{26} + 4 \times \tfrac{1}{26} + 6 \times \tfrac{5}{156} + 9 \times \tfrac{1}{156} = \tfrac{24}{13} = 1\tfrac{11}{13}$

This result gives us $E(XY) = \tfrac{24}{13} = \tfrac{18}{13} \times \tfrac{4}{3} = E(X) \times E(Y)$.

Exercise 7B

1. The bivariate probability distribution of two discrete random variables, X and Y, is displayed in the following table:

		Values of Y	
	0	1	2
Values of X 0	0.12	0.08	0.10
1	0.10	0.12	0.12
2	0.16	0.14	0.06

(i) Illustrate the bivariate distribution in a diagram.

(ii) Find the marginal probabilities for X and Y.

(iii) Find $E(X)$ and $E(Y)$.

(iv) Find $P(X = 1 \mid Y = 0)$, $P(X = 1 \mid Y = 1)$ and $P(X = 1 \mid Y = 2)$.

What do you conclude about the random variables X and Y?

2. Using the bivariate distribution for the FA Premier League, developed at the beginning of this chapter, construct the conditional distribution of Y for each value of X.

3. A bag contains four discs, marked 1, 2, 3 and 4. Two are selected at random. Let X represent the higher of the two numbers drawn and Y the lower of the two numbers drawn.

(i) Explain why there are six possible selections, and from this complete the following table of joint and marginal probabilities for X and Y:

		Values of Y		$P(X = x)$
	1	2	3	
Values of X 2				0
3				
4	$\tfrac{1}{6}$			
$P(Y = y)$				1

(ii) Are X and Y independent? Explain your reasoning.

4. A jar contains ten sweets, identical in shape, but four are toffees, three are humbugs and three are milk chocolates. Let X represent the number of toffees and Y the number of humbugs selected when three are chosen at random.

(i) Explain why the bivariate probability distribution for X and Y is given by:

$$P(X = x, Y = y) = \frac{{}^{4}C_x \times {}^{3}C_y \times {}^{3}C_{(3-x-y)}}{{}^{10}C_3}$$

for $X = 0, 1, 2, 3$ and $Y = 0, 1, 2, 3$

subject to $0 \leqslant x + y \leqslant 3$

(ii) Construct a bivariate probability distribution for X and Y by completing the following table:

	Values of Y			
	0	1	2	3
Values of X 0				
1		$\tfrac{3}{10}$		0
2			0	0
3		0	0	0

   (iii) Find the marginal probabilities for X and Y.

   (iv) Find the conditional distribution of X for each value of Y.

5. Two fair dice are thrown and the scores noted. Let X represent the larger of the two scores and Y the absolute difference between the two scores.

   (i) Construct separate probability distributions for the random variables X and Y.

   (ii) Construct a bivariate probability distribution for X and Y.

   (iii) Find the marginal probabilities for X and Y and show that they correspond to the distributions found in (i).

   (iv) Calculate the conditional probabilities $P(Y = y \mid X = 4)$. Compare them with $P(Y = y)$ found in (i). Are X and Y independent?

6. Three fair coins are tossed. Let X represent the number of heads and Y the number of 'runs', e.g. the outcome **HTT** would result in $x = 1$, $y = 2$ and the outcome **HHH** would result in $x = 3$, $y = 1$.

   (i) Construct a bivariate probability distribution for X and Y.

   (ii) Find the marginal probabilities for X and Y and obtain $E(X)$ and $E(Y)$.

   (iii) Are X and Y independent? Give a reason for your answer.

7. X and Y are discrete random variables whose joint distribution is shown in the table:

		Values of Y		
		1	2	3
	1	$\frac{1}{4}$	$\frac{1}{4}$	0
Values of X	2	$\frac{1}{8}$	$\frac{1}{12}$	$\frac{1}{24}$
	3	$\frac{1}{4}$	0	0

   (i) Find the distributions of X and Y. Obtain $E(X)$ and $\text{Var}(X)$.

   (ii) Find the conditional distribution of X for each value of Y.

   (iii) Are X and Y independent? Justify your answer.

   (iv) Obtain $E[X \mid Y = 1]$, i.e. the expected value

of X conditional on $Y = 1$; obtain similarly $E[X \mid Y = 2]$ and $E[X \mid Y = 3]$.

Show how these three expected values, together with the distribution of Y, can be used to obtain $E[X]$.

[MEI]

8. X and Y are discrete random variables whose joint distribution is shown in the table:

		Values of Y		
		1	2	3
	1	0.20	0.10	0.05
Values of X	2	0.05	0.20	0.10
	3	0.15	0.10	0.05

   (i) Find the distributions of X and Y. Obtain $E(X)$ and $E(Y)$.

   (ii) Are X and Y independent? Justify your answer.

   (iii) Find the distributions of:

     (a) $X + Y$;

     (b) $X - Y$;

     (c) XY.

   (iv) Using (iii), determine which of the following statements are true and which are false, stating clearly a reason in each case:

     (a) $E(X + Y) = E(X) + E(Y)$;

     (b) $E(X - Y) = E(X) - E(Y)$;

     (c) $E(XY) = E(X)E(Y)$.

9. X and Y are random variables which take six possible pairs of values with the probabilities shown:

		Values of Y		
		-1	0	1
Values of X	0	$\frac{1}{56}$	$\frac{3}{56}$	$\frac{3}{56}$
	1	$\frac{1}{4}$	$\frac{1}{8}$	$\frac{1}{2}$

   (i) Find the probability that $X = 1$, and the probability that $Y = 1$.

   (ii) Calculate $E(X)$, $E(Y)$ and $E(XY)$.

   (iii) Are X and Y independent random variables? Give the reason for your answer.

[O&C, SMP]

Covariance and correlation

In the last section we took a close look at the idea of independence for two discrete random variables. For the cases where the two variables were not independent, to what extent does one variable influence the other? In *Statistics 2* we studied closely the idea of correlation for a bivariate sample and used a hypothesis test to determine whether the correlation coefficient was significantly different from zero. In this section we examine the degree to which two random variables are correlated, by calculating the population equivalent to the sample product moment correlation coefficient.

Just as with the sample correlation coefficient, we first need to define the *covariance* between two random variables:

$$\text{Cov}\,(X, Y) = \text{E}[(X - \mu_X)(Y - \mu_Y)]$$

where $\mu_X = \text{E}(X)$ and $\mu_Y = \text{E}(Y)$. As the square root of the variance is the standard deviation, a useful short-hand for the standard deviation of X is σ_X, i.e. $\sigma_X^2 = \text{Var}\,(X)$. Similarly, the standard deviation of Y is denoted by σ_Y, i.e. $\sigma_Y^2 = \text{Var}\,(Y)$.

In the same way that the formula for the variance has an alternative form which is usually easier to work with, so too does the covariance, which can be seen by the following algebraic manipulation:

$$\text{Cov}\,(X, Y) = \text{E}([X - \mu_X][Y - \mu_Y])$$

$$= \text{E}(XY - \mu_X Y - \mu_Y X + \mu_X \mu_Y)$$

$$- \text{E}(XY) - \mu_X \text{E}(Y) - \mu_Y \text{E}(X) + \text{E}(\mu_X \mu_Y)$$

$$= \text{E}(XY) - \mu_X \mu_Y - \mu_Y \mu_X + \mu_X \mu_Y$$

$$= \text{E}(XY) - \mu_X \mu_Y$$

i.e. the alternative form for the covariance is $\text{E}(XY) - \mu_X \mu_Y$ or $\text{E}(XY) - \text{E}(X)\text{E}(Y)$.

When expressed in this form we can see that whenever random variables X and Y are independent then the covariance will be zero as $\text{E}(XY) = \text{E}(X)\text{E}(Y)$ for independent variables. However, the implication is one way only, and a zero covariance will not necessarily mean that the variables are independent.

Continuing our analogy with the correlation coefficient for a bivariate sample, the definition of the product moment correlation coefficient for a bivariate probability distribution is:

$$\rho = \frac{\text{Cov}\,(X, Y)}{\sigma_X \sigma_Y}$$

The following example illustrates the way in which both the covariance $\text{Cov}\,(X, Y)$ and the product moment correlation coefficient ρ may be evaluated.

A bivariate distribution is defined by the following joint and marginal probabilities:

		Values of Y				
		1	2	3	4	$P(X = x)$
Values of X	1	0	0	0	0.2	0.2
	2	0	0.2	0	0.1	0.3
	3	0.1	0	0.2	0	0.3
	4	0.2	0	0	0	0.2
	$P(Y = y)$	0.3	0.2	0.2	0.3	1

(i) Illustrate the distribution using a suitable diagram.

(ii) Find $E(X)$, $Var(X)$, $E(Y)$ and $Var(Y)$.

(iii) Tabulate the probability distribution for XY and hence find $E(XY)$.

(iv) Find the values of $Cov(X, Y)$ and the correlation coefficient ρ.

Solution:

(i)

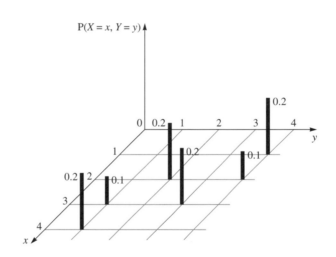

Figure 7.2

(ii) $E(X) = 1 \times 0.2 + 2 \times 0.3 + 3 \times 0.3 + 4 \times 0.2 = 2.5$

$Var(X) = 1^2 \times 0.2 + 2^2 \times 0.3 + 3^2 \times 0.3 + 4^2 \times 0.2 - 2.5^2 = 7.3 - 6.25 = 1.05$

$E(Y) = 1 \times 0.3 + 2 \times 0.2 + 3 \times 0.2 + 4 \times 0.3 = 2.5$

$Var(Y) = 1^2 \times 0.3 + 2^2 \times 0.2 + 3^2 \times 0.2 + 4^2 \times 0.3 - 2.5^2 = 7.7 - 6.25 = 1.45$

(iii) The probability distribution for XY is:

xy	1	2	3	4	6	8	9	12	16
$P(XY - xy)$	0	0	0.1	0.6	0	0.1	0.2	0	0

Thus $E(XY) = 3 \times 0.1 + 4 \times 0.6 + 8 \times 0.1 + 9 \times 0.2 = 5.3$

(iv) Using values from (i) and (ii) we can deduce:

$$\text{Cov}(X, Y) = E(XY) - E(X)E(Y) = 5.3 - 2.5^2 = -0.95 \text{ and}$$

$$\rho = \frac{\text{Cov}(X, Y)}{\sigma_X \sigma_Y} = \frac{-0.95}{\sqrt{1.05}\sqrt{1.45}} = -0.770 \text{ (to 3 sf)}$$

The correlation is negative because of the 'inverse' nature of the relationship; i.e. X tends to be large when Y is small, and vice versa. This may be seen clearly in the diagram on page 117.

When working with sample product-moment correlation coefficients in *Statistics 2* we saw that r must satisfy the inequality $-1 \leqslant r \leqslant 1$, i.e. the magnitude of r cannot exceed 1. We now show why this must also be true for the population correlation coefficient ρ, i.e. $|\rho| < 1$.

Suppose X and Y are random variables, then let $U = X - \mu_X$ and $V = Y - \mu_Y$.

For any real z, we have:

$$0 \leqslant E([V - zU]^2)$$

$$= E(V^2 - 2zUV + z^2U^2)$$

$$= E(V^2) - 2zE(UV) + z^2E(U^2)$$

$$= az^2 + bz + c$$

where $a = E(U^2)$, $b = -2E(UV)$ and $c = E(V^2)$.

As this quadratic is non-negative for all real z, the discriminant $(b^2 - 4ac)$ must be non-positive, for if it were positive there would be two real zeros, in which case the quadratic would be negative for some values of z.

Thus:

$$b^2 - 4ac = 4[E(UV)]^2 - 4E(U^2)E(V^2) \leqslant 0$$

$$\Rightarrow \quad [E(UV)]^2 \leqslant E(U^2)E(V^2)$$

$$\Rightarrow \quad [E((X - \mu_X)(Y - \mu_Y))]^2 \leqslant E((X - \mu_X)^2)E((Y - \mu_Y)^2)$$

$$\Rightarrow \quad [\text{Cov}(X, Y)]^2 \leqslant \text{Var}(X)\text{Var}(Y)$$

$$\Rightarrow \quad \frac{[\text{Cov}(X, Y)]^2}{\text{Var}(X)\text{Var}(Y)} \leqslant 1$$

$$\Rightarrow \quad \rho^2 \leqslant 1$$

$$\Rightarrow \quad -1 \leqslant \rho \leqslant 1$$

Coding

Suppose random variables X and Y are connected to random variables X' and Y' using the coding $X = aX' + b$ and $Y = cY' + d$, then $E(X) = aE(X') + b$ and $E(Y) = cE(Y') + d$.

Then:

$$\text{Cov}(X, Y) = E([X - \mu_X][Y - \mu_Y])$$

$$= E([aX' + b - a\mu_{X'} - b][cY' + d - c\mu_{Y'} - d])$$

$$= E([aX' - a\mu_{X'}][cY' - c\mu_{Y'}])$$

$$= E(ac[X' - \mu_{X'}][Y' - \mu_{Y'}])$$

$$= ac\,E([X' - \mu_{X'}][Y' - \mu_{Y'}])$$

$$\Rightarrow \quad \text{Cov}(X, Y) = ac\,\text{Cov}(X', Y')$$

Similarly, as $\text{Var}(X) = \text{Var}(aX' + b) = a^2\,\text{Var}(X)$ and $\text{Var}(Y) = \text{Var}(cY' + d) = c^2\,\text{Var}(Y')$, the link between the correlation coefficient for X and Y, denoted by ρ_{XY} and the correlation coefficient for X' and Y', denoted by $\rho_{X'Y'}$ may be established:

$$\rho_{XY} = \frac{\text{Cov}(X, Y)}{\sqrt{\text{Var}(X)}\sqrt{\text{Var}(Y)}} = \frac{ac\,\text{Cov}(X', Y')}{ac\sqrt{\text{Var}(X')}\sqrt{\text{Var}(Y')}}$$

$$= \frac{\text{Cov}(X', Y')}{\sqrt{\text{Var}(X')}\sqrt{\text{Var}(Y')}} = \rho_{X'Y'}$$

provided $ac > 0$.

EXAMPLE A bivariate distribution is defined by the following joint probabilities:

		Values of Y		
		1	2	3
	1	0.3	0.05	0
Values of X	2	0.05	0.2	0.05
	3	0	0.05	0.3

(i) Illustrate the distribution using a suitable diagram.

(ii) Find $\text{Cov}(X, Y)$ and the correlation coefficient between X and Y.

(iii) Deduce the covariance and correlation coefficients between random variables U and V, where $U = 2X + 1$, $V = 3X - 2$.

Solution:

(i)

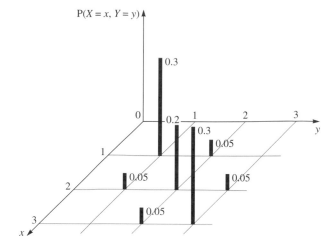

Figure 7.3

(ii) The table of joint and marginal probabilities is given by:

		Values of Y			
		1	2	3	$P(X = x)$
Values of X	1	0.3	0.05	0	0.35
	2	0.05	0.2	0.05	0.3
	3	0	0.05	0.3	0.35
	$P(Y = y)$	0.35	0.3	0.35	1

Using the marginal probabilities we may deduce:

$$E(X) = E(Y) = 1 \times 0.35 + 2 \times 0.3 + 3 \times 0.35 = 2$$

$$E(X^2) = E(Y^2) = 1 \times 0.35 + 4 \times 0.3 + 9 \times 0.35 = 4.7$$

$$\text{Var}\,(X) = \text{Var}\,(Y) = 4.7 - 4 = 0.7$$

The distribution of XY is given by:

xy	1	2	3	4	6	9
$P(XY = xy)$	0.3	0.1	0	0.2	0.1	0.3

Therefore $E(XY) = 1 \times 0.3 + 2 \times 0.1 + 4 \times 0.2 + 6 \times 0.1 + 9 \times 0.3 = 4.6$
and so:

$$\text{Cov}\,(X, Y) = E(XY) - E(X)E(Y) = 4.6 - 2 \times 2 = 0.6$$

$$\Rightarrow \quad \rho_{X,Y} = \frac{\text{Cov}\,(X, Y)}{\sigma_X \sigma_Y} = \frac{0.6}{0.7} = \frac{6}{7}$$

(iii) As $U = 2X + 1$ and $V = 3X - 2$:

$$\text{Cov}(U, V) = 2 \times 3 \times \text{Cov}(X, Y) = 6 \times 0.6 = 3.6$$

$$\rho_{U,V} = \rho_{X,Y} = \tfrac{6}{7}$$

Exercise 7C

1. X and Y are discrete random variables whose joint distribution is shown in the table:

		Values of Y	
		-1	0	1
	1	$\frac{1}{4}$	0	$\frac{1}{8}$
Values of X	2	$\frac{1}{8}$	$\frac{1}{4}$	0
	3	0	$\frac{1}{12}$	$\frac{1}{6}$

(i) Find the distributions of X and Y. Obtain $\text{E}(X)$ and $\text{Var}(X)$.

(ii) Find the conditional distribution of X for each value of Y.

(iii) Are X and Y independent? Justify your answer.

(iv) Obtain the covariance of X and Y.

[MEI]

2. X and Y are discrete random variables whose joint distribution is shown in the table:

		Values of Y	
		0	1	2
	-1	p	0	p
Values of X	0	q	p	q
	1	p	0	p

(i) Giving a reason, state whether X and Y are independent.

(ii) Show that the covariance of X and Y is 0.

(iii) Given that $\text{Var}(Y) = \frac{5}{6}$, find values for p and q.

(iv) With p and q having the values found in (iii), find the conditional distribution of X for each value of Y.

[Cambridge]

3. The random variables X and Y take a finite number of discrete values.

(i) Define $\text{Cov}(X, Y)$, and prove that if X and Y are independent then $\text{Cov}(X, Y) = 0$.

(ii) In a particular case, X and Y each take values 1, 2 and 3. The probability that $X = i$ and $Y = j$ is denoted by p_{ij}. The values of $p_{12}, p_{21}, p_{23}, p_{32}$, are each 0.25, and the values of all the other p_{ij} are zero. Show that X and Y are not independent. Calculate $\text{Cov}(X, Y)$ and comment on your answer.

[Cambridge]

4. (*Numerical answers in this question should be given as fractions in their lowest terms.*)

X and Y are discrete random variables whose joint distribution is given in the table:

		Values of Y	
		1	2	3
	-1	$\frac{1}{9}$	$\frac{1}{6}$	0
Values of X	0	0	$\frac{1}{4}$	$\frac{1}{6}$
	1	$\frac{1}{9}$	0	$\frac{7}{36}$

(i) Find $\text{P}(X + Y > 1)$.

(ii) Find the distribution of X and the distribution of Y, i.e. the two marginal distributions for the table above. Find the mean and variance of the marginal distribution of X and the mean of the marginal distribution of Y.

(iii) Find the conditional distribution of X given for each value of Y.

(iv) Are X and Y independent? Justify your answer, based on your solutions to (ii) and/or (iii).

(v) Obtain the covariance of X and Y.

[MEI Statistics, 6 June 1993]

5. Jim and Kate have been invited to come round tonight to watch a video. Jim might bring X friends $(X = 0, 1, 2)$ and Kate might bring Y friends $(Y = 0, 1, 2)$. The joint probability distribution of X and Y is given in the table:

Exercise 7C continued

	Values of Y		
	0	1	2
Values of X 0	0.05	0.03	0.02
1	0.25	0.15	0.10
2	0.20	0.12	0.08

(i) Show that X and Y are independent, carefully explaining the steps of your argument.

(ii) Let T be the *total* number of persons who come to watch the video. Find the expected value and the variance of T.

(iii) Construct a table showing the joint probability distribution of X and T.

(iv) From this, or otherwise, find $\mathrm{Cov}\,(X, T)$.
[MEI Statistics, 6 June 1993]

6. (*Numerical answers in this question, except for the final answer in part (v), should be given as fractions in their lowest terms.*)

X and Y are discrete random variables whose joint distribution is given in the table:

	Values of Y			
	2	4	6	8
−2	$\frac{3}{32}$	$\frac{1}{32}$	0	$\frac{1}{16}$
−1	$\frac{1}{16}$	0	$\frac{3}{32}$	$\frac{3}{32}$
Values of X 0	$\frac{1}{16}$	$\frac{1}{16}$	$\frac{1}{16}$	$\frac{1}{16}$
1	$\frac{5}{32}$	0	0	$\frac{5}{32}$

(i) Find $\mathrm{P}(X + Y > 3)$.

(ii) Find the marginal distribution of X and its mean and variance. Find also the marginal distribution of Y.

(iii) Give a justification for the statement that X and Y are not independent.

(iv) Find the conditional distribution of X given that $Y = 8$.

(v) Find the correlation coefficient for X and Y.
[MEI Statistics, 6 June 1995]

7. A trial consists of throwing two distinguishable dice and noting the individual scores. Random variables X, Y, U, V are defined as follows:

X: score on first die;
Y: score on second die;
U: sum of scores of the two dice;
V: (score on first die) − (score on second die).

(i) Give the probability distribution of X and use it to find $\mathrm{E}(X)$ and $\mathrm{E}(X^2)$.

(ii) Use the result $uv = x^2 - y^2$ to find $\mathrm{E}(UV)$, and from this show that $\mathrm{E}(UV) - \mathrm{E}(U)\mathrm{E}(V)$, the covariance of U and V, is equal to zero.

(iii) Show, by considering the probability $\mathrm{P}(U = 3)$ and the conditional probability $\mathrm{P}(U = 3 \mid V = 1)$, that the variables U and V are *not* independent (despite them having zero covariance).
[O&C, SMP]

Variances of linear combinations

In this final section we will develop the general formula for the variance of a linear combination of two discrete random variables, X and Y. We have seen examples where, for independent random variables X and Y,

$$\mathrm{Var}\,(X \pm Y) = \mathrm{Var}\,(X) + \mathrm{Var}\,(Y)$$

But what happens when X and Y are *not* independent?

Using the notation $\mathrm{E}(X) = \mu_X$ and $\mathrm{E}(Y) = \mu_Y$ then by definition:

$$\mathrm{Var}\,(X + Y) = \mathrm{E}([X + Y - \mathrm{E}(X + Y)]^2)$$

$$= \mathrm{E}([X + Y - (\mu_X + \mu_Y)]^2)$$

$$= \mathrm{E}([(X - \mu_X) + (Y - \mu_Y)]^2)$$

Now expand the square of the sum in brackets:

$$[(X - \mu_X) + (Y - \mu_Y)]^2 = (X - \mu_X)^2 + 2(X - \mu_X)(Y - \mu_Y) + (Y - \mu_Y)^2$$

Using the notion that the expectation of the sum is the sum of the expectations gives:

$$\begin{aligned}
\text{Var}(X + Y) &= E((X - \mu_X)^2 + 2(X - \mu_X)(Y - \mu_Y) + (Y - \mu_Y)^2) \\
&= E((X - \mu_X)^2) + 2E((X - \mu_X)(Y - \mu_Y)) + E((Y - \mu_Y)^2) \\
&= \text{Var}(X) + 2\,\text{Cov}(X, Y) + \text{Var}(Y)
\end{aligned}$$

For *independent* variables X and Y, we note that $\text{Cov}(X, Y) = 0$, from which we derive the special result:

$$\text{Var}(X + Y) = \text{Var}(X) + \text{Var}(Y).$$

Two counters are drawn from a bag with four counters, numbered 1, 2, 3 and 4. Let X and Y denote, respectively, the larger and smaller of the numbers drawn. The joint distribution and marginal probabilities are shown in the following table:

		Values of Y			
		1	2	3	$P(X = x)$
Values of X	2	$\frac{1}{6}$	0	0	$\frac{1}{6}$
	3	$\frac{1}{6}$	$\frac{1}{6}$	0	$\frac{1}{3}$
	4	$\frac{1}{6}$	$\frac{1}{6}$	$\frac{1}{6}$	$\frac{1}{2}$
	$P(Y = y)$	$\frac{1}{2}$	$\frac{1}{3}$	$\frac{1}{6}$	1

(i) Are variables X and Y independent?

(ii) Find $E(X + Y)$ and $\text{Var}(X + Y)$ from the distributions of X and Y.

(iii) Verify the answers to (ii) by first tabulating the probability distribution for $X + Y$.

Solution:

(i) Variables X and Y are *not* independent, as for all values of X and Y:

$$P(X = x, Y = y) \neq P(X = x) \times P(Y = y).$$

(ii) Using the marginal distributions:

$$E(X) = 2 \times \tfrac{1}{6} + 3 \times \tfrac{1}{3} + 4 \times \tfrac{1}{2} = \tfrac{10}{3} \text{ and } E(Y) = 1 \times \tfrac{1}{2} + 2 \times \tfrac{1}{3} + 3 \times \tfrac{1}{6} = \tfrac{5}{3}$$

$$\text{Var}(X) = 4 \times \tfrac{1}{6} + 9 \times \tfrac{1}{3} + 16 \times \tfrac{1}{2} - (\tfrac{10}{3})^2 = \tfrac{35}{3} - \tfrac{100}{9} = \tfrac{5}{9}$$

$$\text{Var}(Y) = 1 \times \tfrac{1}{2} + 4 \times \tfrac{1}{3} + 9 \times \tfrac{1}{6} - (\tfrac{5}{3})^2 = \tfrac{10}{3} - \tfrac{25}{9} = \tfrac{5}{9}$$

$$E(XY) = (2 + 3 + 4 + 6 + 8 + 12) \times \tfrac{1}{6} = \tfrac{35}{6}$$

From these values we can deduce:

$$E(X + Y) = E(X) + E(Y) = \tfrac{10}{3} + \tfrac{5}{3} = 5$$

$$\text{Cov}(X, Y) = E(XY) - E(X)E(Y) = \tfrac{35}{6} - \tfrac{5}{3} \times \tfrac{10}{3} = \tfrac{5}{18}$$

and so

$$\text{Var}(X + Y) = \text{Var}(X) + 2\,\text{Cov}(X, Y) + \text{Var}(Y) = \tfrac{5}{9} + 2 \times \tfrac{5}{18} + \tfrac{5}{9} = \tfrac{5}{3}$$

7

(iii) The probability distribution of $X + Y$ is given by:

$x + y$	3	4	5	6	7
$P(X = x, Y = y)$	$\frac{1}{6}$	$\frac{1}{6}$	$\frac{1}{3}$	$\frac{1}{6}$	$\frac{1}{6}$

from which we can deduce $E(X + Y) = 5$ (by symmetry) and:

$$\text{Var}(X + Y) = 9 \times \tfrac{1}{6} + 16 \times \tfrac{1}{6} + 25 \times \tfrac{1}{3} + 36 \times \tfrac{1}{6} + 49 \times \tfrac{1}{6} - 25 = \tfrac{5}{3}$$

The result for the variance of the sum of two random variables, X and Y, can be generalised to a linear combination of them as follows:

$$\text{Var}(aX + bY) = E([aX + bY - E(aX + bY)]^2)$$
$$= E([(aX - a\mu_X) + (bY - b\mu_Y)]^2)$$
$$= E((aX - a\mu_X)^2 + 2(aX - a\mu_X)(bY - b\mu_Y) + (bY - b\mu_Y)^2)$$
$$= a^2 E((X - \mu_X)^2) + 2ab E((X - \mu_X)(Y - \mu_Y)) + b^2 E((Y - \mu_Y)^2)$$
$$= a^2 \text{Var}(X) + 2ab \text{Cov}(X, Y) + b^2 \text{Var}(Y)$$

In particular, when $a = 1$ and $b = -1$:

$$\text{Var}(X - Y) = \text{Var}(X) - 2\text{Cov}(X, Y) + \text{Var}(Y)$$

and for *independent* variables X and Y, for which $\text{Cov}(X, Y) = 0$,

$$\text{Var}(X - Y) = \text{Var}(X) + \text{Var}(Y)$$

Exercise 7D

1. Random variables X and Y are such that $\text{Var}(X) = \text{Var}(Y) = \text{Cov}(X, Y) = 1$. Find:

(i) $\text{Var}(X + 2)$;

(ii) $\text{Var}(3Y - 5)$;

(iii) $\text{Var}(X + Y)$;

(iv) $\text{Var}(3X - 2Y)$;

(v) $\text{Var}(X + 4Y - 7)$;

(vi) $\text{Cov}(X, X + Y)$.

2. A discrete random variable, X, takes values 0, 1, 2, 3 and a discrete random variable, Y, takes values 0, 1, 2. The joint probability distribution of X and Y is given by the following table:

		Values of Y		
		0	1	2
Values of X	0	0	0.1	0.1
	1	0.1	0.2	0
	2	0.1	0.2	0
	3	0	0	0.2

(i) Show that $\text{Cov}(X, Y) = 0.15$.

(ii) Calculate:

(a) $\text{Var}(2X - 7)$;

(b) $E(X + Y)$;

(c) $\text{Var}(X + Y)$.

[Cambridge]

3. A bag contains five discs, marked 1, 2, 3, 4 and 5. Two are selected at random. Let X represent the higher of the two numbers drawn and Y the lower of the two numbers drawn.

(i) Form a table of joint and marginal probabilities for X and Y.

(ii) Find $\text{Var}(X + Y)$ and $\text{Var}(X - Y)$.

(iii) Are X and Y independent? Explain your reasoning.

4. Four fair coins are tossed. Let X represent the number of tails and Y the number of 'runs', e.g. the outcome **HTTT** would result in $X = 3$, $Y = 2$

and the outcome **THHT** would result in $X = 2$, $Y = 3$.

(i) Construct a bivariate probability distribution for X and Y.

(ii) Find the marginal probabilities for X and Y and obtain $E(X)$ and $E(Y)$.

(iii) Find $\text{Var}(X + Y)$. Are X and Y independent? Give a reason for your answer.

5. (i) Three random variables are X, Y and Z. Find expressions for $E(X + Y + Z)$ and $\text{Var}(X + Y + Z)$.

(ii) Three fair dice are thrown. Let X, Y and Z represent the scores on the first, second and third die respectively.

Find expressions for (a) $E(X + Y + Z)$ and (b) $\text{Var}(X + Y + Z)$.

6. (i) Use the properties of the expectation operation E to show that if X and Y are random variables and λ is a constant,

$\text{Var}(X + \lambda Y)$

$= \text{Var}(X) + 2\lambda \text{Cov}(X, Y) + \lambda^2 \text{Var}(Y)$

(ii) Assuming $\text{Var}(X)$ and $\text{Var}(Y)$ are both greater than zero, find the value of λ which makes $\text{Var}(X + \lambda Y)$ as small as possible and deduce that the absolute value of the correlation between X and Y cannot be greater than unity.

(iii) The temperatures in $°C$ at 6 am and 12 noon on the same day were measured at seven different weather stations. The mean temperatures were $7°C$ and $24°C$ respectively and the sample standard deviations were $2°C$ and $5°C$ respectively. The sample correlation coefficient between the temperatures at the two different times was 0.8. Find the sample correlation coefficient between the rise in temperature and the temperature at 6 am and test whether this differs significantly from zero.

[O&C]

7. The variables X and Y are distributed independently with the same variance, σ^2 (where $\sigma^2 \neq 0$), but with (possibly) different means, μ, ν, respectively. A linear transformation is now made

to variables Z and W, defined by:

$$z = ax + by;$$
$$w = cx + dy;$$

where a, b, c, d are constants. Find an expression for $E(ZW) - E(Z)E(W)$ in terms of (some or all of) a, b, c, d, μ, ν, σ^2 and show that $E(ZW) = E(Z)E(W)$ if, and only if, $ac + bd = 0$.

[O&C, SMP]

8. Given that X, Y and Z are discrete random variables, prove that:

(i) $\text{Cov}(X + Y, Z) = \text{Cov}(X, Z) + \text{Cov}(Y, Z)$

(ii) $\text{Var}(X - Y) = \text{Var}(X) + \text{Var}(Y) - 2\text{Cov}(X, Y)$

(iii) The mutually independent random variables $X_1, X_2, \ldots, X_n$, are such that:

$$\text{Var}(X_i) = \sigma^2, \text{ for } i = 1, 2, \ldots, n$$

The random variable $\bar{X}$ is given by:

$$\bar{X} = \frac{1}{n}(X_1 + X_2 + \cdots + X_n).$$

Find the linear correlation coefficient between X_1 and $\bar{X}$.

[Cambridge]

9. (i) Prove that:

(a) $\text{Var}(X \pm Y) = \text{Var}(X) + \text{Var}(Y) \pm 2\text{Cov}(X, Y)$;

(b) $\text{Cov}(X + Y, X + Z) = \text{Var}(X) + \text{Cov}(Y, Z) + \text{Cov}(X, Y) + \text{Cov}(X, Z)$;

(c) $\text{Var}\left(\sum_{i=1}^{n} X_i\right) = \sum_{i=1}^{n} \text{Var}(X_i)$

if the X_i are mutually independent random variables.

(ii) If $\bar{X} = \frac{1}{n}\sum_{i=1}^{n} X_i$ where the X_i are mutually independent variates with common mean and variance,

(a) show that the product moment correlation coefficient between X_1 and $(X_2 - \bar{X})$ is $-\sqrt{1 - \frac{1}{n}}$

(b) find the correlation coefficient between $(X_1 - \bar{X})$ and $(X_2 - 2\bar{X})$.

[MEI]

KEY POINTS

- For discrete random variables X and Y, their *joint distribution* may be defined by a table of joint probabilities or a definition in the form $P(X = x, Y = y) = \cdots$

- Marginal probabilities are found by summing rows and columns:

$$P(X = x) = \sum_{y} P(X = x, Y = y) \text{ and } P(Y = y) = \sum_{x} P(X = x, Y = y)$$

- For any X and Y: $E(aX + bY) = aE(X) + bE(Y)$

- The *conditional probability* of X, given Y is defined by:

$$P(X = x | Y = y) = \frac{P(X = x, Y = y)}{P(Y = y)}$$

- Two random variables, X and Y, are *independent* if and only if:

$$P(X = x, Y = y) = P(X = x, Y = y) \times P(X = x, Y = y)$$

$$\text{for all values of } X \text{ and } Y.$$

If X and Y are independent, then $E(XY) = E(X)E(Y)$.

- The covariance of X and Y: $\text{Cov}(X, Y) = E(XY) - E(X)E(Y)$

If X and Y are independent, then $\text{Cov}(X, Y) = 0$.

- The *product moment correlation coefficient* between X and Y is ρ, where:

$$\rho = \frac{\text{Cov}(X, Y)}{\sigma_X \sigma_Y}$$

and σ_X and σ_Y are the standard deviations of X and Y respectively.

- If $X = aX' + b$ and $Y = cY' + d$, then:

$$\text{Cov}(X, Y) = ac\,\text{Cov}(X', Y') \text{ and } \rho_{X,Y} = \rho_{X',Y'}$$

- For any X and Y:

$$\text{Var}(aX + bY) = a\,\text{Var}(X) + 2ab\,\text{Cov}(X, Y) + b\,\text{Var}(Y)$$

If X and Y are independent, then $\text{Var}(aX \pm bY) = a\,\text{Var}(X) + b\,\text{Var}(Y)$ and, in particular:

$$\text{Var}(X \pm Y) = \text{Var}(X) + \text{Var}(Y)$$

8 Markov chains

I can see looming ahead one of those terrible exercises in probability where six men have white hats and six men have black hats and you have to work out by mathematics how likely it is that the hats will get mixed up and in what proportion.

Agatha Christie

In November 1996 the people of the USA re-elected a Democratic president for a second term, the three previous presidential terms, each of four years in length, having been held by the Republicans. For the past 140 years the president of the USA has come from either the Democratic or the Republican Party. Each time there is an election, how likely is the current government to remain in power and how likely is it that there will be a change of party in power?

The outcome of the last 36 presidential elections in the USA has resulted in the following pattern of results (where D represents Democrat and R represents Republican).

D R R R R R D R D R R
R R D D R R R D D D D D
R R D D R R D R R D D

You can check that, of the 35 handovers of power from one president to the next, the following pattern emerges:

		To		
		Democrat	Republican	Total
From	Democratic	8	7	15
	Republican	6	14	20

These results can be used to generate *empirical* probabilities of the four patterns of handovers:

| | | To | | |
		Democrat	Republican	Total
From	Democratic	$\frac{8}{15}$	$\frac{7}{15}$	1
	Republican	$\frac{3}{10}$	$\frac{7}{10}$	1

This table is very informative as it tells us that, over the last 140 years, whenever the Democrats have held office, on about half of these occasions they have lost the presidency at the next election. However, when there has been a Republican president, the party has retained the presidency, on average, seven times out of ten.

The fractions in the table are called *transition probabilities* as they give the probabilities of moving from one state (a Democratic or Republican president) to the next state (a Democratic or Republican president). An alternative representation of these probabilities is a *transition state diagram.*

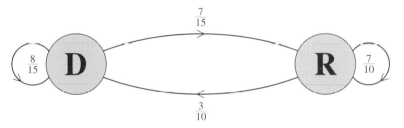

Figure 8.1

To see how transition probabilities may be used to find the probability of states in the future (beyond the next state), we shall look at another example which follows a similar pattern.

Building a Markov chain

Tony is an amateur weather forecaster. For several months he has kept a note of whether any particular day is *fine* or *wet*. If it rains during daylight hours, he classifies the day as *wet*, otherwise the day is said to be *dry*. He notes that if it is fine one day, it is often fine the next day. Similarly, a wet day is often followed by another wet day.

From his records over the past year, Tony suggests the following model:

If a day is fine, then the probability that the next day is fine is $\frac{2}{3}$.

If a day is wet, then the probability that the next day is wet is $\frac{3}{4}$.

Monday is fine. What is the probability that:

(a) it is wet on Wednesday;

(b) it is fine on Thursday?

This situation can be illustrated by a tree diagram:

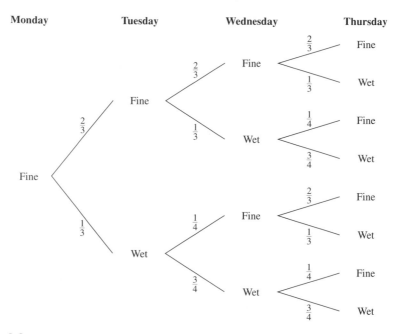

Figure 8.2

Given that Monday is fine, the probability that it is wet on Wednesday is found from the diagram:

$$\tfrac{2}{3} \times \tfrac{1}{3} + \tfrac{1}{3} \times \tfrac{3}{4} = \tfrac{17}{36}$$

The probability that it is fine on Thursday is:

$$\tfrac{2}{3} \times \tfrac{2}{3} \times \tfrac{2}{3} + \tfrac{2}{3} \times \tfrac{1}{3} \times \tfrac{1}{4} + \tfrac{1}{3} \times \tfrac{1}{4} \times \tfrac{2}{3} + \tfrac{1}{3} \times \tfrac{3}{4} \times \tfrac{1}{4} = \tfrac{203}{432}$$

In the above example it was assumed that the probability of a day being fine or wet depends only on the previous day's weather. This is an example of a *Markov chain*, where the probability of a particular outcome, or state, at a given time (e.g. fine or wet tomorrow) is dependent only on the state at the previous time (e.g. fine or wet today).

The four conditional probabilities:

P(fine tomorrow | today is fine) $= \tfrac{2}{3}$ P(wet tomorrow | today is fine) $= \tfrac{1}{3}$

P(fine tomorrow | today is wet) $= \tfrac{1}{4}$ P(wet tomorrow | today is wet) $= \tfrac{3}{4}$

are the transition probabilities.

It is convenient to summarise this information by arranging such probabilities into a matrix, called a *transition matrix*, which is denoted by **P**.

S6

Tomorrow

$$\begin{array}{c}\text{Today} \end{array} \begin{array}{cc} & \begin{array}{cc} Fine & Wet \end{array} \\ \begin{array}{c} Fine \\ Wet \end{array} & \begin{bmatrix} \frac{2}{3} & \frac{1}{3} \\ \frac{1}{4} & \frac{3}{4} \end{bmatrix} \end{array} = \mathbf{P}$$

The entries in the first row correspond to the possible weather conditions on the following day, given that it is fine at present; and the entries in the second row correspond to the possible weather conditions on the following day, given that it is wet at present. Each row of a transition matrix is known as a *probability vector* and it is not difficult to see that the sum of the terms in each row must equal 1.

Given that it is fine on Monday, the probability that it is wet on Wednesday is given by:

$$\tfrac{2}{3} \times \tfrac{1}{3} + \tfrac{1}{3} \times \tfrac{3}{4} = \underline{\tfrac{17}{36}}$$

Similarly, given that it is fine on Monday, the probability that it is fine on Wednesday is given by:

$$\tfrac{2}{3} \times \tfrac{2}{3} + \tfrac{1}{3} \times \tfrac{1}{4} = \underline{\tfrac{19}{36}}$$

To complete the picture, suppose that Monday is wet. The corresponding probabilities of it being wet or fine on Wednesday are given by:

$$\tfrac{1}{4} \times \tfrac{1}{3} + \tfrac{3}{4} \times \tfrac{3}{4} = \underline{\tfrac{31}{48}} \quad \text{and} \quad \tfrac{1}{4} \times \tfrac{2}{3} + \tfrac{3}{4} \times \tfrac{1}{4} = \underline{\tfrac{17}{48}} \text{ respectively.}$$

The four underlined probabilities are the entries in the two-step transition matrix, which can easily be found by squaring matrix **P** (multiplying **P** by itself), i.e.:

$$\mathbf{P} \times \mathbf{P} = \begin{bmatrix} \frac{2}{3} & \frac{1}{3} \\ \frac{1}{4} & \frac{3}{4} \end{bmatrix} \times \begin{bmatrix} \frac{2}{3} & \frac{1}{3} \\ \frac{1}{4} & \frac{3}{4} \end{bmatrix} = \begin{bmatrix} \frac{19}{36} & \frac{17}{36} \\ \frac{17}{48} & \frac{31}{48} \end{bmatrix} = \mathbf{P}^2$$

Notice that each row of $\mathbf{P}^2$ satisfies the condition to be a probability vector as the sum of the terms in each row equals 1.

A natural extension of the analysis is to cube the transition matrix to give the three-step transition matrix, from which we can read off various probabilities for Thursday:

$$\mathbf{P} \times \mathbf{P} \times \mathbf{P} = \begin{bmatrix} \frac{2}{3} & \frac{1}{3} \\ \frac{1}{4} & \frac{3}{4} \end{bmatrix} \times \begin{bmatrix} \frac{2}{3} & \frac{1}{3} \\ \frac{1}{4} & \frac{3}{4} \end{bmatrix} \times \begin{bmatrix} \frac{2}{3} & \frac{1}{3} \\ \frac{1}{4} & \frac{3}{4} \end{bmatrix}$$

$$= \begin{bmatrix} \frac{19}{36} & \frac{17}{36} \\ \frac{17}{48} & \frac{31}{48} \end{bmatrix} \times \begin{bmatrix} \frac{2}{3} & \frac{1}{3} \\ \frac{1}{4} & \frac{3}{4} \end{bmatrix} = \begin{bmatrix} \frac{203}{432} & \frac{229}{432} \\ \frac{229}{576} & \frac{347}{576} \end{bmatrix} = \mathbf{P}^3$$

Check that each row of $\mathbf{P}^3$ is a probability vector.

Among others, the probability of it being fine on Thursday, given that it was fine on Monday (found earlier), is given by the top left-hand entry of matrix $\mathbf{P}^3$. Check that the top right-hand entry of matrix $\mathbf{P}^3$ gives the probability of it being wet on Thursday, given that it was fine on Monday. Once again, to complete the picture, suppose that Monday was wet. Then the corresponding probabilities of it being wet or fine on Thursday are given by the bottom right-hand and bottom left-hand entries of $\mathbf{P}^3$, respectively.

Although the tree diagram only takes us to Thursday, higher powers of matrix $\mathbf{P}$ ($\mathbf{P}^4$, $\mathbf{P}^5$, etc.) may be used to calculate conditional weather probabilities for succeeding days.

Exercise 8A

1. For each of the following transition matrices, work out $\mathbf{P}^2$, $\mathbf{P}^3$ and $\mathbf{P}^4$

   (i) $\quad \mathbf{P} = \begin{bmatrix} \frac{5}{8} & \frac{3}{8} \\ \frac{3}{4} & \frac{1}{4} \end{bmatrix}$

   (ii) $\quad \mathbf{P} = \begin{bmatrix} \frac{1}{3} & \frac{2}{3} \\ \frac{3}{4} & \frac{1}{4} \end{bmatrix}$

   (iii) $\quad \mathbf{P} = \begin{bmatrix} \frac{1}{6} & \frac{5}{6} \\ \frac{5}{6} & \frac{1}{6} \end{bmatrix}$

   (iv) $\quad \mathbf{P} = \begin{bmatrix} 0.7 & 0.3 \\ 0.1 & 0.9 \end{bmatrix}$

2. Ruth fancies herself as a weather forecaster. She classifies each day as either *sunny* or *cloudy*. If today is *sunny*, she thinks there is a 70% chance that tomorrow will be *sunny*. If today is *cloudy*, she reckons that there is an 80% chance that tomorrow will be *cloudy*.

   (i) Form a 2 by 2 transition matrix, $\mathbf{P}$.

   (ii) Today is Saturday and it is *sunny*. Use suitable powers of $\mathbf{P}$ to find the probability that it is:

     (a) *sunny* on Monday;

     (b) *cloudy* on Tuesday;

     (c) *sunny* on Wednesday.

3. (i) Write down the probabilities for the changeover of presidents in the USA in a transition matrix, $\mathbf{P}$.

   Given that a Democratic president was re-elected in November 1996, find the probability that:

   (ii) the US president to be elected in 2000 will be a Republican;

   (iii) a Democratic president will be elected in 2004.

4. On a Saturday night Tina goes to either the disco or the cinema. If she has been to the disco the previous Saturday then there is a probability of 0.5 that she will go to the disco again. However, if she has been to the cinema the previous Saturday there is a probability of 0.75 that she will go to the disco.

   (i) Write down the transition matrix $\mathbf{P}$ for the problem.

   (ii) On the first Saturday in February Tina went to the disco.

     Find the probability that Tina goes to:

     (a) the disco on the third Saturday in February;

     (b) the cinema on the fourth Saturday in February.

   (iii) On the first Saturday in March Tina went to the cinema. Find the probability that Tina goes to the disco on the first Saturday in April.

   (*Note: there are two possible answers.*)

5. A tennis player hits either to his opponent's forehand or to his opponent's backhand. If he has previously hit to the forehand then he has a probability of $\frac{4}{5}$ of hitting to the backhand on the next shot. If, however, he has previously hit to the backhand, there is a probability of $\frac{2}{3}$ that he will again hit to the backhand.

   (i) Write down the transition matrix for the problem.

   (ii) If his first shot is to his opponent's backhand, calculate the probability that the third shot will also be to the backhand.

   (iii) What is the probability that his fourth shot will be to his opponent's backhand if his first shot is to the:

     (a) backhand;

     (b) forehand?

6. Since the university boat race began, whenever Oxford win there seems to be a $\frac{3}{5}$ chance that they will also win the following year. For Cambridge the corresponding probability is $\frac{2}{3}$.

Exercise 8A continued

(i) Write down the transition matrix for the problem.

(ii) Find out which team won the last race and so calculate the probability of each team winning the race after next.

7. If I am late for school, I make a greater effort to arrive on time on the next school day. If I arrive on time, I am liable to be less careful the next day.

Consequently, if I am late one day, the probability that I am on time the next day is 0.75. If I am on time one day, the probability that I am late the next day is 0.5. I am on time on Monday.

(i) Write down the transition matrix for the problem.

(ii) Calculate the probability that in the same week I shall be on time:

    (a) on the Wednesday;

    (b) on the Friday.

8. A 2 by 2 transition matrix, $\mathbf{P}$, is given by $\begin{bmatrix} a & b \\ c & d \end{bmatrix}$ where $0 \leqslant a, b, c, d \leqslant 1$.

(i) Write down two equations satisfied by some of a, b, c, d.

(ii) Find $\mathbf{P}^2$ in terms of a, b, c, d and therefore show that each row of $\mathbf{P}^2$ is a probability vector, i.e. that $\mathbf{P}^2$ is a transition matrix.

(iii) Show that $\mathbf{P}^3$ is also a transition matrix.

3 by 3 transition matrices

Markov chains can have three or more states at each stage of the process. If there are, say, three possible outcomes, then a 3 by 3 matrix will be required to store the nine possible transition probabilities.

EXAMPLE

Bob has a very unreliable car. Every morning he goes out to the garage hoping to start it – some days it starts by itself, some days it starts if he gets a push from a neighbour, but on other days no amount of pushing is effective and the service station must be called. If it starts one day, the chances for the next day are $\frac{1}{2}$ it will start, $\frac{1}{3}$ it must be pushed and $\frac{1}{6}$ the service station must be called. If it is pushed one day, the chances on the next day are $\frac{1}{3}$ it will start and $\frac{2}{3}$ the service station must be called. (It is never pushed two days in a row.) If the service station is called one day, the chances on the next day are $\frac{5}{6}$ it will start and $\frac{1}{6}$ it must be pushed.

On Monday morning the car started by itself. What is the probability that it will start by itself on:

(i) Wednesday morning;

(ii) Friday morning?

Solution:

First, form a 3 by 3 transition matrix:

$$
\begin{array}{c}
\\
\textbf{Today}
\end{array}
\begin{array}{c}
\\
\textit{Starts} \\
\textit{Push} \\
\textit{Service}
\end{array}
\overset{\displaystyle \textbf{Tomorrow}}{
\overset{\textit{Starts} \quad \textit{Push} \quad \textit{Service}}{
\begin{bmatrix}
\frac{1}{2} & \frac{1}{3} & \frac{1}{6} \\
\frac{1}{3} & 0 & \frac{2}{3} \\
\frac{5}{6} & \frac{1}{6} & 0
\end{bmatrix}}} = \mathbf{P}
$$

For Wednesday's probabilities we require the two-step transition matrix which can be found by squaring matrix $\mathbf{P}$, i.e.:

$$\mathbf{P} \times \mathbf{P} = \begin{bmatrix} \frac{1}{2} & \frac{1}{3} & \frac{1}{6} \\ \frac{1}{3} & 0 & \frac{2}{3} \\ \frac{5}{6} & \frac{1}{6} & 0 \end{bmatrix} \times \begin{bmatrix} \frac{1}{2} & \frac{1}{3} & \frac{1}{6} \\ \frac{1}{3} & 0 & \frac{2}{3} \\ \frac{5}{6} & \frac{1}{6} & 0 \end{bmatrix} = \begin{bmatrix} \frac{1}{2} & \frac{7}{36} & \frac{11}{36} \\ \frac{13}{18} & \frac{2}{9} & \frac{1}{18} \\ \frac{17}{36} & \frac{5}{18} & \frac{1}{4} \end{bmatrix} = \mathbf{P}^2$$

Therefore the probability that the car will start by itself on Wednesday morning is still $\frac{1}{2}$. But will this remain the same for Friday morning? We need to compute the four-step transition matrix, $\mathbf{P}^4$, which we do in two stages, first calculating $\mathbf{P}^3$, i.e.:

$$\mathbf{P}^2 \times \mathbf{P} = \begin{bmatrix} \frac{1}{2} & \frac{7}{36} & \frac{11}{36} \\ \frac{13}{18} & \frac{2}{9} & \frac{1}{18} \\ \frac{17}{36} & \frac{5}{18} & \frac{1}{4} \end{bmatrix} \times \begin{bmatrix} \frac{1}{2} & \frac{1}{3} & \frac{1}{6} \\ \frac{1}{3} & 0 & \frac{2}{3} \\ \frac{5}{6} & \frac{1}{6} & 0 \end{bmatrix} = \begin{bmatrix} \frac{41}{72} & \frac{47}{216} & \frac{23}{108} \\ \frac{13}{27} & \frac{1}{4} & \frac{29}{108} \\ \frac{29}{54} & \frac{43}{216} & \frac{19}{72} \end{bmatrix} = \mathbf{P}^3$$

$$\mathbf{P}^3 \times \mathbf{P} = \begin{bmatrix} \frac{41}{72} & \frac{47}{216} & \frac{23}{108} \\ \frac{13}{27} & \frac{1}{4} & \frac{29}{108} \\ \frac{29}{54} & \frac{43}{216} & \frac{19}{72} \end{bmatrix} \times \begin{bmatrix} \frac{1}{2} & \frac{1}{3} & \frac{1}{6} \\ \frac{1}{3} & 0 & \frac{2}{3} \\ \frac{5}{6} & \frac{1}{6} & 0 \end{bmatrix} = \begin{bmatrix} \frac{77}{144} & \frac{73}{324} & \frac{311}{1296} \\ \frac{355}{648} & \frac{133}{648} & \frac{20}{81} \\ \frac{719}{1296} & \frac{289}{1296} & \frac{2}{9} \end{bmatrix} = \mathbf{P}^4$$

From the top left-hand corner entry of $\mathbf{P}^4$ we can see that the probability of the car starting by itself has increased slightly to $\frac{77}{144} \approx 0.535$. The most useful aspect of computing successive transition matrices is that, at a glance, we can see what happens to certain probabilities over a period of time. For example, if Bob needs to take his car to the service station on Monday morning, the probability that he needs to take it in on Tuesday morning is 0. The probability that he needs to take it in on Wednesday, however, is $\frac{1}{4} = 0.25$; for Thursday it is $\frac{19}{72} \approx 0.264$; and for Friday it is $\frac{2}{9} \approx 0.222$.

Exercise 8B

1. For each of the following transition matrices, work out $\mathbf{P}^2$, $\mathbf{P}^3$ and $\mathbf{P}^4$:

(i) $\quad \mathbf{P} = \begin{bmatrix} 0 & \frac{1}{2} & \frac{1}{2} \\ \frac{3}{4} & 0 & \frac{1}{4} \\ \frac{5}{6} & 0 & \frac{1}{6} \end{bmatrix}$

(ii) $\quad \mathbf{P} = \begin{bmatrix} 0.5 & 0.45 & 0.05 \\ 0.25 & 0.5 & 0.25 \\ 0.3 & 0.3 & 0.4 \end{bmatrix}$

(iii) $\quad \mathbf{P} = \begin{bmatrix} \frac{1}{2} & \frac{1}{3} & \frac{1}{6} \\ \frac{1}{3} & \frac{1}{3} & \frac{1}{3} \\ \frac{1}{6} & \frac{1}{3} & \frac{1}{2} \end{bmatrix}$

2. Every year the Smith family goes on vacation – a camping trip (preferred by the children), a visit to the city (preferred by Mrs Smith) or a winter vacation (preferred by Mr Smith). They never take the same kind of vacation two years in a row. Each year they toss a coin to decide which of the two types of vacation that they did not take the previous year they will take this year.

(i) Form a 3 by 3 transition matrix, $\mathbf{P}$.

(ii) This year the Smith family spent their vacation on a visit to the city.

Use suitable powers of $\mathbf{P}$ to find the probability that:

(a) the year after next the Smiths spend their vacation in the city;

Exercise 8B continued

(b) the year after next they spend their vacation on a camping trip;

(c) the Smiths go on a winter vacation in three years' time.

3. In a particular area, three weekly newspapers, the *Herald*, the *Tribune* and the *Gazette*, have, between them, a fixed number of subscribers. During any month the *Herald* retains $\frac{7}{8}$ of its subscribers and loses $\frac{1}{8}$ of them to the *Tribune*; the *Tribune* retains $\frac{1}{12}$ of its subscribers and loses $\frac{1}{12}$ of them to the *Herald* and the rest of them to the *Gazette*; the *Gazette* retains $\frac{1}{3}$ of its subscribers and loses $\frac{1}{2}$ of them to the *Herald* and the rest of them to the *Tribune*.

(i) Write down the transition matrix, **P**, for the problem.

(ii) On 1 September Liam is a *Tribune* subscriber. Find the probability that:

(a) on 1 October he subscribes to the *Gazette*;

(b) on 1 November he subscribes to the *Tribune* once more;

(c) on 1 January he is still subscribing to the *Tribune*.

4. A sports correspondent has to write a background article each day in a daily paper. He writes about athletics, cricket or tennis, and arranges his writing as follows.

He never writes about athletics on two consecutive days. After a day writing about athletics, he writes about cricket the next day with a probability of $\frac{2}{3}$. After a day writing about cricket, he has a probability of $\frac{1}{3}$ of again writing about cricket the next day and a probability of $\frac{1}{2}$ of writing about tennis the next day. After a day writing about tennis, he writes about athletics the next day with a probability of $\frac{1}{2}$ and is otherwise equally likely to write again about tennis or about cricket.

(i) Form a 3 by 3 transition matrix, **P**, for this problem.

(ii) On the Tuesday of a certain week, he writes about athletics. Find the probabilities of him writing about each sport on:

(a) the Thursday;

(b) the Friday of that week. **[MEI]**

5. Consider the following simple model of the demand for cars. There are three makes, A, B and C, of similar type. Market research has estimated that owners who buy a new car every year do so according to the following scheme:

New car

		A	B	C
	A	$\frac{1}{2}$	$\frac{1}{4}$	$\frac{1}{4}$
Old car B		$\frac{1}{6}$	$\frac{1}{2}$	$\frac{1}{3}$
	C	$\frac{1}{4}$	$\frac{1}{4}$	$\frac{1}{2}$

(i) Which make of car is a person most likely to own in 1999 if he owned a car of make B in 1996?

(ii) In a certain district there are 1000 such owners of make A, 600 of make B and 400 of make C in 1996. What are the total sales of each make from 1996 to 1999 inclusive? **[MEI]**

6. A 3 by 3 transition matrix, **P**, is given by
$$\begin{bmatrix} a & b & c \\ d & e & f \\ g & h & i \end{bmatrix} \quad \text{where: } 0 \leqslant a, b, c, d, e, f, g, h, i \leqslant 1.$$

(i) Write down three equations satisfied by some of $a, b, c, d, e, f, g, h, i$.

(ii) Find $\mathbf{P}^2$ in terms of $a, b, c, d, e, f, g, h, i$ and therefore show that $\mathbf{P}^2$ is a transition matrix.

7. A drunk is struggling up a flight of three steps. When he is on level S_i $(i = 0, 1, 2)$ the probability that he next occupies level S_{i+1} is p, while the probability that he next occupies level S_0 is $q = 1 - p$. If he is on level S_3, however, he remains there with a probability of 1.

(i) Write down the transition matrix corresponding to the Markov chain with states S_0, S_1, S_2, S_3.

(ii) Suppose that he starts on the bottom level, S_0, and let f_n denote the probability that he is on level S_0 after n transitions. Show that $f_1 = f_2 = f_3$, but that if $0 < p < 1$, then $f_4 < f_3$. (*Hint: You may wish to use* $(1 - x)(1 + x + x^2) = 1 - x^3$.)

[O&C, SMP]

Investigation

(You will need a graphic calculator (or computer program) that performs matrix arithmetic.)

Take the 2 by 2 transition matrix $\mathbf{P}$ as $\begin{bmatrix} \frac{2}{3} & \frac{1}{3} \\ \frac{1}{4} & \frac{3}{4} \end{bmatrix}$ as used by Tony for his weather forecasting.

Use your calculator to find successive powers of matrix $\mathbf{P}$, i.e. $\mathbf{P}^2, \mathbf{P}^3, \mathbf{P}^4, \mathbf{P}^5, \mathbf{P}^6, \ldots$
Continuing the sequence we began earlier, you should be able to obtain:

Friday: $\quad \mathbf{P}^4 = \begin{bmatrix} 0.4457 & 0.5542 \\ 0.4156 & 0.5843 \end{bmatrix}$ 　　　 Saturday: $\mathbf{P}^5 = \begin{bmatrix} 0.4357 & 0.5642 \\ 0.4231 & 0.5768 \end{bmatrix}$

Sunday: $\quad \mathbf{P}^6 = \begin{bmatrix} 0.4315 & 0.5684 \\ 0.4263 & 0.5736 \end{bmatrix}$ 　　　 Monday: $\mathbf{P}^7 = \begin{bmatrix} 0.4298 & 0.5701 \\ 0.4276 & 0.5723 \end{bmatrix}$

(Note: For convenience the probabilities are given as decimals to 4 dp.)

By inspecting matrix $\mathbf{P}^7$ you will see that the pair of probabilities in the two rows are roughly equal. Show that, by taking successively higher powers of matrix $\mathbf{P}$, the two rows do, in fact, become closer to each other.

Show also that the probabilities in each row tend towards 0.4286 and 0.5714 (to 4 dp).

Using transition probabilities from $\mathbf{P}$, evaluate: $\dfrac{\frac{1}{4}}{\frac{1}{3}+\frac{1}{4}}$ and $\dfrac{\frac{1}{3}}{\frac{1}{3}+\frac{1}{4}}$ as fractions and decimals. What do you notice?

Repeat the activities above with other 2 by 2 transition matrices you have met so far.

Take the 3 by 3 transition matrix $\mathbf{P}$ as $\begin{bmatrix} \frac{1}{2} & \frac{1}{3} & \frac{1}{6} \\ \frac{1}{3} & 0 & \frac{2}{3} \\ \frac{5}{6} & \frac{1}{6} & 0 \end{bmatrix}$ used for starting Bob's car. Use your calculator to find successive powers of matrix $\mathbf{P}$, i.e. $\mathbf{P}^2, \mathbf{P}^3, \mathbf{P}^4, \mathbf{P}^5, \mathbf{P}^6, \ldots$
Confirm that you obtain:

Saturday: $\mathbf{P}^5 = \begin{bmatrix} 0.5424 & 0.2182 & 0.2393 \\ 0.5480 & 0.2237 & 0.2281 \\ 0.5369 & 0.2219 & 0.2411 \end{bmatrix}$

Sunday: $\quad \mathbf{P}^6 = \begin{bmatrix} 0.5434 & 0.2207 & 0.2358 \\ 0.5387 & 0.2207 & 0.2405 \\ 0.5433 & 0.2191 & 0.2374 \end{bmatrix}$

Show that, by taking successively higher powers of matrix $\mathbf{P}$, the three rows do, in fact, become closer to each other.

By taking high enough powers of $\mathbf{P}$, show that the probabilities in each row tend towards 0.5424, 0.2203 and 0.2373 (to 4 dp).

Repeat the above activities with other 3 by 3 transition matrices you have met so far.

The limiting probabilities met in these two examples are known as steady-state or **equilibrium** *probabilities. They indicate that, 'in the long run', the probability of any of the three events (car starts on its own, needs a push, or needs a service) are independent of what happened on the first day. Can you explain why you would expect this to happen?*

Equilibrium probabilities

In the problems discussed so far it has been assumed that, initially, a particular state exists, and probabilities of future events, based on the initial state, have been calculated. In other words, we have found *conditional probabilities*, dependent on the initial state.

- In the first example, the initial state was that it was *fine* on Monday.

- In Exercise 8A, Question 2, the initial state was that it was *sunny* on Saturday.

- In the second example, the initial state was that Bob's car *started by itself* on Monday.

- In Exercise 8B, Question 2, the initial state was that, in 1993, the Smiths spent their vacation *in the city*.

Now consider the situation where we attach probabilities to the initial states. These may be 1 or 0, reflecting a known initial state, or values between 0 and 1, reflecting an uncertain initial state.

Let's return to Tony's weather forecasting. It was assumed that it was fine on Monday, therefore:

$$P(\text{Fine on Monday}) = 1 \quad \text{and} \quad P(\text{Wet on Monday}) = 0$$

These two 'probabilities' can be represented by a *row matrix*: [1 0]. Now multiply this row matrix by the transition matrix to obtain a second row matrix:

$$[1 \quad 0]\begin{bmatrix} \frac{2}{3} & \frac{1}{3} \\ \frac{1}{4} & \frac{3}{4} \end{bmatrix} = [\frac{2}{3} \quad \frac{1}{3}]$$

The second row matrix simply gives the probabilities of it being fine or wet on Tuesday. By repeating the process, to obtain further row matrices, you automatically generate probabilities of it being fine or wet on Wednesday, Thursday, etc.:

$$[\frac{2}{3} \quad \frac{1}{3}]\begin{bmatrix} \frac{2}{3} & \frac{1}{3} \\ \frac{1}{4} & \frac{3}{4} \end{bmatrix} = [\frac{19}{36} \quad \frac{17}{36}]$$

$$[\frac{19}{36} \quad \frac{17}{36}]\begin{bmatrix} \frac{2}{3} & \frac{1}{3} \\ \frac{1}{4} & \frac{3}{4} \end{bmatrix} = [\frac{203}{432} \quad \frac{229}{432}]$$

Notice that since the first row matrix was [1 0], successive row matrices are just the top rows of **P**, **P**^{2}, **P**^{3}, etc. If it had been wet on Monday, our initial row matrix would have been [0 1], with successive row matrices being the bottom rows of $\mathbf{P}$, $\mathbf{P}^2$, $\mathbf{P}^3$, etc.:

$$[0 \quad 1]\begin{bmatrix} \frac{2}{3} & \frac{1}{3} \\ \frac{1}{4} & \frac{3}{4} \end{bmatrix} = [\frac{1}{4} \quad \frac{3}{4}]$$

$$[\frac{1}{4} \quad \frac{3}{4}]\begin{bmatrix} \frac{2}{3} & \frac{1}{3} \\ \frac{1}{4} & \frac{3}{4} \end{bmatrix} = [\frac{17}{48} \quad \frac{31}{48}]$$

$$[\frac{17}{48} \quad \frac{31}{48}]\begin{bmatrix} \frac{2}{3} & \frac{1}{3} \\ \frac{1}{4} & \frac{3}{4} \end{bmatrix} = [\frac{229}{576} \quad \frac{347}{576}]$$

Let us now suppose that there is a 50 : 50 chance of it being fine or wet on Monday. In this case the initial probabilities, in row matrix form, become $[\frac{1}{2} \quad \frac{1}{2}]$. These can be used to generate further row matrices as follows:

$$[\frac{1}{2} \quad \frac{1}{2}]\begin{bmatrix} \frac{2}{3} & \frac{1}{3} \\ \frac{1}{4} & \frac{3}{4} \end{bmatrix} = [\frac{11}{24} \quad \frac{13}{24}]$$

$$[\frac{11}{24} \quad \frac{13}{24}]\begin{bmatrix} \frac{2}{3} & \frac{1}{3} \\ \frac{1}{4} & \frac{3}{4} \end{bmatrix} = [\frac{127}{288} \quad \frac{161}{288}]$$

Converting to decimal notation for the row matrices, the next four row matrices are found:

$$[0.4410 \quad 0.5590]\begin{bmatrix} \frac{2}{3} & \frac{1}{3} \\ \frac{1}{4} & \frac{3}{4} \end{bmatrix} = [0.4337 \quad 0.5663]$$

$$[0.4337 \quad 0.5663]\begin{bmatrix} \frac{2}{3} & \frac{1}{3} \\ \frac{1}{4} & \frac{3}{4} \end{bmatrix} = [0.4307 \quad 0.5693]$$

$$[0.4307 \quad 0.5693]\begin{bmatrix} \frac{2}{3} & \frac{1}{3} \\ \frac{1}{4} & \frac{3}{4} \end{bmatrix} = [0.4295 \quad 0.5705]$$

$$[0.4295 \quad 0.5705]\begin{bmatrix} \frac{2}{3} & \frac{1}{3} \\ \frac{1}{4} & \frac{3}{4} \end{bmatrix} = [0.4289 \quad 0.5711]$$

By continuing in this way, you will notice that the probabilities in the row matrices seem to be converging towards particular values. They are called steady-state or *equilibrium probabilities*, as referred to in the investigation. By continuing the sequence of row matrices, you can see that the probabilities converge towards [0.4286   0.5714]. Therefore multiplying this row matrix by the transition matrix leaves the row matrix unchanged.

$$[0.4286 \quad 0.5714]\begin{bmatrix} \frac{2}{3} & \frac{1}{3} \\ \frac{1}{4} & \frac{3}{4} \end{bmatrix} = [0.4286 \quad 0.5714]$$

It can be shown that whatever the values of the probabilities in our initial row matrix, the sequence of row matrices generated by repeated multiplication by $\mathbf{P}$, the transition matrix, converge on the same equilibrium row matrix.

The equilibrium row matrix has the property that it remains unchanged when it is multiplied by the transition matrix. Using this property we can calculate the equilibrium row matrix directly, rather than by iteration, as follows:

Let the steady-state row matrix be $[p_1 \quad p_2]$, then:

$$[p_1 \quad p_2] \begin{bmatrix} \frac{2}{3} & \frac{1}{3} \\ \frac{1}{4} & \frac{3}{4} \end{bmatrix} = [p_1 \quad p_2]$$

Multiplying out, this gives:

$$\tfrac{2}{3} p_1 + \tfrac{1}{4} p_2 = p_1$$
$$\tfrac{1}{3} p_1 + \tfrac{3}{4} p_2 = p_2$$

Collecting like terms:

$$-\tfrac{1}{3} p_1 + \tfrac{1}{4} p_2 = 0$$
$$\tfrac{1}{3} p_1 - \tfrac{1}{4} p_2 = 0$$

Notice that both equations give the same information! However we also know that $p_1 + p_2 = 1$, therefore we can solve the simultaneous equations:

$$\tfrac{1}{3} p_1 - \tfrac{1}{4} p_2 = 0 \tag{1}$$
$$p_1 + p_2 = 1 \tag{2}$$

to find the values of p_1 and p_2.

$$4 \times (1) + (2): \quad \tfrac{7}{3} p_1 = 1$$
$$\Rightarrow \quad p_1 = \tfrac{3}{7}, \ p_2 = \tfrac{4}{7}$$

Check that these values for p_1 and p_2 correspond to the equilibrium probabilities found by the iteration above.

A similar technique may be used to find the equilibrium probabilities for a 3 by 3 transition matrix directly. The transition matrix for Bob's unreliable car leads to the steady-state situation:

$$[p_1 \quad p_2 \quad p_3] \begin{bmatrix} \frac{1}{2} & \frac{1}{3} & \frac{1}{6} \\ \frac{1}{3} & 0 & \frac{2}{3} \\ \frac{5}{6} & \frac{1}{6} & 0 \end{bmatrix} = [p_1 \quad p_2 \quad p_3]$$

Multiplying out, this gives:

$$\tfrac{1}{2} p_1 + \tfrac{1}{3} p_2 + \tfrac{5}{6} p_3 = p_1$$
$$\tfrac{1}{3} p_1 \qquad\quad + \tfrac{1}{6} p_3 = p_2$$
$$\tfrac{1}{6} p_1 + \tfrac{2}{3} p_2 \qquad\quad = p_3$$

Collecting like terms:

$$-\tfrac{1}{2} p_1 + \tfrac{1}{3} p_2 + \tfrac{5}{6} p_3 = 0$$
$$\tfrac{1}{3} p_1 - \ p_2 + \tfrac{1}{6} p_3 = 0$$
$$\tfrac{1}{6} p_1 + \tfrac{2}{3} p_2 - \ p_3 = 0$$

These three equations are dependent on each other, i.e. any one of them may be obtained from a linear combination of the other two, so only two of them may be used in order to find p_1, p_2 and p_3.

However, we also know that $p_1 + p_2 + p_3 = 1$, therefore we need to solve the simultaneous equations:

$$\tfrac{1}{3}p_1 - p_2 + \tfrac{1}{6}p_3 = 0 \tag{1}$$

$$\tfrac{1}{6}p_1 + \tfrac{2}{3}p_2 - p_3 = 0 \tag{2}$$

$$p_1 + p_2 + p_3 = 1 \tag{3}$$

First eliminate p_1 from equations (1), (2) and (3):

$$(3) - 3 \times (1) \qquad 4p_2 + \tfrac{1}{2}p_3 = 1 \tag{4}$$

$$(3) - 6 \times (2) \qquad -3p_2 + 7p_3 = 1 \tag{5}$$

Now eliminate p_2 from equations (4) and (5):

$$3 \times (4) + 4 \times (5) \qquad 29\tfrac{1}{2}p_3 = 7$$

$$p_3 = \tfrac{14}{59}$$

Substituting for p_3 into (4) gives:

$$4p_2 + \tfrac{1}{2} \times \tfrac{14}{59} = 1$$

$$4p_2 = 1 - \tfrac{7}{59}$$

$$p_2 = \tfrac{13}{59}$$

Substituting for p_2 and p_3 into (3) gives:

$$p_1 + \tfrac{13}{59} + \tfrac{14}{59} = 1$$

$$p_1 = 1 - \tfrac{27}{59}$$

$$p_1 = \tfrac{32}{59}$$

Therefore the equilibrium probabilities are:

$$p_1 = \tfrac{32}{59} \approx 0.5424, \qquad p_2 = \tfrac{13}{59} \approx 0.2203, \qquad p_3 = \tfrac{14}{59} \approx 0.2373$$

Comparing these probabilities with the values obtained in the investigation, you can see that this direct method gives the steady-state probabilities, irrespective of the values of the initial state row matrix.

Exercise 8C

1. Look back at the transition matrix for each of the following and, using the direct method, calculate the steady-state probabilities:

(i) Exercise 8A, Questions 1–5;

(ii) Exercise 8B, Questions 1–4.

2. Each year in the community of Gardenville, 5% of the residents in the city proper move to the suburbs and 2% of the people in the suburbs move to the city. Assuming that the total number of people in the community remains constant, determine the long-run proportions of city and suburban residents.

3. A country has a three-party political system and the results of elections follow a definite pattern: if a party wins an election, its chance of winning the next election are $50:50$ and if it loses the next election, each of the other two parties has a $50:50$ chance of winning.

What proportion of the elections does each party win over a long period of time?

4. A firm hires out specialist earth-moving equipment to two large construction companies, A and B. One particular piece of equipment is hired out for a week at a time, but sometimes has to spend a whole week undergoing maintenance. (The piece of equipment is never idle; it is always either out on hire or undergoing maintenance.) It is found that, after a week on hire to company A, this piece of equipment has a probability of $\frac{1}{2}$ of again being hired to A for the next week and a probability of $\frac{1}{6}$ of needing maintenance for the next week. After a week on hire to company B, it has a probability of $\frac{1}{4}$ of again being hired to B for the next week and a probability of $\frac{1}{2}$ of needing maintenance for the next week. After a week undergoing maintenance, it will certainly be back on hire in the next week and is equally likely to be with either A or B.

(i) Write down the transition matrix to describe this situation.

(ii) In a certain week (week 1), this piece of equipment is on hire to company B. Find the probabilities of it being with A, B and under maintenance in the second subsequent week (week 3).

(iii) Find the long-run proportions of weeks spent with A and B and under maintenance.

[MEI]

5. A 2 by 2 transition matrix, **P**, is given by
$\begin{bmatrix} a & b \\ c & d \end{bmatrix}$ where $0 \leqslant a, b, c, d \leqslant 1$.

Show that equilibrium probabilities p_1 and p_2 are given by

$$p_1 = \frac{c}{b+c}, \quad p_2 = \frac{b}{b+c}, \text{ provided } b + c \neq 0.$$

6. A maintenance team divides its time between three places, its base A, a nearby plant at B and a more distant plant at C, spending a whole number of days in each. After a day at A they go to B with a probability of $\frac{3}{4}$. After a day at B they go to C with a probability of $\frac{2}{3}$. After a day at C they go back to B with a probability of $\frac{1}{2}$. They

never go directly from A to C or vice versa and they never spend two consecutive days at B.

(i) Write down the transition matrix for this Markov chain.

(ii) If the team spends Monday at A, find the probability of them being at C on Thursday.

(iii) Find the proportions of its time that the team spends in each place, over a long period.

[O&C]

7. A school canteen has been provided with an automatic hot drink dispenser. The beverages available are tea, coffee or chocolate. The tea is so awful that only 20% of those having it on any one day have it again the next day, the remainder changing with equal probability to the other two drinks. The coffee drinkers have coffee again with the same probability that they change to chocolate, and this change is twice as likely as a change to tea. The chocolate is so popular that 60% of those drinking it have it again the next day; the remainder change in equal numbers to one of the other two drinks.

(i) Set up a transition matrix for this system.

(ii) If 800 pupils buy hot drinks every day, how many drinks of the tea type should the school budget for in the long run?

(iii) Show that, after a week, demand can be expected to have settled down to a steady state.

[O&C SMP]

8. A crane spends each working day in one of three states: working, under repair, or waiting for work. On each day its state depends only on the state it was in on the previous day. After working for a day, the probability of working next day is 0.8 and of being under repair is 0.125. After days spent on repairs or waiting for work, the probabilities of working next day are 0.5 and 0.9, respectively; neither of these states is ever followed by the other.

(i) Write down the transition matrix for this Markov chain.

(ii) If the crane is under repair on Monday, find the probability that it will be under repair on the following Wednesday.

(iii) If it is under repair on both a Monday and the following Wednesday, find the probability that it was also under repair on the intervening Tuesday.

(iv) Deduce the proportions of its time that the crane spends over a long period in working, being repaired and waiting for work.

[O&C]

Six chairs, labelled 1–6, are placed clockwise, in order, around the sides of a hexagonal table. Peter has a biased coin which shows a head with probability p and a tail with probability $q(= 1 - p)$; he tosses it once each second and moves one place clockwise or anticlockwise depending on whether a head or tail appears. Therefore his positions at successive times form a six-state Markov chain.

(i) Write down the transition matrix of the chain.

(ii) Peter starts on chair 1 at time 0. Explain why his positions at times $0, 2, 4, 6, \ldots$ form a three-state Markov chain, and deduce the transition matrix of this chain.

(iii) Show that, after $2n$ seconds (n large), he is equally likely to be on chairs 1, 3 or 5.

[Oxford]

Secret tunnels connect the four rooms on the ground floor of a castle. There are four tunnels between rooms A and B, three tunnels between A and C, two tunnels between B and D, and three tunnels between C and D. Robert and Daniel are initially in rooms A and B, respectively; once every minute, John blows a whistle, whereupon Robert and Daniel each select one tunnel at random in the room they are in, and travel along it to its end in another room. Therefore each of their positions at times $0, 1, 2, \ldots$ form a four-state Markov chain.

(i) Write down its transition matrix.

(ii) Find the probability distributions of the rooms Robert and Daniel are in after two movements.

(iii) Explain why they will never be in the same room at the same time.

(iv) Show that if Peter enters one of the four rooms at random, and moves according to the same rules, the long-term probability of him being in a given room is proportional to the number of tunnels in that room.

[Oxford]

11. A Markov chain has two states, A and B. The probability of a transition from A to B is $p_1 \ (\neq 0)$ and the probability of a transition from B to A is $p_2 \ (\neq 0)$.

(i) Write down the transition matrix $\mathbf{P}$.

(ii) The system is initially in state A. Show that the probability that the system is in state B after n transitions is

$$\frac{p_1[1 - (1 - p_1 - p_2)^n]}{p_1 + p_2}.$$

(iii) Find also the proportions of time that the system spends in states A and B over a long period.

Run lengths in Markov chains

Let us return again to Tony's weather forecasting problem. We know that it is fine on Monday. What is the probability that it is fine for the rest of the week (Tuesday to Friday inclusive), but wet on Saturday? This can easily be found from an extended tree-diagram by the appropriate multiplication of probabilities:

$$\tfrac{2}{3} \times \tfrac{2}{3} \times \tfrac{2}{3} \times \tfrac{2}{3} \times \tfrac{1}{3} = \left(\tfrac{2}{3}\right)^4 \times \tfrac{1}{3} = \tfrac{16}{243}$$

This gives us the probability of exactly four further consecutive fine days, given that Monday was fine. Similarly, we can find the probability of any number of further consecutive fine days: the probability that, after Monday, the next seven days will be fine and the following Tuesday wet is:

$$\tfrac{2}{3} \times \tfrac{2}{3} \times \tfrac{2}{3} \times \tfrac{2}{3} \times \tfrac{2}{3} \times \tfrac{2}{3} \times \tfrac{2}{3} \times \tfrac{1}{3} = \left(\tfrac{2}{3}\right)^7 \times \tfrac{1}{3} = \tfrac{128}{6561}$$

We can formalise this idea in the following way. Let X represent the number of further consecutive days on which it is fine, given that Monday is fine, then:

$$P(X = x) = \left(\tfrac{2}{3}\right)^x \times \tfrac{1}{3}, \qquad x = 0, 1, 2, 3, 4, \ldots$$

We have defined a discrete probability distribution with an infinite sample space. In appearance it is not unlike the geometric distribution. We can construct a table of probabilities as follows:

x	0	1	2	3	4	$\cdots$
$P(X = x)$	$\tfrac{1}{3}$	$\tfrac{2}{3} \times \tfrac{1}{3}$	$\left(\tfrac{2}{3}\right)^2 \times \tfrac{1}{3}$	$\left(\tfrac{2}{3}\right)^3 \times \tfrac{1}{3}$	$\left(\tfrac{2}{3}\right)^4 \times \tfrac{1}{3}$	$\cdots$

To find the mean and variance of this distribution we will find its probability generating function, $G(t)$, and use results for the mean and variance:

$$G(t) = \tfrac{1}{3} + \tfrac{2}{3} \times \tfrac{1}{3} t + \left(\tfrac{2}{3}\right)^2 \times \tfrac{1}{3} t^2 + \left(\tfrac{2}{3}\right)^3 \times \tfrac{1}{3} t^3 + \left(\tfrac{2}{3}\right)^4 \times \tfrac{1}{3} t^4 + \cdots$$

$$= \tfrac{1}{3} \times \left(1 + \tfrac{2}{3} t + \left(\tfrac{2}{3} t\right)^2 + \left(\tfrac{2}{3} t\right)^3 + \left(\tfrac{2}{3} t\right)^4 + \cdots\right)$$

$$- \tfrac{1}{3} \times \dfrac{1}{1 - \tfrac{2}{3} t} - \dfrac{\tfrac{1}{3}}{1 - \tfrac{2}{3} t}$$

sum to infinity of a geometric progression

Differentiating with respect to t:

$$G'(t) = \dfrac{\tfrac{2}{9}}{\left(1 - \tfrac{2}{3} t\right)^2} \quad \Rightarrow \quad G'(1) = \dfrac{\tfrac{2}{9}}{\left(1 - \tfrac{2}{3}\right)^2} = 2$$

Therefore the expected (mean) number of further consecutive days on which it will be fine is 2.

Further differentiation with respect to t gives:

$$G''(t) = \dfrac{\tfrac{8}{27}}{\left(1 - \tfrac{2}{3} t\right)^3} \quad \Rightarrow \quad G''(1) = \dfrac{\tfrac{8}{27}}{\left(1 - \tfrac{2}{3}\right)^3} = 8$$

Therefore $\sigma^2 = G''(1) - [G'(1)]^2 = 8 - 4 = 4 \Rightarrow \sigma = 2$.

Having examined a specific case, we now generalise for a Markov chain with two, three or any number of states. For any state A, let α be the probability that the system remains in that state at the next stage. Therefore the probability that it changes from state A to state A' in one step is $1 - \alpha$.

Let X represent the number of further consecutive stages in which the state of the system is A, given that it is initially in state A, then:

$$P(X = x) = \alpha^x (1 - \alpha), \qquad x = 0, 1, 2, 3, 4, \ldots$$

From the definition we derive:

x	0	1	2	3	4	$\cdots$
$P(X = x)$	$1 - \alpha$	$\alpha(1 - \alpha)$	$\alpha^2(1 - \alpha)$	$\alpha^3(1 - \alpha)$	$\alpha^4(1 - \alpha)$	$\cdots$

The probability generating function, $G(t)$, is given by:

$$G(t) = (1 - \alpha) + \alpha(1 - \alpha)t + \alpha^2(1 - \alpha)t^2 + \alpha^3(1 - \alpha)t^3 + \alpha^4(1 - \alpha)t^4 + \cdots$$

$$= (1 - \alpha)(1 + \alpha t + (\alpha t)^2 + (\alpha t)^3 + (\alpha t)^4 + \cdots)$$

$$= \frac{1 - \alpha}{1 - \alpha t}$$

Differentiating with respect to t:

$$G'(t) = \frac{\alpha(1 - \alpha)}{(1 - \alpha t)^2} \quad \Rightarrow \quad G'(1) = \frac{\alpha(1 - \alpha)}{(1 - \alpha)^2} = \frac{\alpha}{1 - \alpha}$$

Therefore $E(X) = \dfrac{\alpha}{1 - \alpha}$.

Further differentiation with respect to t gives:

$$G''(t) = \frac{2\alpha^2(1 - \alpha)}{(1 - \alpha t)^3} \quad \Rightarrow \quad G''(1) = \frac{2\alpha^2(1 - \alpha)}{(1 - \alpha)^3} = \frac{2\alpha^2}{(1 - \alpha)^2}$$

Therefore

$$\sigma^2 = G''(1) - [G'(1)]^2 = \frac{2\alpha^2}{(1 - \alpha)^2} - \left(\frac{\alpha}{1 - \alpha}\right)^2 = \frac{\alpha^2}{(1 - \alpha)^2} = \left(\frac{\alpha}{1 - \alpha}\right)^2$$

$$\Rightarrow \quad \sigma = \frac{\alpha}{1 - \alpha}$$

Thus both the mean and standard deviation of X are the same.

EXAMPLE

Look again at the three-state Markov chain concerning Bob's old car. The only event that could take place two days running is that the car starts by itself. Given that the car starts by itself one day, find the mean and standard deviation of the number of further consecutive days on which it starts by itself.

Solution:

The probability that it starts by itself the next day is $\frac{1}{2}$. Therefore $\alpha = \frac{1}{2}$.

Let X represent the number of further consecutive days on which the car starts by itself, given that it starts by itself on Monday, then:

$$P(X = x) = (\tfrac{1}{2})^x \times \tfrac{1}{2} = (\tfrac{1}{2})^{x+1}, \text{ for } x = 0, 1, 2, 3, \ldots$$

$$\Rightarrow \quad E(X) = \frac{\alpha}{1 - \alpha} = \frac{\frac{1}{2}}{1 - \frac{1}{2}} = 1$$

Therefore the mean and standard deviation of the number of further consecutive days on which it starts by itself is 1.

Exercise 8D

1. For each of the following, given the initial state, find the expected number of consecutive further stages when the initial state remains unchanged.

Initial state

(i)   Exercise 8A   Question 2:   weather is sunny
(ii) Exercise 8A   Question 2:   weather is cloudy
(iii) Exercise 8A   Question 3:   Tina goes to the disco
(iv) Exercise 8A   Question 4:   Tina goes to the cinema
(v)   Exercise 8A   Question 5:   shot to opponent's backhand
(vi) Exercise 8A   Question 4:   shot to opponent's forehand
(vii) Exercise 8B   Question 3:   subscribes to *Tribune*
(viii) Exercise 8B Question 3:   subscribes to *Herald*
(ix) Exercise 8B   Question 3:   subscribes to *Gazette*
(x)   Exercise 8B   Question 4:   writes about tennis

2. A trucking company offers its drivers three approved routes between two cities: over the Mystic Bridge, on the Interstate Parkway, or on Route 1. If a trucker goes on the Mystic Bridge the chance of getting into a traffic jam is $\frac{1}{3}$; if he does get in a traffic jam, the next day he takes the Interstate Parkway with a probability of $\frac{2}{3}$ or Route 1 with a probability of $\frac{1}{3}$. If he doesn't get in a traffic jam on day one, the next day he takes the Mystic Bridge again, with a probability of $\frac{1}{2}$, the Interstate Parkway with a probability of $\frac{1}{6}$, or Route 1 with a probability of $\frac{1}{3}$. If he takes the Interstate Parkway, the chance of him getting into a traffic jam is $\frac{1}{2}$; if he does get in a traffic jam, the next day he takes the Mystic Bridge; if he doesn't get in a traffic jam, the next day he takes the Mystic Bridge, the Interstate Parkway or Route 1 with equal probability. If he takes Route 1, the trucker is invariably late, so he never takes Route 1 two days in a row and the next day he takes the Mystic Bridge with a probability of $\frac{1}{3}$ or the Interstate Parkway with a probability of $\frac{2}{3}$.

(i)   Form a 3 by 3 transition matrix, **P**, for the problem.

(ii) On Monday, the trucker takes Route 1. Find the probability that he takes:

   (a) Route 1 on Wednesday;

   (b) Interstate Parkway on Wednesday;

   (c) Mystic Bridge on Thursday;

   (d) Route 1 on Friday.

(iii) In the long run, what proportion of the time does the trucker go on the Mystic Bridge, the Interstate Parkway and Route 1, respectively?

(iv) One day the trucker takes the Interstate Parkway. Find the expected number of consecutive further days on which he takes the Interstate Parkway.

3. A TV news camera team may be allocated for a whole day to either of two reporters A or B, and the team also sometimes spend a day on stand-by to cover any sudden unexpected news items.

After a day on stand-by, the team are always allocated to one of the reporters on the next day, and are equally likely to be with either reporter. After a day with either reporter, the team have a probability of 0.6 of being allocated to the same reporter for the next day; after a day with reporter A, the probability of being allocated to stand-by on the next day is 0.25, but after a day with reporter B this probability is only 0.1.

(i)   Model this situation as a Markov chain.

(ii) On a certain Monday, the team are on stand-by. For the immediately following Tuesday and Wednesday, find the probabilities that they are on stand-by, with reporter A, or with reporter B.

(iii) On a certain day, the team are with one of the reporters. Find the expected number of consecutive further days that they will remain with this reporter.

[MEI]

4. An aircraft is based at airport A. It serves two routes, one between airport A and airport B and the other between airport A and airport C. On each route, it makes one out-and-back journey in a day. The aircraft also sometimes has to spend a whole day at airport A undergoing maintenance.

After a day operating the route to airport B, the probability that the aircraft will require maintenance on the next day is $\frac{1}{6}$; but after a day operating the route to airport C, the probability of requiring maintenance on the next day is $\frac{1}{3}$. After a day undergoing maintenance, the aircraft will certainly be back in operation on the next day, with, respectively, probabilities of $\frac{3}{5}$ and $\frac{2}{5}$ of serving the routes to airports B and C. After a day in operation on either route, the probability of operating the airport B route on the next day is $\frac{1}{2}$.

(i) Model this situation as a Markov chain.

(ii) On the Wednesday of a certain week, the aircraft is undergoing maintenance. For the Thursday and Friday of that week, find the probabilities that it is undergoing maintenance, operating the route to airport B, or operating the route to airport C. Find also the long-run proportions of days spent under maintenance and operating the routes to airports B and C.

(iii) On a certain day, the aircraft is operating the route to airport C. What is the expected number of consecutive *further* days that it operates this route?

[MEI]

5. In a study of the climate in Tel Aviv, it was found that during a certain part of the year the occurrence of dry and wet days was well modelled by a Markov chain with just two states, 'dry day' and 'wet day', with transition probabilities P(wet day follows dry day) $= 0.250$ and P(dry day follows wet day) $= 0.338$.

(i) Write down the transition matrix.

(ii) Obtain the equilibrium probabilities of a day being 'dry' or 'wet'.

(iii) Show that, in this model, no matter what the climate is on the current day, the equilibrium conditions will be very nearly reached after only about ten days.

(iv) Given that the current day (day 1) is wet, show that the probability that the next dry day occurs on day $n + 1$ is $(0.662)^{n-1}(0.338)$. In this way find the expected length of a 'wet spell' (i.e. a period of successive wet days after which the next day is dry). In a similar way, find the expected length of a 'dry spell'. Deduce that the expected length of a 'weather cycle' (i.e. a wet spell followed by a dry spell) is very nearly one week.

[MEI Statistics, 6 June 1994]

6. On any day, a factory machine may be in working order, requiring minor service, or requiring major service. If it is in working order, the probability that on the following day it requires minor service is 0.1 and the probability that it requires major service is also 0.1. If it is in the state of requiring minor service, the probability that on the following day it is still in this state is 0.2 and the probability that it is in working order is 0.6. If it is requiring major service, the probability that on the following day it is still requiring major service is 0.4 and the probability that it is in working order is 0.3.

(i) Write down the transition matrix for the Markov chain model of this situation.

(ii) Given that on day 1 the machine is in working order, use the Markov chain model to find the probability that the machine is in each possible state on day 3.

(iii) Over a long period, what are the proportions of days that the machine spends in working order, requiring minor service and requiring major service?

(iv) Given that on day 1 the machine is in working order, find the probability distribution of N, the number of *further* days before the day on which the first service of any kind is needed. Obtain the expected value of N.

[MEI Statistics, 6 June 1993]

7. A three-state Markov chain has transition matrix:

$$\mathbf{P} = \begin{pmatrix} 0.9 & 0 & 0.1 \\ 0.25 & 0.5 & 0.25 \\ 0.1 & 0 & 0.9 \end{pmatrix}$$

where, for example, the entry 0.25 in the $(2, 1)$ position is the transition probability from state 2 to state 1. Obtain the transition matrices for two steps of the process and for three steps of the process. Deduce the probabilities of being in each state after three steps if the process is initially in state 2. Also find the equilibrium probabilities of being in each state.

Suppose, instead, that the transition matrix is:

$$\mathbf{Q} = \begin{pmatrix} 1 & 0 & 0 \\ 0.25 & 0.5 & 0.25 \\ 0 & 0 & 1 \end{pmatrix}$$

Exercise 8D continued

(i) Describe what happens after the system enters:

    (a) state 1;

    (b) state 2;

    (c) state 3.

(ii) Explain what will happen to the system eventually if it starts in state 2.

[MEI Statistics, 6 June 1995]

KEY POINTS

- A sequence of events, where the probability of an outcome at one stage depends only on the outcome of the event at the previous stage, is known as a *Markov chain*.

- The conditional probabilities of passing from one stage to the next are called *transition probabilities*. They are most usefully arranged in a *transition matrix*, **P**, which is always a square matrix. Each row of **P** is a *probability vector*.

- Powers of the transition matrix, **P**, give conditional probabilities of moving from one outcome to another over 2, 3, 4, etc. steps.

- In the long run, successive powers of **P** converge towards an *equilibrium matrix*, each probability vector of which is the same. The entries in any row are called *equilibrium probabilities*.

- The equilibrium probabilities may be found directly by solving the equation:

$$\mathbf{pP} = \mathbf{p}$$

where **P** is the transition matrix, and **p** is a row matrix of equilibrium probabilities.

- Given an initial state, with probability α, the number of further consecutive stages, X, in which the state of the system remains in the initial state is given by:

$$P(X = x) = \alpha^x(1 - \alpha), \text{ for } x = 0, 1, 2, 3, \ldots$$

$$E(X) = \frac{\alpha}{1 - \alpha} \quad \text{and} \quad \text{Var}(X) = \left(\frac{\alpha}{1 - \alpha}\right)^2$$

Analysis of variance

The control of large numbers is possible, and like unto that of small numbers, if we subdivide them.

Sun Tse Ping Fa

ABC Engineering Company produce many component parts for the motor vehicle industry. In one particular workshop three machines each produce a particular component. The quality control inspector suspects that the outputs from three processing machines are different. From each machine he takes five components at random, all produced during the same shift. The measurements in the samples from the three machines were as follows:

| | Machine | | |
	A	B	C
	31	28	29
	32	27	28
Output	28	27	29
	29	28	30
	30	30	29

This may be illustrated diagramatically:

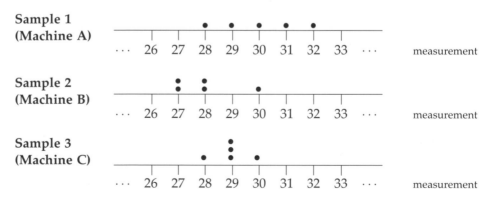

Figure 9.1

There is evidently some variation in the measurements, from 27 to 32. But how much of the variation is due to *within sample variation*, that is, variation due to chance fluctuations in the performance of each machine, and how much is due to *between sample variation*, that is, due to at least one of the machines consistently producing measurements that are different from those of the other(s)?

A technique used to analyse the source of variation is called the *analysis of variance* (commonly written as *ANOVA* for short). Certain assumptions are made before the analysis begins:

- The three samples are drawn from populations which are Normally distributed.

- The populations have a common variance, σ^2.

A null hypothesis is set up which claims that each of the three populations also has the same mean, μ, i.e. the samples are effectively drawn from one Normal population with mean μ and variance σ^2. ANOVA uses the within sample variation and the between sample variation to produce two unbiased estimates of the common population variance σ^2. These estimates of σ^2 are then compared.

If it should prove that the *between sample* variation is significantly greater than the *within sample* variation, then we should suspect that, in fact, the samples were *not* drawn from the same population, but from populations whose means differed, so that on top of the *within population variation* there also existed a *between population variation*.

Formally, we set up a hypothesis test as follows. Let μ_1, μ_2, μ_3 represent the means of the three Normal populations from which the samples are drawn. The null and alternative hypotheses are given by:

$$H_0: \quad \mu_1 = \mu_2 = \mu_3 = \mu$$

$$H_1: \quad \text{not all population means are the same.}$$

Let the *within sample* and *between sample* estimates of the common population variance be denoted by s_w^2 and s_b^2. To compare these two estimates of the population we use the *F*-test developed in *Statistics 5*.

Now select a significance level, e.g. 5%. If the value of the variance ratio $\dfrac{s_b^2}{s_w^2}$ exceeds the critical value, then we reject H_0 at the 5% level, i.e. we accept that not all the population means are the same. If the variance ratio does not exceed the critical value, then we conclude that all the sample observations might well have come from the same Normal population.

Both the notation and the method are most easily explained by applying them to our example. The notation used here and in subsequent work is:

k = number of samples	x_{ij} = jth member of the ith sample
n_i = number of observations in the ith sample	n = total sample size
$\bar{x}_i$ = mean of the ith sample	$\bar{x}$ = overall sample mean
s_i^2 = variance of the ith sample	s^2 = overall sample variance

As we have three samples, $k = 3$. The remaining statistics are summarised in the table:

Machine	A	B	C	Overall
Sample size	$n_1 = 5$	$n_2 = 5$	$n_3 = 5$	$n = 15$
Sample mean	$\bar{x}_1 = 30$	$\bar{x}_2 = 28$	$\bar{x}_3 = 29$	$\bar{x} = 29$
Sample variance	$s_1^2 = 2.5$	$s_2^2 = 1.5$	$s_3^2 = 0.5$	$s^2 = 2$

NOTE

All of the statistics in the table can be found by entering the sample data (the three samples separately followed by the overall sample) into a scientific calculator in statistics mode. The sample sizes and sample means are self-explanatory. The sample variance is the **unbiased** *estimate of the population variance, found by squaring the standard deviation with divisor 'n − 1' denoted by σ_{n-1} or similar symbol on your calculator.*

Enter the data yourself and confirm that the results obtained are correct.

The *within groups* estimate s_w^2

Whether or not the null hypothesis is true, an unbiased estimate of the population variance is given by pooling the three sample variances:

$$s_w^2 = \frac{(n_1 - 1)s_1^2 + (n_2 - 1)s_2^2 + (n_3 - 1)s_3^2}{n_1 + n_2 + n_3 - 3}$$

$$= \frac{4 \times 2.5 + 4 \times 1.4 + 4 \times 0.5}{5 + 5 + 5 - 3} = \frac{18}{12} = 1.5$$

Note that this can also be given by:

$$s_w^2 = \frac{\sum_j (x_{1j} - \bar{x}_1)^2 + \sum_j (x_{2j} - \bar{x}_2)^2 + \sum_j (x_{3j} - \bar{x}_3)^2}{n_1 + n_2 + n_3 - 3} = \frac{\sum_i \sum_j (x_{ij} - \bar{x}_i)^2}{n - k}$$

The numerator is known as the *within samples sum of squares* (of deviations from the sample means) and the denominator is the number of *degrees of freedom*.

The *between samples* estimate s_b^2

Provided the null hypothesis is true, an unbiased estimate of the population variance is also given by replacing every item in a sample by the sample mean and considering the variance of the deviations of the sample means from the overall mean:

$$s_b^2 = \frac{n_1(\bar{x}_1 - \bar{x})^2 + n_2(\bar{x}_2 - \bar{x})^2 + n_3(\bar{x}_3 - \bar{x})^2}{3 - 1}$$

$$= \frac{5 \times (1)^2 + 5 \times (-1)^2 + 5 \times (0)^2}{3 - 1} = \frac{10}{2} = 5$$

Note that this can also be given by:

$$s_b^2 = \frac{\sum_i n_i(\bar{x}_i - \bar{x})^2}{3 - 1} = \frac{\sum_i n_i(\bar{x}_i - \bar{x})^2}{k - 1}$$

The numerator is known as the *between samples sum of squares* (of deviations of the sample means from the overall mean) and the denominator is the number of *degrees of freedom*.

Summary

The results obtained so far can be summarised in the following table:

Source of variation	Sum of squares	Degrees of freedom	Variance estimate
Between samples	10	2	$s_b^2 = 5$
Within samples	18	12	$s_w^2 = 1.5$

Applying the hypothesis test

The *F*-test statistic may now be calculated:

$$F = \frac{s_b^2}{s_w^2} = \frac{5}{1.5} = 3.33$$

If H_0 is true, the computed F value should not be significantly greater than 1. If H_0 is false, then s_b^2 will overestimate σ^2 and so F will be significantly greater than 1. Consider a one-tailed test at the 5% level of significance. From the F distribution table (*MEI Tables*, page 28) the critical value is 3.89, based on the respective degrees of freedom, $\nu_1 = 2$ and $\nu_2 = 12$.

As our calculated value is less than the critical value, the result is not significant and we accept the null hypothesis H_0 and conclude that all 15 observations might well have come from the same Normal population with common mean as well as common variance. The evidence suggests that there is no significant difference between the measurements obtained from the three samples.

Extending our example

Suppose that it is found that the measurement of 28 from machine A was, in fact, from machine B. Does this information affect our previous conclusion?

The data now read:

	Machine		
	A	B	C
	31	28	29
	32	27	28
Output	29	27	29
	30	28	30
		30	29
		28	

The summary statistics for the newly grouped data become:

Machine	A	B	C	Overall
Sample size	$n_1 = 4$	$n_2 = 6$	$n_3 = 5$	$n = 15$
Sample mean	$\bar{x}_1 = 30.5$	$\bar{x}_2 = 28$	$\bar{x}_3 = 29$	$\bar{x} = 29$
Sample variance	$s_1^2 = 1.67$	$s_2^2 = 1.2$	$s_3^2 = 0.5$	$s^2 = 2$

The *within samples* estimate:

$$s_w^2 = \frac{(n_1 - 1)s_1^2 + (n_2 - 1)s_2^2 + (n_3 - 1)s_3^2}{n_1 + n_2 + n_3 - 3}$$

$$= \frac{3 \times 1.67 + 5 \times 1.2 + 4 \times 0.5}{4 + 6 + 5 - 3} = \frac{13}{12} = 1.0833 \text{ (5 sf)}$$

The *between samples* estimate:

$$s_b^2 = \frac{n_1(\bar{x}_1 - \bar{x})^2 + n_2(\bar{x}_2 - \bar{x})^2 + n_3(\bar{x}_3 - \bar{x})^2}{3 - 1}$$

$$= \frac{4 \times (1.5)^2 + 6 \times (-1)^2 + 5 \times (0)^2}{3 - 1} = \frac{15}{2} = 7.5$$

The results obtained so far can again be summarised in a table:

Source of variation	Sum of squares	Degrees of freedom	Variance estimate
Between samples	15	2	$s_b^2 = 7.5$
Within samples	13	12	$s_w^2 = 1.0833$

Finally, calculate the *F*-test statistic:

$$F = \frac{s_b^2}{s_w^2} = \frac{7.5}{1.0833} = 6.92$$

As the degrees of freedom are once again $\nu_1 = 2$ and $\nu_2 = 12$, the critical value for a 5% level of significance is again 3.89. As the calculated value is greater than the critical value, the result is significant and we reject the null hypothesis H_0 in favour of the alternative hypothesis H_1. We conclude that there is sufficient evidence to suggest that the differences between the means as reflected in the between samples estimate of the population variance are too large to be accounted for by chance fluctuations, i.e. not all of the population means are the same.

Exercise 9A

1. Tests were carried out by a chemist to measure the percentage of impurity in a chemical solution, using five different methods on samples of four. The percentage of impurity was recorded as follows:

Method	% impurity			
1	25	19	20	21
2	27	28	24	28
3	21	18	21	17
4	20	21	21	17
5	24	27	21	24

The chemist wishes to test, at the 5% significance level, to see if there is any significant difference between the mean percentages obtained by the different methods.

(i)   State suitable null and alternative hypotheses for an analysis of variance test.

(ii) Copy and complete the following table of summary statistics:

Method	1	2	3	4	5	Overall
Sample size	$n_1 =$	$n_2 =$	$n_3 =$	$n_4 =$	$n_5 =$	$n =$
Sample mean	$\bar{x}_1 =$	$\bar{x}_2 =$	$\bar{x}_3 =$	$\bar{x}_4 =$	$\bar{x}_5 =$	$\bar{x} =$
Sample variance	$s_1^2 =$	$s_2^2 =$	$s_3^2 =$	$s_4^2 =$	$s_5^2 =$	$s^2 =$

(iii) Construct a summary table of sums of squares, degrees of freedom and variance estimates for within samples and between samples variation.

(iv) Calculate the F-ratio and compare it with the critical value obtained from tables.

(v)   State your conclusions.

2. The times, to the nearest minute, taken by Alex, Bobby and Carol to complete a random sample of crosswords were as follows:

Alex	77	81	71	76	80
Bobby	72	58	74	66	70
Carol	76	85	82	80	77

At the 5% level, test whether the differences in times they take to do crosswords are significant.
[MEI]

3. Four machines, each dispensing sugar in nominal quantities of 1 kg, produce the following quantities when five measures are taken from each:

Dispenser	Mass of sugar (g)				
1	998	1002	1000	1011	1003
2	1006	1010	1014	997	1005
3	991	1001	999	998	993
4	1006	984	993	1001	998

Test to see if the quantities produced by the machines are significantly different:

(i)   at the 5% level;

(ii) at the 1% level.

4. Samples of four different varieties of wheat, planted in similar ground, gave the following yields in kg:

Variety	Yield (kg)			
A	40	42	44	
B	46	44	46	46
C	35	38		
D	37	49	37	

Are the mean yields significantly different at the 5% level?

5. A catering firm wished to buy a meat tenderiser, but was concerned with the effect on the weight loss of meat during cooking. The following results were obtained for the weight loss of steaks of the same pre-cooked weight when three different tenderisers were used:

Tenderiser	Weight loss in grams			
A	36	28	42	58
B	17	59	33	
C	36	74	29	55	48

Carry out an analysis of variance to test, at the 5% level of significance, whether there is a difference in weight loss between tenderisers.
[AEB]

Exercise 9A continued

6. An experiment was conducted to study the effects of various diets on pigs. A total of 24 similar pigs were selected and randomly allocated to one of the five groups so that the control group, which was fed a normal diet, contained eight pigs and each of the other groups, to which the new diets were given, contained four pigs each. After a fixed time the gains in mass, in kg, of the pigs were measured. Unfortunately, by this time two pigs had died, one of which was on diet A and the other on diet C. The gains in mass of the remaining pigs are recorded below:

Diet	Gains in mass (kg)							
Normal	23.1	9.8	15.5	22.6	14.6	11.2	15.7	10.5
A	21.9	13.2	19.7					
B	16.5	22.8	18.3	31.0				
C	30.9	21.9	29.8					
D	21.0	25.4	21.5	21.2				

Test:

(i) at the 5% level of significance;

(ii) at the 1% level of significance;

for differences between diets.

[AEB]

The *total* estimate s^2

Although we compare s_w^2 and s_b^2 using the F-test, a third method of estimating the common population variance is to regard all the observations as one sample.

Provided the null hypothesis is true, that the populations from which the samples are drawn all have the same mean, μ, then s^2 also gives an unbiased estimate of σ^2.

Returning to our first example, the table of results gives $s^2 = 2$.

Note that s^2 is given by:

$$s^2 = \frac{\sum_i \sum_j (x_{ij} - \bar{x})^2}{n - 1}$$

The numerator is known as the *total sum of squares* (of deviations from the overall mean) and the denominator is the number of *degrees of freedom*.

As $s^2 = 2$ and $n - 1 = 14$, this must mean that $\sum_i \sum_j (x_{ij} - \bar{x})^2 = 28$.

Check this last result by computing:

$$\begin{aligned}
\sum_i \sum_j (x_{ij} - \bar{x})^2 = {} & (31 - 29)^2 + (32 - 29)^2 + (28 - 29)^2 \\
& + (29 - 29)^2 + (30 - 29)^2 \qquad \text{sample 1} \\
& + (28 - 29)^2 + (27 - 29)^2 + (27 - 29)^2 \\
& + (28 - 29)^2 + (30 - 29)^2 \qquad \text{sample 2} \\
& + (29 - 29)^2 + (28 - 29)^2 + (29 - 29)^2 \\
& + (30 - 29)^2 + (29 - 29)^2 \qquad \text{sample 3}
\end{aligned}$$

You have now discovered three ways of estimating the population variance σ^2, all of which produce unbiased estimates, given that the null hypothesis is true. The results now obtained can be summarised in the table:

Source of variation	Sum of squares	Degrees of freedom	Variance estimate
Between samples	10	2	$s_b^2 = 5$
Within samples	18	12	$s_w^2 = 1.5$
Total	28	14	$s^2 = 2$

Two very important properties are illustrated here:

Total sum of squares =

within samples sum of squares + between samples sum of squares.

Total degrees of freedom =

within samples degrees of freedom + between samples degrees of freedom.

The second equation is easy to follow as, using the generalised form for the degrees of freedom:

$$n - 1 = (n - k) + (k - 1)$$

The first equation in generalised form gives:

$$\sum_{i=1}^{k} \sum_{j=1}^{n_i} (x_{ij} - \bar{x})^2 = \sum_{i=1}^{k} \sum_{j=1}^{n_i} (x_{ij} - \bar{x}_i)^2 + \sum_{i=1}^{k} n_i(\bar{x}_i - \bar{x})^2$$

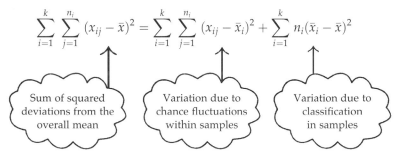

Sum of squared deviations from the overall mean

Variation due to chance fluctuations within samples

Variation due to classification in samples

The formulae for the *total* sum of squares and the *between samples* sum of squares can be awkward to evaluate directly if the population mean is, for example, a recurring decimal. Alternative versions, involving sample and grand totals, can be derived by simple algebraic manipulation.

Let T_i represent the total of the ith sample and let T represent the overall sample total, i.e.:

$$T_i = \sum_{j} x_{ij} \quad \Rightarrow \quad \bar{x}_i = \frac{T_i}{n_i} \quad \text{and} \quad T = \sum_{i} \sum_{j} x_{ij} \quad \Rightarrow \quad \bar{x} = \frac{T}{n}$$

then:

Between samples sum of squares

$$\sum_i n_i(\bar{x}_i - \bar{x})^2 = \sum_i n_i(\bar{x}_i - \bar{x})(\bar{x}_i - \bar{x})$$

$$= \sum_i n_i(\bar{x}_i^2 - 2\bar{x}\bar{x}_i + \bar{x}^2)$$

$$= \sum_i n_i\bar{x}_i^2 - 2\bar{x}\sum_i n_i\bar{x}_i + \bar{x}^2\sum_i n_i$$

$$= \sum_i \frac{T_i^2}{n_i} - \frac{2T^2}{n} + \frac{T^2}{n}$$

$$= \sum_i \frac{T_i^2}{n_i} - \frac{T^2}{n}$$

Total sum of squares

$$\sum_i \sum_j (x_{ij} - \bar{x})^2 = \sum_i \sum_j (x_{ij} - \bar{x})(x_{ij} - \bar{x})$$

$$= \sum_i \sum_j (x_{ij}^2 - 2\bar{x}x_{ij} + \bar{x}^2)$$

$$= \sum_i \sum_j x_{ij}^2 - 2\bar{x}\sum_i \sum_j x_{ij} + n\bar{x}^2$$

$$= \sum_i \sum_j x_{ij}^2 - \frac{2T^2}{n} + \frac{T^2}{n}$$

$$= \sum_i \sum_j x_{ij}^2 - \frac{T^2}{n}$$

Within samples sum of squares

This may now be obtained by subtraction:

Within samples sum of squares =

total sum of squares − between samples sum of squares

$$= \sum_i \sum_j x_{ij}^2 - \frac{T^2}{n} - \left(\sum_i \frac{T_i^2}{n_i} - \frac{T^2}{n}\right) = \sum_i \sum_j x_{ij}^2 - \sum_i \frac{T_i^2}{n_i}$$

Returning to our extended example on page 150, the alternative sum of squares formulae can be used to produce the variance estimates s_b^2 and s_w^2.

The **summary statistics** for the grouped data become:

Machine	A	B	C	Overall
Sample size	$n_1 = 4$	$n_2 = 6$	$n_3 = 5$	$n = 15$
Sample total	$T_1 = 122$	$T_2 = 168$	$T_3 = 145$	$T = 435$
$\sum_i \sum_j x_{ij}^2 = 31^2 + 32^2 + 28^2 + \cdots + 29^2 + 30^2 + 29^2 = 12\,643$				

The *between samples* estimate:

$$s_b^2 = \frac{\sum_i \dfrac{T_i^2}{n_i} - \dfrac{T^2}{n}}{k - 1} = \frac{\dfrac{122^2}{4} + \dfrac{168^2}{6} + \dfrac{145^2}{5} - \dfrac{435^2}{15}}{3 - 1}$$

$$= \frac{3721 + 4704 + 4205 - 12\,615}{2} = \frac{15}{2} = 7.5$$

The *within samples* estimate:

$$s_w^2 = \frac{\sum_i \sum_j x_{ij}^2 - \sum_i \dfrac{T_i^2}{n_i}}{n - k} = \frac{12\,643 - \left(\dfrac{122^2}{4} + \dfrac{168^2}{6} + \dfrac{145^2}{5}\right)}{15 - 3} = \frac{13}{12} = 1.0833$$

For Discussion

Compare the two computational methods for finding s_b^2 and s_w^2. What are the advantages of either method?

The ANOVA model

The general form of the hypothesis for the analysis of variance is:

$$H_0: \quad \mu_1 = \mu_2 = \cdots = \mu_k = \mu$$
$$H_1: \quad \text{not all population means are the same;}$$

where $x_{ij} \sim N(\mu_i, \sigma^2)$.

Each observation may be written in the form $x_{ij} = \mu_i + e_{ij}$ where e_{ij} represents the *experimental error*, i.e. the measure of the deviation of the jth observation of the ith sample (x_{ij}) from the corresponding population mean μ_i. It is also assumed that $e_{ij} \sim N(0, \sigma^2)$.

An alternative and preferred form of this equation is obtained by substituting $\mu_i = \mu + \alpha_i$, where μ is defined to be the mean of all the μ_i; i.e. $\mu = \dfrac{1}{k} \sum_i \mu_i$

Therefore we may write $x_{ij} = \mu + \alpha_i + e_{ij}$ subject to the restriction that $\sum_i \alpha_i = 0$. It is customary to refer to α_i as the *treatment effect* of the ith population. The null hypothesis, that the k population means are equal against the alternative that at least two of the means are unequal, may now be replaced by the equivalent statements:

$$H_0: \quad \alpha_1 = \alpha_2 = \cdots = \alpha_k = 0;$$
$$H_1: \quad \text{not all the } \alpha_i \text{ are zero.}$$

The t-test for the difference between population means

The analysis of variance tests whether there are any overall differences among the population means. To see whether two particular means, μ_i and μ_j, are the same, we may, of course, use an ordinary two-sample t-test:

$$H_0: \quad \mu_i = \mu_j$$
$$H_1: \quad \mu_i \neq \mu_j$$

As $\text{Var}\,(\bar{X}_i) = \dfrac{\sigma^2}{n_i}$ and $\text{Var}\,(\bar{X}_j) = \dfrac{\sigma^2}{n_j}$, then:

$$\text{Var}\,(\bar{X}_i - \bar{X}_j) = \frac{\sigma^2}{n_i} + \frac{\sigma^2}{n_j} = \sigma^2\left(\frac{1}{n_i} + \frac{1}{n_j}\right)$$

so if we knew σ^2 we could take as our test statistic:

$$\frac{\bar{x}_i - \bar{x}_j}{\sigma\sqrt{\dfrac{1}{n_i} + \dfrac{1}{n_j}}}$$

and refer this to $N(0, 1)$. However, the population variance σ^2 is unknown. An unbiased estimator for σ^2 is given by s_w^2, regardless of any hypothesis about the population means, so we use the test statistic:

$$\frac{\bar{x}_i - \bar{x}_j}{s_w\sqrt{\dfrac{1}{n_i} + \dfrac{1}{n_j}}}$$

and refer to t_{n-k}.

There is, however, the difficulty that there will usually be many pairs of means and we could well find one pair (or more) to give a significant result by chance (a type I error). With k samples there are ${}^kC_2$ possible t-tests, and by considering every one, the probability of such an occurrence at the 5% level is given by:

$$P(\text{at least one type I error}) = 1 - P(\text{no type I error } {}^kC_2 \text{ in tests})$$

$$= 1 - (0.95)^{{}^kC_2}$$

In the extension of our original example, it would seem sensible to compare A with B or C. For example, consider A and B. The test statistic, taking $i = 1$ and $j = 2$, is:

$$\frac{\bar{x}_1 - \bar{x}_2}{s_w\sqrt{\dfrac{1}{n_1} + \dfrac{1}{n_2}}} = \frac{30.5 - 28}{\sqrt{1.0833}\sqrt{\frac{1}{4} + \frac{1}{6}}} = 3.72$$

which we compare with t_{12}. The result is significant, even at the 1% level, for which the critical value is 3.055. By rejecting the null hypothesis for the F-test we came to the conclusion that there was sufficient evidence to suggest that not all population means, μ_i, were equal. By rejecting the null hypothesis for the t-test we come to the conclusion that there is sufficient evidence to suggest that $\mu_1 \neq \mu_2$.

A similar t-test applied to A and C produces a t-statistic of 2.15. By comparison with the critical value, we would not reject the null hypothesis at the 1% level. That is, there is not enough evidence to reject the null hypothesis that $\mu_1 = \mu_3$.

Exercise 9B

1. As part of a project to improve the steerability of trucks, a manufacturer took three trucks of the same model and fitted them with soft, standard and hard front springs respectively. The turning radius (the radius of the circle in which the truck could turn full circle) was measured for each truck using a variety of drivers, speeds and conditions. The following results are available:

Source of variation	Sum of squares	Degrees of freedom
Between springs	37.9	2
Within springs	75.6	18
Total	113.5	20

(i) How many observations were made altogether?

(ii) Assuming that each truck underwent the same number of tests, how many was this?

(iii) Carry out a one-way analysis of variance at the 5% significance level to test for a difference in the springs.

[AEB]

2. A batch of bricks was randomly divided into three parts and each part was stored by a different method. After a week the percentage water content of a number of bricks stored by each method was measured.

Method of storage	% water content					
1	7.4	8.5	7.1	6.2	7.8	
2	5.5	7.1	5.6			
3	4.8	5.1	6.2	4.9	6.1	7.1

(i) Copy and complete the following table of summary statistics:

Method of storage	1	2	3	Overall
Sample size	$n_1 =$	$n_2 =$	$n_3 =$	$n =$
Sample mean	$\bar{x}_2 =$	$\bar{x}_2 =$	$\bar{x}_3 =$	$\bar{x} =$
Sample variance	$s_1^2 =$	$s_2^2 =$	$s_3^2 =$	$s^2 =$

(ii) Construct a summary table of sums of squares, degrees of freedom and variance estimates for within samples and between samples variation.

(iii) Use the analysis of variance to test, at the 5% level of significance, for differences between methods of storage.

[AEB]

3. Eastside Area Health Authority has a policy whereby any patient admitted to a hospital with a suspected heart attack is automatically placed in the intensive care unit. The table below gives the number of hours spent in intensive care by such patients at five hospitals in the area:

(i) Use a one-way analysis of variance to test, at the 1% level of significance, for differences between hospitals.

Hospital				
A	B	C	D	E
30	42	65	67	70
25	57	46	58	63
12	47	55	81	80
23	30	27		
16				

(ii) Write down an estimate, with its standard error, of the mean time spent in intensive care by this type of patient in hospital C.

[AEB]

4. A commuter in a large city can travel to work by car, bicycle or bus. She times four journeys by each method, with the following results (in minutes):

Car	Bicycle	Bus
27	34	26
45	38	41
33	43	35
31	42	46

(i) Carry out an analysis of variance at the 5% significance level to find whether there are differences in the mean journey times for the three methods of transport.

(ii) The time of day at which she travels to work varies. Bearing in mind that this is likely to affect the time taken for the journey, suggest a better design for her experiment and explain briefly why you believe it to be better.

(iii) Suggest a factor, other than leaving time, which is likely to affect the journey time and two factors, other than journey time, which might be considered when choosing the method of transport.

[AEB]

5. An archaeological team unearthed human skulls at three different locations. It was known that certain different subspecies of 'early man' differed in the length of their skulls, so it was decided to examine whether or not the average skull lengths of the underlying population of 'early man' at these three locations could be assumed to be the same. The lengths in mm of the skulls found at the locations were as follows:

Location								
1	188	179	183	171	187	172	176	174
2	176	193	181	191	178			
3	180	159	175	170	169	166		

(i) Carry out a one-way analysis of variance using a 5% significance level, carefully displaying your working.

(ii) State carefully the null and alternative hypotheses and the critical value of your test statistic.

(iii) Discuss briefly your conclusions. What are the assumptions underlying your analysis?

[MEI, June 1992]

6. (i) In a one-way analysis of variance, k treatments are being compared. There are n_i observations on the ith treatment, and x_{ij} represents the jth observation on the ith treatment ($i = 1, 2, \ldots, k$; $j = 1, 2, \ldots, n_i$). A suitable statistical model is:

$$x_{ij} = \mu + \alpha_i + e_{ij}$$

$$i = 1, 2, \ldots, k; \quad j = 1, 2, \ldots, n_i$$

where μ represents the overall population mean for the whole situation, α_i represents the population mean amount by which the ith treatment differs from the overall mean, and e_{ij} represents the 'experimental error'.

(a) State carefully the statistical properties that the e_{ij} need to possess for the usual analysis of variance to be applicable.

(b) Explain why the null hypothesis customarily tested can be written as $\alpha_1 = \alpha_2 = \cdots = \alpha_k = 0$.

(ii) At an agricultural research station, four different fertilisers are being compared. Each is applied to a number of similar plots of soil and a standard variety of wheat is grown under carefully controlled conditions. The yields of wheat, measured in a convenient unit, from the plots are as follows:

Fertiliser 1	23.7	24.2	24.9	24.6	
Fertiliser 2	22.9	23.7	23.6	24.4	23.4
Fertiliser 3	22.9	23.6	22.4		
Fertiliser 4	24.3	24.9	24.5	24.0	

(a) Carry out the customary one-way analysis of variance using a 5% significance level, carefully displaying your working and stating the critical value of your test statistic.

(b) Discuss briefly your conclusions.

[MEI, June 1993]

7. At a chemical plant, trials are being conducted concerning the production of a particular chemical. Four processes for making this chemical are being compared in terms of the purity of the product. The following data show the percentages of impurity in the product in a number of experimental runs using each process.

Process A   6.21   5.64   7.47   7.36
Process B   11.55   10.63   5.62   7.57   8.13
Process C   9.31   7.46   11.13   10.22
Process D   9.06   5.59   5.72   3.60   7.23

NOTE: $(6.21)^2 + (5.64)^2 + \cdots + (7.23)^2 = 1163.6658$.

(i) State the conditions that are necessary for it to be appropriate to analyse these data using the customary one-way analysis of variance.

(ii) Assuming these conditions are satisfied, carry out the analysis of variance using a 5% significance level, stating the null and alternative hypotheses and the critical value of the test statistic.

(iii) Process A is the standard process and process C the cheapest. Use a t-test to examine, at the 5% significance level, whether the mean percentage impurities for these two processes differ.

[MEI, June 1994]

8. (i) In a one-way analysis of variance situation, k treatments are being compared. There are n_i observations on the ith treatment; the jth observation on the ith treatment is denoted by x_{ij} $(i = 1, 2, \ldots, k; j = 1, 2, \ldots, n_i)$. A statistical model commonly used for this situation is:

$$x_{ij} = \mu + \alpha_i + e_{ij}$$

$$i = 1, 2, \ldots, k; \quad j = 1, 2, \ldots, n_i$$

where e_{ij} represents the experimental error.

(a) State carefully the statistical properties that the e_{ij} need to possess for the usual analysis of variance to be applicable. Interpret the parameters μ and α_i in the model.

(b) State, in terms of the α_i the null hypothesis that is customarily tested.

(ii) In an engineering development laboratory, prototypes of a casting are being made by three processes. A critical dimension is measured for each casting and the results (in cm), for a random sample of four castings made by each process, are as follows:

Process A   9.68   9.54   9.95   9.83
Process B   10.12   9.78   10.02   9.94
Process C   9.63   9.68   9.51   9.48

Carry out the customary one-way analysis of variance using a 1% significance level, stating the critical value of the test statistic.

[MEI, June 1995]

9. A food manufacturer has been attempting to improve a breakfast cereal. Four new recipes (A, B, C, D) have been developed. Members of a tasting panel have assigned 'scores' to random samples produced by the four recipes as follows:

A	28.7	29.4	30.5	29.0
B	31.1	30.4	30.2	31.5
C	27.7	33.6	32.2	32.8
D	33.0	33.6	32.2	32.8

NOTE: *The sum of these scores is 484.2 and the sum of their squares is 14 711.22.*

(i) Carry out the customary one-way analysis of variance to examine whether or not it may be assumed that there are differences between the recipes.

Use a 0.1% significance level, display your results carefully and state the critical value of your test statistic.

(ii) Let x_{ij} denote the jth observation on the ith treatment in a one-way analysis of variance situation (such as that in (i)), where, in general, $i = 1, 2, \ldots, k$ and $j = 1, 2, \ldots, n_i$. State a suitable statistical model on which the one-way analysis of variance can be based. Interpret the parameters of your model and state the statistical properties of any terms representing experimental error. State, in terms of the parameters of your model, the null hypothesis that is customarily used.

[MEI, June 1996]

10. At an agricultural research station, a trial of four varieties of carrots is being carried out under carefully controlled conditions. The yields, in kg per plot, at the end of the trial are as follows:

Variety A   44.2   43.8   45.6   42.2
Variety B   46.7   45.0   45.8   43.6
Variety C   50.2   48.8   46.4   48.6
Variety D   41.3   39.9   42.6

NOTE: $(44.2)^2 + (43.8)^2 + \cdots + (42.6)^2 = 30\,465.63$.

(i) Carry out the customary one-way analysis of variance to examine whether it may be assumed that there are differences between the varieties. Use a 1% significance level. Display your working carefully.

(ii) Let x_{ij} denote the jth observation on the ith treatment in a general one-way analysis of variance situation $(i = 1, 2, \ldots, k; j = 1, 2, \ldots, n_i)$ and let σ^2 denote the common population variance underlying all the observations. Denote the within-samples sum of squares by W and the sample variance for the ith sample

by s_i^2, so that

$$W = \sum_{i=1}^{k} \sum_{j=1}^{n_i} (x_{ij} - \bar{x}_i)^2$$

and

$$s_i^2 = \frac{1}{n_i - 1} \sum_{j=1}^{n_i} (x_{ij} - \bar{x}_i)^2$$

where: $\bar{x}_i = \dfrac{1}{n_i} \sum_{j=1}^{n_i} x_{ij}$

Use the result that the underlying distribution of s_i^2 is $\dfrac{\sigma^2}{n_i - 1} \chi^2_{n_i-1}$ to deduce that $\sum_{j=1}^{n_i} (x_{ij} - \bar{x}_i)^2$ has the underlying distribution $\sigma^2 \chi^2_{n_i-1}$

(iii) The additive property of χ^2 states that the random variable, which is the sum of independent random variables each having χ^2 distributions, has itself a χ^2 distribution; and, further, its number of degrees of freedom is the sum of the numbers of degrees of freedom of the random variables in the sum. Use this result to deduce that the distribution underlying W is $\sigma^2 \chi^2_{n-k}$ where $n = \sum_{i=1}^{k} n_i$

KEY POINTS

- The general form of the hypothesis for the analysis of variance is:

$$H_0: \quad \mu_1 = \mu_2 = \cdots = \mu_k = \mu$$
$$H_1: \quad \text{not all population means are the same;}$$

where $x_{ij} \sim N(\mu_i, \sigma^2)$.

- Each observation may be written in the form $x_{ij} = \mu_i + e_{ij}$, where e_{ij} measures the experimental error, i.e. the deviation of the jth observation of the ith sample (x_{ij}) from the corresponding population mean μ_i. It is also assumed that $e_{ij} \sim N(0, \sigma^2)$.

- The test statistic is $F = \dfrac{S_b^2}{S_w^2}$

Source of variation	Sum of squares	Degress of freedom	Variance estimate
Between samples	$\displaystyle\sum_{i=1}^{k} n_i(\bar{x}_i - \bar{x})^2$	$k - 1$	$s_b^2 = \dfrac{\displaystyle\sum_{i=1}^{k} n_i(\bar{x}_i - \bar{x})^2}{k-1}$
Within samples	$\displaystyle\sum_{i=1}^{k}\sum_{j=1}^{n_i} (x_{ij} - \bar{x}_i)^2$	$n - k$	$s_w^2 = \dfrac{\displaystyle\sum_{i=1}^{k}\sum_{j=1}^{n_i} (x_{ij} - \bar{x}_i)^2}{n-k}$

k = number of samples $\qquad x_{ij} = j$th member of the ith sample

n_i = size of the ith sample $\qquad n$ = total sample size

$\bar{x}_i$ = mean of the ith sample $\qquad \bar{x}$ = overall sample mean

s_i^2 = variance of the ith sample $\quad s^2$ = overall sample variance

10 Regression

She knew only that if she did or said thus-and-so, men would unerringly respond with the complimentary thus-and-so. It was like a mathematical formula and no more difficult ...

Margaret Mitchell
(Scarlett O'Hara in *Gone With The Wind*)

The Cheapotel Company operates basic accommodation for motorists. It owns hotels near main roads all over the country, and is looking for guidelines on the cost of building new hotels. The analyst assigned to this project has data for the cost of the 38 hotels built so far and the number of rooms in each hotel. The data are given in the table below and also illustrated in figure 10.1.

	Number of rooms	Building cost (£000)		Number of rooms	Building cost (£000)		Number of rooms	Building cost (£000)
1	81	2095	14	122	2076	27	197	2420
2	98	1758	15	206	2545	28	50	1701
3	244	2558	16	113	2762	29	53	1954
4	72	1492	17	82	1843	30	68	2316
5	262	2433	18	199	2762	31	52	1931
6	65	1526	19	46	1819	32	30	1862
7	39	1649	20	77	2605	33	63	1780
8	36	1894	21	210	2310	34	249	2506
9	88	2344	22	29	1569	35	60	1880
10	43	2094	23	56	2235	36	134	2263
11	280	1902	24	94	2371	37	83	1848
12	75	2068	25	182	2631	38	51	2129
13	160	2362	26	46	1807			

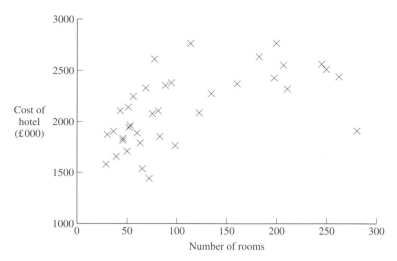

Figure 10.1

We can model the relationship between the number of rooms in the hotel and the cost of construction as the sum of three terms. There will be a fixed cost for acquiring and preparing the site and building the administrative and public areas. Added to this will be the cost of building the rooms, which we might expect to be proportional to the number of rooms. Finally, an additional amount will need to be added or subtracted depending on all the other factors which affect the cost – for instance, labour and land costs will depend on where in the country the hotel is. The key part of the modelling, which turns this into a statistical question, is that we take this additional amount to be a random variable, that is, we model our *ignorance* of the other factors by *randomness*.

We can write this symbolically as:

$$Y = \alpha + \beta x + E$$

where

Y is the variable recording the cost of building a hotel;

α is the fixed cost;

x is the number of rooms in the hotel;

β is the constant of proportionality giving the extra cost of building each room;

E is the additional amount added or subtracted to account for all the other effects on the cost.

You should note that E is a random variable and so, therefore, is Y, but x is non-random as the number of rooms was presumably decided by the company before building.

This model contains two unknown parameters, α and β, whose values determine the relationship we need between number of rooms and cost. The data we have enable us to estimate the values of these parameters.

The method of least squares

Our model for the process which generates the data says that when a value of x is selected by the 'experimenter' (in this case, the hotel company), a corresponding value, y, of the random variable Y is generated. This comes from a value, e, of the random variable E, which is the *residual*, added to the *trend* value implied by the selected x, which is $\alpha + \beta x$. Because we do not know the values α and β, we have to estimate them: these estimates are called a and b. Using these values enables us, for a given x value and the corresponding y that is generated, to calculate the estimated or observed residual, as:

$$\hat{e} = y - (a + bx)$$

By choosing the model above, we are explaining some of the variation in building costs by its dependence on the number of rooms. By then estimating particular values, a and b, for the parameters of our model, we are trying to explain exactly how building costs are affected by the number of rooms.

The estimated residual then measures that part of the cost which is not explained by the model and must be explained by the factors of which we are ignorant, those modelled as random variation. The least squares estimation strategy is to choose the parameters of the model to make the sum over the sample of the squares of the unexplained residuals as small as possible: that is, to maximise, within the sample, the explanatory power of the model.

As an example, suppose that data are generated by the process $Y = 90 + 10x + E$, so that $\alpha = 90$ and $\beta = 10$. A sample of size 4 has been taken.

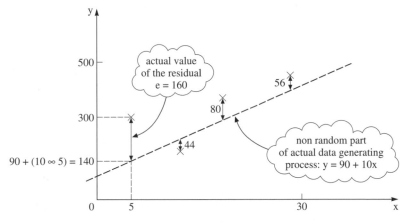

Figure 10.2

Suppose we estimated α and β by the values $a = 150$ and $b = 8$.

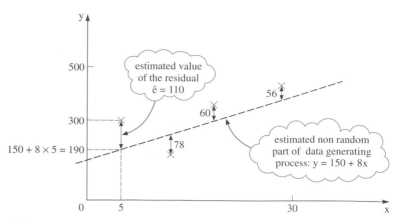

Figure 10.3

$$\text{Sum of squares of estimated residuals} = 110^2 + 78^2 + 60^2 + 56^2$$

$$= 24\,920$$

Alternatively, we might estimate α and β by the values $a = 190$ and $b = 7$.

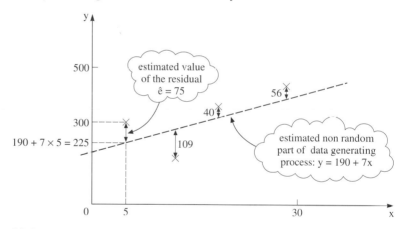

Figure 10.4

$$\text{Sum of squares of estimated residuals} = 75^2 + 109^2 + 40^2 + 56^2$$

$$= 22\,242$$

Note that the sum of the squares of the estimated residuals is smaller in the second case than in the first, so that the least squares criterion would prefer the second estimate. However, both the estimates a and b are further from the true values in this second case. This illustrates the important point that the least squares method attempts to fit the *sample* data as well (in one particular sense) as possible, but this does not guarantee that it produces a good estimate of the *population* parameters. You saw in *Statistics 4* that a good *estimator* is one which produces estimates which, *on the whole*, are near the true values of the parameter being estimated, not the one which gives the best *estimate* from a particular sample which happens to have arisen.

Of course, guessing values for a and b and calculating the sum of the squares of the estimated residuals only enables us to decide which of the two sets of estimates is preferred by the least squares criterion. What we need is an efficient way of calculating which estimates a and b will give the least possible value for the sum of the squares of the estimated residuals. In the next section, you will see how to do this for the hotel data.

Calculating the least squares estimates

In *Statistics 4*, you saw how, in general, the process of sampling from a population described by a random variable, V, can be modelled. A sample of size n corresponds to n independent variables V_i, where i runs from 1 to n, and where each V_i has the same distribution as V.

Here we use the subscript i, with $n = 38$ in this case, to distinguish the random variables relating to different hotels, so that for each i we have variables E_i and Y_i, with E_i a Normal random variable with distribution $N(0, \sigma^2)$ and:

$$Y_i = \alpha + \beta x_i + E_i$$

We are to estimate α and β by the values of a and b which minimise the sum:

$$R[a, b] \equiv \sum_{i=1}^{n} \hat{e}_i^2 = \sum_{i=1}^{n} (y_i - a - bx_i)^2$$

A standard method for simplifying sums of this type is to refer each term to its sample average. That is, given that:

$$\bar{x} = \frac{1}{n} \sum_{i=1}^{n} x_i \text{ and } \bar{y} = \frac{1}{n} \sum_{i=1}^{n} y_i$$

we rewrite the bracket $(y_i - a - bx_i)$ as:

$$([y_i - \bar{y}] + [\bar{y} - a - b\bar{x}] - b[x_i - \bar{x}])$$

adding and subtracting terms so that the overall value of the bracket is unchanged.

Squaring this gives:

$$(y_i - a - bx_i)^2 = [y_i - \bar{y}]^2 + [\bar{y} - a - b\bar{x}]^2 + b^2[x_i - \bar{x}]^2 + 2[y_i - \bar{y}][\bar{y} - a - b\bar{x}]$$
$$- 2b[x_i - \bar{x}][\bar{y} - a - b\bar{x}] - 2b[x_i - \bar{x}][y_i - \bar{y}]$$

Summing for values of i from 1 to n gives:

$$\sum_{i=1}^{n} [y_i - \bar{y}]^2 \text{ for which we shall use the notation } S_{YY}$$

$$\sum_{i=1}^{n} [\bar{y} - a - b\bar{x}]^2, \text{ which is just equal to } n \cdot [\bar{y} - a - b\bar{x}]^2, \text{ because each}$$

of the n terms in the sum is identical − that is, independent of i

$$b^2 \sum_{i=1}^{n} [x_i - \bar{x}]^2 = b^2 S_{XX}, \text{ defining the notation } S_{XX} = \sum_{i=1}^{n} [x_i - \bar{x}]^2$$

$$\sum_{i=1}^{n} 2[y_i - \bar{y}][\bar{y} - a - b\bar{x}] = 2[\bar{y} - a - b\bar{x}] \sum_{i=1}^{n} [y_i - \bar{y}] = 0$$

since $[\bar{y} - a - b\bar{x}]$ is constant — that is, independent of i,

and since $\sum_{i=1}^{n} [y_i - \bar{y}] = \sum_{i=1}^{n} \bar{y} = n \cdot \bar{y} - n \cdot \bar{y} = 0$ (which should not be surprising: intuitively, the sum of the deviations from the mean must be zero)

$$\sum_{i=1}^{n} 2b[x_i - \bar{x}][\bar{y} - a - b\bar{x}] = 0, \text{ by identical reasoning;}$$

$$2b \sum_{i=1}^{n} [x_i - \bar{x}][y_i - \bar{y}] = 2bS_{XY}, \text{ defining the notation } S_{XY} = \sum_{i=1}^{n} [x_i - \bar{x}][y_i - \bar{y}]$$

Finally, therefore:

$$R[a, b] = S_{YY} + n \cdot [\bar{y} - a - b\bar{x}]^2 + b^2 S_{XX} - 2bS_{XY}$$

$$= S_{YY} + n \cdot [\bar{y} - a - b\bar{x}]^2 + S_{XX}\left[b - \frac{S_{XY}}{S_{XX}}\right]^2 - \frac{S_{XY}^2}{S_{XX}}$$

where, in the last simplification, the technique of 'completing the square' has been used. You should check, by multiplying out the brackets, that:

$$S_{XX}\left[b - \frac{S_{XY}}{S_{XX}}\right]^2 - \frac{S_{XY}^2}{S_{XX}} = b^2 S_{XX} - 2bS_{XY}$$

It is now easy to see how to make the expression for $R[a, b]$ as small as possible by suitable choice of a and b. Neither of the terms involving a and b can be negative, because they are both squares, so that they are minimised by making each equal to zero. The least squares estimates a and b of α and β therefore satisfy the equations:

$$b = \frac{S_{XY}}{S_{XX}}$$

$$\bar{y} - a - b\bar{x} = 0$$

The second of these equations rearranges as:

$$a = \bar{y} - b\bar{x}$$

so that a can be found once b is determined.

Because of the way these results were derived, it is easy to see what the minimum value of $R[a, b]$ is. Two of the terms in the expression are zero at this minimum so that:

$$R[a, b] = S_{YY} - \frac{S_{XY}^2}{S_{XX}} = S_{YY}\left(1 - \frac{S_{XY}^2}{S_{XX}S_{YY}}\right) = S_{YY}(1 - r^2)$$

where r^2, known as the coefficient of determination, is defined as:

$$r^2 = \frac{S_{XY}^2}{S_{YY}S_{XX}}$$

The hotel data

For the data from Cheapotels, we have:

$$\sum_{i=1}^{n} x_i = 4095, \quad \sum_{i=1}^{n} y_i = 80\,037,$$

$$\sum_{i=1}^{n} x_i^2 = 641\,763, \quad \sum_{i=1}^{n} y_i^2 = 173\,278\,928, \quad \sum_{i=1}^{n} x_i y_i = 9\,208\,565;$$

so that:

$$\bar{x} = 107.76, \quad \bar{y} = 2106.24,$$

$$S_{XX} = \sum_{i=1}^{n} x_i^2 - n\bar{x}^2 = 200\,472.87, \quad S_{YY} = \sum_{i=1}^{n} y_i^2 - n\bar{y}^2 = 4\,712\,150.87,$$

$$S_{XY} = \sum_{i=1}^{n} x_i y_i - n\bar{x}\bar{y} = 583\,525.13;$$

and therefore:

$$b = \frac{S_{XY}}{S_{XX}} = 2.9107$$

$$a = \bar{y} - b\bar{x} = 1792.6$$

$$r^2 = \frac{S_{XY}^2}{S_{XX} \cdot S_{YY}} = 0.360\,45$$

Figure 10.5 repeats the scatter diagram for these data, with the regression line $y = a + bx$ added.

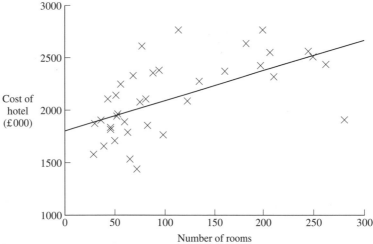

Figure 10.5

Partial differentiation

The equations for a and b are important enough to see a second method for deriving them, using the technique of partial differentiation. This relies on the fact that a minimum of a function of two variables occurs at the point where the derivative of the function with respect to each variable (treating the other temporarily as a constant) is zero. That is, in this case, the minimum of $R[a, b]$ occurs at the values of a and b where:

$$\frac{\partial}{\partial a} R[a, b] = 0 \quad \text{and} \quad \frac{\partial}{\partial b} R[a, b] = 0$$

where the notation $\dfrac{\partial}{\partial a}$ is used to mean 'differentiate with respect to a, treating b temporarily as a constant'.

The differentiation goes as follows:

$$\frac{\partial}{\partial a} R[a, b] = \frac{\partial}{\partial a} \sum_{i=1}^{n} (y_i - a - bx_i)^2 = \sum_{i=1}^{n} \frac{\partial}{\partial a} (y_i - a - bx_i)^2$$

$$= \sum_{i=1}^{n} 2(y_i - a - bx_i) \frac{\partial}{\partial a} (y_i - a - bx_i)$$

$$= \sum_{i=1}^{n} 2(y_i - a - bx_i)(-1)$$

For a minimum, we need to set this expression equal to 0, obtaining:

$$\sum_{i-1}^{n} (y_i - a - bx_i) = \sum_{i-1}^{n} y_i - \sum_{i-1}^{n} a - b \sum_{i-1}^{n} x_i = 0$$

or:

$$\sum_{i=1}^{n} y_i - na - b \sum_{i=1}^{n} x_i = 0$$

Similarly:

$$\frac{\partial}{\partial b} R[a, b] = \frac{\partial}{\partial b} \sum_{i=1}^{n} (y_i - a - bx_i)^2 = \sum_{i=1}^{n} \frac{\partial}{\partial b} (y_i - a - bx_i)^2$$

$$= \sum_{i=1}^{n} 2(y_i - a - bx_i) \frac{\partial}{\partial b} (y_i - a - bx_i)$$

$$= \sum_{i=1}^{n} 2(y_i - a - bx_i)(-x_i)$$

Setting this also equal to 0, as the condition for a minimum:

$$\sum_{i=1}^{n} (y_i - a - bx_i)x_i = \sum_{i=1}^{n} y_i x_i - a \sum_{i=1}^{n} x_i - b \sum_{i=1}^{n} x_i^2 = 0$$

The two equations:

$$\sum_{i=1}^{n} y_i - na - b \sum_{i=1}^{n} x_i = 0$$

$$\sum_{i=1}^{n} y_i x_i - a \sum_{i=1}^{n} x_i - b \sum_{i=1}^{n} x_i^2 = 0$$

are simultaneous equations in a and b, called the *normal equations* for the problem, whose solutions are our least squares estimates. Dividing the first equation by n gives:

$$\bar{y} - a - b\bar{x} = 0 \quad \text{or} \quad a = \bar{y} - b\bar{x}$$

which can be substituted into the second equation:

$$\sum_{i=1}^{n} y_i x_i - n(\bar{y} - b\bar{x})\bar{x} - b\sum_{i=1}^{n} x_i^2 = 0 \quad \text{or} \quad b\left(\sum_{i=1}^{n} x_i^2 - n\bar{x}^2\right) = \sum_{i=1}^{n} y_i x_i - n\bar{y}\bar{x}$$

We can recognise here the alternative forms for S_{XX} and S_{XY}:

$$S_{XX} = \sum_{i=1}^{n} (x_i - \bar{x})^2 = \sum_{i=1}^{n} x_i^2 - n\bar{x}^2,$$

$$S_{XY} = \sum_{i=1}^{n} (x_i - \bar{x})(y_i - \bar{y}) = \sum_{i=1}^{n} x_i y_i - n\bar{x}\bar{y}$$

so that, finally:

$$b = \frac{S_{XY}}{S_{XX}}$$

as before.

Note that the normal equations can be written, neatly and memorably, as:

$$\sum_{i=1}^{n} (y_i - a - bx_i) = 0$$

$$\sum_{i=1}^{n} x_i(y_i - a - bx_i) = 0$$

or, in terms of the estimated residuals:

$$\sum_{i=1}^{n} \hat{e}_i = 0$$

$$\sum_{i=1}^{n} x_i \hat{e}_i = 0$$

NOTE *The partial differentiation method for minimising $R[a, b]$ is more sophisticated than the algebraic method, but is considerably simpler and it alone will be used for similar calculations later in this chapter.*

Analysis of variance for regression

The sample y_i-values vary. Our model suggests that some of this variation is explained by the different values of x_i associated with the elements of the sample, via the linear dependence $\alpha + \beta x_i$. Further variation, however, comes from the addition of the random component e_i to the deterministic part of the model. Is it possible to separate out these two effects and measure how much of the variation in the y_i is caused by each component?

The variation in the sample y_i-values about their mean is measured by the expression:

$$S_{YY} = \sum_{i=1}^{n} (y_i - \bar{y})^2$$

which, in this context, is called the *total sum of squares (TSS)*.

For each x-value we can also find the y values predicted by the deterministic part of the model, using the parameters we have estimated. These y values are given by:

$$\hat{y}_i = a + bx_i$$

The sample mean of these estimated y values is:

$$\bar{\hat{y}} = \frac{1}{n} \sum_{i=1}^{n} \hat{y}_i = a + b\frac{1}{n} \sum_{i=1}^{n} x_i = a + b\bar{x} = \bar{y}$$

so that the deviations of the $\hat{y}_i$ from their mean are given by:

$$\hat{y}_i - \bar{y} = (a - bx_i) - (a - b\bar{x}) = b(x_i - \bar{x})$$

and the expression:

$$\sum_{i=1}^{n} (\hat{y}_i - \bar{\hat{y}})^2$$

measures the variation of the predicted $\hat{y}_i$ values from their mean and is called the *explained sum of squares (ESS)*.

Recall also the definition of the estimated residuals, which represent the part of the variation in the y_i attributed to the random component of the model:

$$\hat{e}_i = y_i - \hat{y}_i$$

which have sample mean:

$$\frac{1}{n} \sum_{i=1}^{n} \hat{e}_i = \frac{1}{n} \sum_{i=1}^{n} y_i - a - b\frac{1}{n} \sum_{i=1}^{n} x_i = 0$$

by the first normal equation derived above. The expression:

$$R[a, b] = \sum_{i=1}^{n} \hat{e}_i^2$$

is called the *residual sum of squares (RSS)*.

We shall prove the following important result relating these quantities:

$$\sum_{i=1}^{n} (y_i - \bar{y})^2 = \sum_{i=1}^{n} (\hat{y}_i - \bar{y})^2 + \sum_{i=1}^{n} \hat{e}_i^2$$

Proof

We can write:

$$(y_i - \bar{y}) = (y_i - \hat{y}_i) + (\hat{y}_i - \bar{y}) = \hat{e}_i + (\hat{y}_i - \bar{y})$$

so:

$$\sum_{i=1}^{n} (y_i - \bar{y})^2 = \sum_{i=1}^{n} \{(\hat{y}_i - \bar{y}) + \hat{e}_i\}^2$$

$$= \sum_{i=1}^{n} (\hat{y}_i - \bar{y})^2 + \sum_{i=1}^{n} \hat{e}_i^2 + 2\sum_{i=1}^{n} (\hat{y}_i - \bar{y})\hat{e}_i$$

but the final term in this expression is zero, because:

$$\sum_{i=1}^{n} (\hat{y}_i - \bar{y})\hat{e}_i = \sum_{i=1}^{n} b(x_i - \bar{x})\hat{e}_i = b\sum_{i=1}^{n} x_i\hat{e}_i - b\bar{x}\sum_{i=1}^{n} \hat{e}_i$$

where both terms on the right-hand side are zero, by the normal equations.

The result we have just proved can also be written:

$$\text{TSS} = \text{RSS} + \text{ESS}.$$

The interpretation of this is that the variation of the y values in the samples as measured by the total sum of squares, can be decomposed, as we hoped, into two parts:

• the variation in the y values predicted by the deterministic part of the estimated model, as measured by the explained sum of squares;

• the residual sum of squares, which measures the amount of random variation which we have needed to introduce in order to model the data.

We can rewrite the explained sum of squares, using the result:

$$\hat{y}_i - \bar{y} = b(x_i - \bar{x})$$

derived above, as:

$$\text{ESS} = \sum_{i=1}^{n} (\hat{y}_i - \bar{y})^2 = b^2 \sum_{i=1}^{n} (x_i - \bar{x})^2 = b^2 S_{XX}$$

But we know that:

$$b = \frac{S_{XY}}{S_{XX}}$$

so that:

$$\frac{\text{ESS}}{\text{TSS}} = \frac{b^2 S_{XX}}{S_{YY}} = \frac{S_{XY}^2}{S_{XX}^2}\frac{S_{XX}}{S_{YY}} = \frac{S_{XY}^2}{S_{XX} S_{YY}} = r^2$$

We can use this result to interpret the coefficient of determination, r^2, as a measure of how good our model is in explaining the variation in the dependent variable. The explained sum of squares is a fraction, r^2, of the total sum of squares, so that the deterministic part of our model has explained this fraction of the total variation in sample Y values as a consequence of the different x values with which these Y values are associated. The remaining variation is a consequence of other factors affecting the dependent variable, which we have modelled as a random influence.

The model fits the data well if it explains a high proportion of the observed variation in the dependent variable as a consequence of differences in the independent variable.

NOTE

In some books, $\sum_{i=1}^{n} \hat{e}_i^2$ is called the error sum of squares (ESS) and $\sum_{i=1}^{n} (\hat{y}_i - \bar{\hat{y}})^2$ is then the regression sum of squares (RSS). Life is not always easy!

Cheapotels' data

For the data from Cheapotels, we calculated:

$$r^2 = 0.360\,45$$

so that about 36% of the variation in the cost of the hotels is explained by the model of linear dependence on the number of rooms.

Exercise 10A

1. At a football ground, the number, Y, of minor injuries requiring treatment at the first aid post on a given Saturday is thought to be related to the number, x, of stewards on duty. This relationship is modelled as:

$$Y = \alpha - \beta x + E.$$

(i) Estimate α and β, from the data given in the tables.

Number, x, of stewards on duty	Number, y, of minor injuries
28	61
56	20
33	34
49	40
27	66
60	31
45	52
41	38
52	46
24	49
37	38
22	56
58	42
49	62
34	54
54	40

(ii) Plot a scatter diagram and calculate the value of r for these data.

(iii) Is this a good model?

2. The daily number, Y, of bottles of mineral water sold at a kiosk is related to the temperature. This relationship is modelled as:

$$Y = \alpha + \beta x + E.$$

where x is the temperature at noon on the relevant day.

(i) Estimate α and β from the sample of 30 summer days summarised by these figures.

$$\sum_{i=1}^{30} x_i = 668, \qquad \sum_{i=1}^{30} x_i^2 = 17\,356;$$

$$\sum_{i=1}^{30} y_i = 19\,408, \qquad \sum_{i=1}^{30} y_i^2 = 13\,470\,302;$$

$$\sum_{i=1}^{30} x_i y_i = 468\,159.$$

(ii) Calculate r^2.

(iii) Is this a useful model?

3. The analysis in the text is sometimes carried out using a different notation. Using this notation, the data generating process is modelled by the equation:

$$Y_i = \gamma + \mu(x_i - \bar{x}) + E_i$$

where γ and μ are the unknown parameters.

Use the method of least squares to derive estimates c and m for γ and μ respectively.

4. In some situations, the intercept of the deterministic part of the data generating process may be known to be zero. This occurs, for instance, if a scientific law requires y to be directly proportional to x, but the y values can only be measured imprecisely. Then the measured Y values are modelled by the equation:

$$Y = \beta X + E,$$

Exercise 10A continued

where E represents the random errors made in measuring Y.

For example, the initial rate, y, at which a particular chemical reaction proceeds is proportional to the concentration, x, of one of the reagents. This concentration can be measured precisely, but measurements of the initial rate of reaction are difficult to obtain and involve random errors, so that the equation above gives a sensible model for the measured initial rate of reaction Y.

(i) Show that, in this case, a least squares estimate of β, based on a sample of size n, is given by:

$$b = \frac{\sum\limits_{i=1}^{n} x_i y_i}{\sum\limits_{i=1}^{n} x_i^2}$$

(ii) Show also that:

$$\text{RSS} = \sum_{i=1}^{n} y_i^2 - \frac{\left(\sum\limits_{i=1}^{n} x_i y_i\right)^2}{\sum\limits_{i=1}^{n} x_i^2}$$

(iii) Use the data below to estimate β, using the formula above.

Concentration of reagent $x\,(\text{mol}\,1^{-1})$	Initial rate of reaction $y\,(\text{mol}\,1^{-1}\,\text{s}^{-1})$
0.02	0.007
0.04	0.015
0.06	0.019
0.08	0.022
0.10	0.032
0.12	0.035
0.14	0.038
0.16	0.046
0.18	0.056
0.2	0.057

(iv) Suppose, instead, that the model:

$$Y = \alpha + \beta x + E$$

was appropriate for these data.

Estimate α and β using the formulae derived in the text. Is $a = 0$? Are the values of b the same in each case? Explain.

(v) In which case is the RSS less? Does a smaller RSS imply a better model?

The method of least squares

The method of least squares is more widely applicable than the use you saw above. Suppose that you have modelled the process by which a set of data was generated and that you need to estimate the parameters of this model. The least squares strategy is as follows:

1. Calculate, as a function of the parameters, the values that would be expected on the basis of the model for the variables measured in the sample.

2. Calculate the residuals: the differences between those expected and the actual values of the variables measured in the sample.

3. Construct the sum of the squares of these residuals.

4. Choose the estimates of the parameters to be those values which make this residual sum of squares as small as possible.

If you have studied the chapter on estimation, you should see a similarity between the method of least squares and the maximum likelihood method. Both methods use the principle that good estimates of the parameters are those which make the actual outcome close, in some sense, to the predictions of the model with those parameter values. The methods do not, however, use the same criterion of closeness and will not, in general, give the same estimates.

F, G and H are triangulation points and the triangle FGH has its angles measured by a surveyor. The results she obtains, which are subject to an error symmetrically distributed either side of zero, are $f°$, $g°$, and $h°$ for angles F, G and H respectively. The true angles of the triangle are $\phi°$, $\gamma°$ and $(180 - (\phi + \gamma))°$, as these angles must, of course, sum to 180°. Construct least squares estimators for ϕ and γ.

Solution:

1. Because the surveyor's errors are symmetrically distributed, the expected values of f, g, and h are just ϕ, γ and $180 - (\phi + \gamma)$.

2. Therefore, the residuals are $(f - \phi)$, $(g - \gamma)$ and $(h - (180 - (\phi + \gamma)))$.

3. So the residual sum of squares is:

$$R[\phi, \gamma] = (f - \phi)^2 + (g - \gamma)^2 + (h - (180 - (\phi + \gamma)))^2$$

$$= 2\phi^2 + 2\phi\gamma + 2\gamma^2 + 2(h - f - 180)\phi + 2(h - g - 180)\gamma + (h - 180)^2$$

4. The partial derivatives of R with respect to ϕ and γ are:

$$\frac{\partial R}{\partial \phi} = 4\phi + 2\gamma + 2(h - f - 180)$$

$$\frac{\partial R}{\partial \gamma} = 2\phi + 4\gamma + 2(h - g - 180)$$

Equating these to zero, as a condition for R to be a minimum, gives the simultaneous equations:

$$2\hat{\phi} + \hat{\gamma} = 180 + f - h$$

$$\hat{\phi} + 2\hat{\gamma} = 180 + g - h$$

for the estimates $\hat{\phi}$ and $\hat{\gamma}$ of ϕ and γ.

Solving these equations simultaneously gives the estimates:

$$\hat{\phi} = 60 + \tfrac{1}{3}(2f - g - h), \qquad \hat{\gamma} = 60 + \tfrac{1}{3}(2g - f - h)$$

It is worth noting that the minimum value of R is:

$$R[\hat{\phi}, \hat{\gamma}] = \tfrac{1}{3}\{(a + b + c) - 180\}^2$$

which measures the extent to which the measured angles fail to sum to 180°.

Exercise 10B

1. If, in the example above, the triangle FGH is known to be isosceles with angle F = angle G = $\alpha°$, say, show that:

(i) a least squares estimate of α is given by $\hat{\alpha} = 60 + \frac{1}{6}(f + g - 2h)$;

(ii) the minimum value of the sum of the squared residuals is given by:

$$R[\hat{\alpha}] = \frac{1}{3}\{(f + g + h) - 180\}^2 + \frac{1}{2}\{f - g\}^2$$

which measures the extent to which:

(a) the measured angles fail to sum to 180°;

(b) the measured base angles fail to be equal.

2. Genetic theory predicts that a characteristic determined by a single gene will occur in the population in three genotypes, called dd, rd and rr, in the proportions:

dd	p^2
dr	$2p(1 - p)$
rr	$(1 - p)^2$

where p is an unknown parameter.

In an experiment, the number of each type of genotype found is:

dd	a
dr	b
rr	c

where $n = a + b + c$ is the sample size.

(i) Explain why the least squares method leads you to minimise:

$$R[p] = \{a - p^2n\}^2 + \{b - 2p(1 - p)n\}^2 + \{c - (1 - p)^2n\}^2$$

(ii) Differentiate with respect to p to show that the value of p for which a local minimum of this expression occurs must satisfy:

$$6np^3 - 9np^2 + (4n + 3b)p - (2b + a) = 0$$

(iii) In the case where $a = 11$, $b = 14$ and $c = 20$, show that the least squares estimate is $\hat{p} = \frac{1}{3}$.

If you have studied Chapter 6, on estimation, you will have found the maximum likelihood estimate of p to be $\frac{2a + b}{2n}$ which, with the values of a, b and c above, gives $\hat{p} = \frac{2}{5}$.

(iv) Why should these figures be so different? (*Hint: calculate the expected values of* a, b *and* c *when* n = 45, *for different values of* p.)

(v) Which estimate is preferable?

Properties of the estimators of α and β

So far we have used the data in a sample to estimate the gradient and intercept of a straight line. The straight line is related to the *data* in a simple and definite way: it is chosen to minimise the sum of squares of the residuals. We now need to investigate the relationship of this line to the underlying *population* from which the sample was drawn: that is, how the gradient and intercept estimators are related to the parameters of our population model.

There are two ways in which this relationship will not be a definite one.

- First, we will only be able to say that *if the model we have adopted for the process by which the data arises is correct*, then the estimators and parameters have a particular relationship.

- Second, the relationship between the estimators and parameters is, as usual, a *probabilistic rather than a deterministic one*.

We have already modelled the data generating process as follows:

For each of the values x_i, ($i = 1$ to 38) of the number of rooms, a value e_i arises at random according to the distribution of a random variable E_i.

The cost of the hotel is then $y_i = \alpha + \beta x_i + e_i$, where α and β are parameters of the model.

Therefore we can write the cost of a hotel with x_i rooms as the random variable $Y_i = \alpha + \beta x_i + E_i$.

We now need to make further assumptions about the model, as follows:

each of the variables E_i has the same distribution;

which is Normal with mean zero and variance σ^2;

and the variables E_i and E_j are independent (when i and j are distinct).

The assumption of zero mean is intuitively sensible. If the 'random extra effects' modelled by E_i are not equally likely to be positive or negative, then they involve a systematic extra effect which can be included in the model by adding it to the value of α, rather than including it within the E_i.

The other assumptions are necessary in order to simplify the analysis. If they are not justified then a more sophisticated approach is necessary.

These assumptions imply that each Y_i, which is just a constant, $\alpha + \beta x_i$, added to a Normal random variable, is also Normal. The parameters of its distribution are:

$$E[Y_i] = E[\alpha + \beta x_i + E_i] = \alpha + \beta x_i + E[E_i] = \alpha + \beta x_i$$

$$\mathrm{Var}\,[Y_i] = \mathrm{Var}\,[\alpha + \beta x_i + E_i] = \mathrm{Var}\,[E_i] = \sigma^2$$

so that $Y_i \sim N(\alpha + \beta x_i, \sigma^2)$

The distribution of the estimators of α and β

In this section, we shall write A for the random variable which is the estimator of the intercept α, and B for the random variable which is the estimator of the gradient β.

The formulae we gave earlier for the estimates a and b mean that A and B are given by:

$$B = \frac{1}{S_{XX}} \sum_{i=1}^{n} (x_i - \bar{x})(Y_i - \bar{Y})$$

and

$$A = \bar{Y} - \bar{x}B$$

where

$$\bar{Y} = \frac{1}{n} \sum_{i=1}^{n} Y_i$$

The formula for B can be simplified by noticing that:

$$\sum_{i=1}^{n} (x_i - \bar{x})\bar{Y} = \bar{Y} \sum_{i=1}^{n}(x_i - \bar{x}) = 0$$

because the sum of the deviations of the x_i from their mean is zero by definition:

$$\sum_{i=1}^{n}(x_i - \bar{x}) = 0$$

Thus:

$$B = \frac{1}{S_{XX}}\sum_{i=1}^{n}(x_i - \bar{x})Y_i$$

Despite the apparent complexity of this formula, B is simply the sum of constant multiples of the set of Normally distributed random variables Y_i:

$$B = \sum_{i=1}^{n}c_iY_i, \text{ where } c_i = \frac{(x_i - \bar{x})}{S_{XX}}$$

Therefore B is itself Normally distributed. This means that A is the difference of constant multiples of the Normal random variables $\bar{Y}$ and B and is therefore also Normal.

The complete distributions of A and B are:

$$A \sim N\left(\alpha, \left(\frac{\sum x^2}{S_{XX}}\right)\frac{\sigma^2}{n}\right) \quad \text{and} \quad B \sim N\left(\beta, \frac{\sigma^2}{S_{XX}}\right) \quad \text{with} \quad \text{Cov}[A, B] = -\frac{\bar{x}\sigma^2}{S_{XX}}$$

These results have relatively complicated derivations, and therefore we will wait to prove them until the end of the next section. Note here, however, the conclusion that both A and B are unbiased estimators of the respective population parameters.

Distribution of the residual sum of squares

The residual sum of squares is:

$$\text{RSS} = \sum_{i=1}^{n}(Y_i - A - x_iB)^2 = \sum_{i=1}^{n}\hat{E}_i^2$$

where the variables

$$\hat{E}_i = Y_i - A - x_iB = Y_i - (\bar{Y} - \bar{x}B) - x_iB$$
$$= (Y_i - \bar{Y}) - (x_i - \bar{x})B$$

are the differences between the measured Y values and those predicted by the estimated model line. Note that these are not the same as the variables $E_i = Y_i - \alpha - \beta x_i$, which give the random fluctuations of the measured values about the true model line.

The expectation of the residual sum of squares is:

$$E[\text{RSS}] = (n - 2)\sigma^2$$

Again, the derivation of this result is delayed until the end of the next section.

This means that the statistic:

$$\frac{\text{RSS}}{n-2} = \frac{\sum_{i=1}^{n} e_i^2}{n-2} = \frac{\sum_{i=1}^{n} \{y_i - a - bx_i\}^2}{n-2}$$

is an unbiased estimate of the common variance σ^2 of the random terms E_i in our model.

A convenient formula is derived from the decomposition:

$$\text{TSS} = \text{RSS} + \text{ESS}$$

so that:

$$\text{RSS} = \text{TSS} - \text{ESS} = \text{TSS}\left(1 - \frac{\text{ESS}}{\text{TSS}}\right) = S_{YY}(1 - r^2)$$

using the definition of TSS and the formula derived above for the ratio of ESS to TSS.

For the hotel data, therefore, the unbiased estimate of the Variance of the E_i is:

$$\hat{\sigma}^2 = \frac{\text{RSS}}{36} = \frac{(1 - 0.36045) \times 4\,712\,150.87}{36} = 83\,712.67$$

giving $\hat{\sigma} = 289.33$.

Hypothesis testing

Because the estimators A and B of the parameters α and β in the regression model have distributions:

$$A \sim \text{N}\left(\alpha, \left(\frac{\sum x^2}{S_{XX}}\right)\frac{\sigma^2}{n}\right) \quad \text{and} \quad B \sim \text{N}\left(\beta, \frac{\sigma^2}{S_{XX}}\right)$$

the statistics:

$$\frac{A - \alpha}{\sqrt{\left(\frac{\sum x^2}{S_{XX}}\right)\frac{\sigma^2}{n}}} \quad \text{and} \quad \frac{B - \beta}{\sqrt{\frac{\sigma^2}{S_{XX}}}}$$

both have $\text{N}(0, 1)$ distributions. So, if the value of σ is known, these statistics may be used to test hypotheses about the values of α and β.

In the usual way, if the value of σ is not known, we can use the unbiased estimate $\hat{\sigma}^2$ of σ^2 constructed in the last section, to conclude that:

$$\frac{A - \alpha}{\sqrt{\left(\frac{\sum x^2}{S_{XX}}\right)\frac{\hat{\sigma}^2}{n}}} \quad \text{and} \quad \frac{B - \beta}{\sqrt{\frac{\hat{\sigma}^2}{S_{XX}}}}$$

have t-distributions with $(n - 2)$ degrees of freedom.

Thus hypothesis tests can be conducted in this case as well.

The hotel data

It has been suggested by one of the analyst's colleagues that the fixed cost of a new hotel is £1 600 000. Formally, he is stating that $\alpha = 1600$ (as the cost figures are in thousands of pounds). The analyst sets up the two-tailed hypotheses:

$$H_0: \quad \alpha = 1600;$$
$$H_1: \quad \alpha \neq 1600;$$

and decides to test at the 2% level.

The test statistic is:

$$\frac{A - 1600}{\sqrt{\left(\dfrac{\sum x^2}{S_{XX}}\right)\dfrac{\hat{\sigma}^2}{n}}}$$

and under the null hypothesis $\alpha = 1600$ this has a t-distribution with $38 - 2 = 36$ degrees of freedom.

With the data given, the value of the test statistic is 2.294. The two-tailed critical value for the t-distribution with 36 degrees of freedom at the 2% level is (by interpolation) 2.441.

As $2.294 < 2.441$, we accept the null hypothesis at this significance level.

Confidence intervals

The distributions of A and B can also be used in the construction of confidence intervals for the parameters α and β. As usual, to construct a two-sided symmetrical $(100 - p)\%$ confidence interval, we use the result that, in $(100 - p)\%$ of samples, it will be the case that:

$$-z_p < \frac{a - \alpha}{\sqrt{\left(\dfrac{\sum x^2}{S_{XX}}\right)\dfrac{\sigma^2}{n}}} < z_p$$

and in $(100 - p)\%$ of samples, it will be the case that:

$$-z_p < \frac{b - \beta}{\sqrt{\dfrac{\sigma^2}{S_{XX}}}} < z_p$$

where, in each case, z_p is the two-sided $p\%$ critical value for the Normal distribution.

Rearranging gives the confidence intervals:

$$a - z_p \cdot \sqrt{\left(\frac{\sum x^2}{S_{XX}}\right)\frac{\sigma^2}{n}} < \alpha < a + z_p \cdot \sqrt{\left(\frac{\sum x^2}{S_{XX}}\right)\frac{\sigma^2}{n}}$$

$$b - z_p \cdot \sqrt{\frac{\sigma^2}{S_{XX}}} < \beta < b + z_p \cdot \sqrt{\frac{\sigma^2}{S_{XX}}}$$

If σ is not known, confidence intervals for α and β are constructed in the same way:

$$a - \tau_p \cdot \sqrt{\left(\frac{\sum x^2}{S_{XX}}\right)\frac{\hat{\sigma}^2}{n}} < \alpha < a + \tau_p \cdot \sqrt{\left(\frac{\sum x^2}{S_{XX}}\right)\frac{\hat{\sigma}^2}{n}}$$

$$b - \tau_p \cdot \sqrt{\frac{\hat{\sigma}^2}{S_{XX}}} < \beta < b + \tau_p \cdot \sqrt{\frac{\hat{\sigma}^2}{S_{XX}}}$$

where, in this case, τ_p is the two-sided $p\%$ critical value for the t-distribution and

$$\hat{\sigma}^2 = \frac{\text{RSS}}{n-2} = \frac{(1 - r^2) \cdot S_{YY}}{n-2}$$

as before.

Substituting the values from the hotel data to obtain a 90% confidence interval for β:

$$2.9107 - 1.691 \times \sqrt{\frac{83\,712.67}{200\,472.87}} < \beta < 2.9107 + 1.691 \times \sqrt{\frac{83\,712.67}{200\,472.87}}$$

as the two-tailed 10% critical value for the t-distribution with 36 degrees of freedom is (by interpolation) 1.691. That is:

$$1.818 < \beta < 4.003.$$

Note the considerable width of this interval.

EXAMPLE

It is believed that a certain species of bird lays larger eggs in colder environments. In an experiment, birds from this species were kept at controlled temperatures, and the average volume of the eggs in each clutch measured. The results were as follows.

Bird number	Temperature, t (°C)	Average egg volume, V (cm^3)
1	6	127.1
2	6	83.0
3	8	107.3
4	8	114.8
5	10	118.0
6	10	98.6
7	12	132.4
8	12	97.2
9	14	69.9
10	14	93.2
11	16	68.1
12	16	109.9
13	18	96.8
14	18	111.9

Assuming that the model:

$$V = \alpha + \beta t + E \qquad E \sim N(0, \sigma^2)$$

is appropriate for these data,

(i) test, at the 5% level, the hypothesis $\beta < 0$;

(ii) provide a 95% confidence interval for α.

Solution:

The data are summarised by:

$$\bar{x} = 12, \qquad \bar{y} = 102.0$$

$$\sum x^2 = 2240, \qquad \sum y^2 = 150\,539, \qquad \sum xy = 16\,847$$

so that:

$$S_{XX} = \sum x^2 - 14 \cdot \bar{x}^2 = 224$$

$$S_{YY} = \sum y^2 - 14 \cdot \bar{y}^2 = 4842.2$$

$$S_{XY} = \sum xy - 14 \cdot \bar{x}\bar{y} = -291.8$$

and so:

$$b = \frac{S_{XY}}{S_{XX}} = -1.3027, \qquad a = \bar{y} - b\bar{x} = 117.63$$

$$r^2 = \frac{S_{XY}^2}{S_{XX}\,S_{YY}} = 0.078\,50, \qquad \hat{\sigma}^2 = \frac{(1-r^2)S_{YY}}{n-2} = 371.84$$

(i) The appropriate hypotheses are:

$$H_0: \quad \beta = 0$$
$$H_1: \quad \beta < 0$$

and the test statistic is:

$$\frac{b}{\sqrt{\dfrac{\hat{\sigma}^2}{S_{XX}}}} = -1.0111$$

The critical value for the t-distribution with $(14 - 2) = 12$ degrees of freedom at the one-tailed 5% level is 1.782, but $-1.782 < -1.0111$, so we accept the null hypothesis that $\beta = 0$. That is, the data do not provide good evidence that egg volume decreases with breeding temperature.

(ii) The standard error of A is:

$$\sqrt{\frac{\sum x^2}{S_{XX}} \frac{\hat{\sigma}^2}{n}} = 16.297$$

and the critical value for the t-distribution with 12 degrees of freedom at the two-tailed 5% level is 2.179, so the 95% confidence interval for α is:

$$117.63 - 2.179 \times 16.297 < \alpha < 117.63 + 2.179 \times 16.297$$

or:

$$82.12 < \alpha < 153.14$$

Exercise 10C

1. The viscosity, v, of a sample of nitrogen is related to its pressure, p, by the equation:

$$v = \eta + \lambda p$$

where η and λ are constants. In an experiment, the pressure of the nitrogen sample can be precisely fixed, but the viscosity measurement is subject to error, so that a model for the relationship between measured values of the random variable V and p is:

$$V = \eta + \lambda p + E$$

with $E \sim N(0, 3.5 \times 10^{-12})$

Use the data below to test the hypothesis that $\lambda = 3 \times 10^{-13}\,\text{s}^{-1}$

Pressure, p $(10^7\,\text{Nm}^2)$	Viscosity, v $(10^{-5}\,\text{Nm}^{-2}\,\text{s})$
2.1	2.2
3.2	2.9
4.2	3.0
5.4	3.3
6.3	3.7
7.4	3.9
8.5	4.6
9.7	5.1

2. The expected value of the heart rate, Y, of a particular patient is thought to be linearly related to the concentration, x, of a tachycardiac drug in her bloodstream, so that

$$Y = \alpha + \beta x + E$$

for some value of α and β.

(i) Use the data below to find 95% confidence intervals for α and β.

Drug concentration x $(\mu\text{g}\,\text{l}^{-1})$	Heart rate y (min^{-1})
1.6	67
2.2	81
3.0	93
3.4	102
3.9	100
4.6	122
4.8	119
5.1	125
5.9	127
6.7	129

(ii) State clearly the assumptions you are making about the random variable E.

(iii) Plot the points on a scattergram. Comment on your results.

3. In the example of Exercise 10A Question 1, it is claimed by the organiser of the stewards that each extra steward on duty saves at least two minor injuries. Use the data given in that question to test this hypothesis at the 5% level.

4. The expectation of the length, L, of the paper produced by a paper cutting machine depends linearly on the control setting, c, but there is also a random component to the length which is known to have mean 0 and variance 0.085 cm.

(i) Write down a suitable model for the process which generates values of L at each value of c.

(ii) Use the data summarised below to find a 99% confidence interval for the expected length of the paper when $c = 0$.

$$\sum_{i=1}^{22} c_i - 114, \quad \sum_{i=1}^{22} c_i^2 - 1099;$$

$$\sum_{i=1}^{22} l_i = 654.33, \quad \sum_{i=1}^{22} l_i^2 = 25\,242.45;$$

$$\sum_{i=1}^{22} c_i l_i = 5104.49.$$

5. The yield, Y, in kilograms per pen in a fish farm is thought to be affected by the number of times, n, during one growing period on which the water in the pen is treated with a growth-promoting agent.

(i) Write down a suitable linear model for the process which generates values of Y at each value of n.

(ii) Use the data summarised below to test the null hypothesis that Y is unaffected by n against the alternative that Y increases with increasing n.

$$\sum_{i=1}^{11} n_i = 81, \quad \sum_{i=1}^{11} n_i^2 = 759;$$

$$\sum_{i=1}^{11} y_i = 630.166, \quad \sum_{i=1}^{11} y_i^2 = 43\,307.86;$$

$$\sum_{i=1}^{11} n_i y_i = 5024.987.$$

(iii) State clearly the assumptions you have made in your model.

6. The air pressure, P, (in kiloPascals) depends linearly on the height, h, (in metres) above sea level of the measuring point but also on other factors.

(i) Write down a suitable model for the process which generates values of P at each value of h, stating clearly the assumptions you have made in modelling the other factors affecting the air pressure.

(ii) Use the data summarised below to find a 90% confidence interval for the loss of pressure per metre rise in height of the measuring point.

$$\sum_{i=1}^{15} h_i = 8142, \qquad \sum_{i=1}^{15} h_i^2 = 5\,357\,000;$$

$$\sum_{i=1}^{15} p_i = 1419, \qquad \sum_{i=1}^{15} p_i^2 = 134\,500;$$

$$\sum_{i=1}^{15} h_i p_i = 759\,000.$$

7. Use the results derived in this chapter to find the distribution of the variable:

$$A + 18B$$

where A and B are the estimators of α and β in the linear model:

$$Y = \alpha + \beta x + E.$$

For the example of Question 2 in Exercise 10A, test the claim that, when the noon temperature is 18°, 550 bottles of mineral water are sold, on average.

Derivation of the distributions of *A*, *B* and the RSS

To determine the expectations of *B* and *A*

Because B can be written:

$$B = \sum_{i=1}^{n} c_i Y_i, \text{ where } c_i = \frac{(x_i - \bar{x})}{S_{XX}}$$

we have:

$$E[B] = E\left[\sum_{i=1}^{n} c_i Y_i\right] = \sum_{i=1}^{n} c_i E[Y_i] = \frac{1}{S_{XX}} \sum_{i=1}^{n} (x_i - \bar{x})(\alpha + \beta x_i)$$

$$= \frac{1}{S_{XX}} \sum_{i=1}^{n} (x_i - \bar{x})\{(\alpha + \beta \bar{x}) + \beta(x_i - \bar{x})\}$$

$$= \frac{1}{S_{XX}} \left\{ (\alpha + \beta \bar{x}) \sum_{i=1}^{n} (x_i - \bar{x}) + \beta \sum_{i=1}^{n} (x_i - \bar{x})^2 \right\}$$

But $\sum_{i=1}^{n} (x_i - \bar{x}) = 0$ and $\sum_{i=1}^{n} (x_i - \bar{x})^2 = S_{XX}$

So

$$E[B] = \beta$$

To find the expectation of A, first consider:

$$\bar{Y} = \frac{1}{n} \sum_{i=1}^{n} Y_i.$$

which has expectation:

$$E[\bar{Y}] = \frac{1}{n} \sum_{i=1}^{n} E[Y_i] = \frac{1}{n} \sum_{i=1}^{n} (\alpha + \beta x_i) = \alpha + \beta \bar{x}$$

This means that A itself has expectation:

$$E[A] = E[\bar{Y} - \bar{x}B] = E[\bar{Y}] - \bar{x}E[B] = \alpha + \beta \bar{x} - \bar{x}\beta$$

$$= \alpha$$

To determine the variances of A and B, and the covariance of A and B

We first need to observe that Y_i and Y_j (for distinct i and j) depend only on E_i and E_j respectively. As these are assumed independent, then so are Y_i and Y_j.

Consequently, $\text{Cov}[Y_i, Y_j] = 0$ unless $i = j$, in which case $\text{Cov}[Y_i, Y_i] = \text{Var}[Y_i] = \sigma^2$ and so:

$$\text{Cov}[Y_i, \bar{Y}] = \frac{1}{n} \sum_{j=1}^{n} \text{Cov}[Y_i, Y_j] = \frac{\sigma^2}{n}.$$

We shall also need the results:

$$\text{Cov}[B, Y_i] = \sum_{j=1}^{n} c_j \text{Cov}[Y_j, Y_i] = c_i \sigma^2 = \frac{(x_i - \bar{x})}{S_{XX}} \sigma^2$$

$$\text{Cov}[B, \bar{Y}] = \frac{1}{n} \sum_{i=1}^{n} \text{Cov}[B, Y_i] = \frac{\sigma^2}{n S_{XX}} \sum_{i=1}^{n} (x_i - \bar{x}) = 0.$$

The independence of Y_i and Y_j (for distinct i and j) means that:

$$\text{Var}[B] = \text{Var}\left[\sum_{i=1}^{n} c_i Y_i \right] = \sum_{i=1}^{n} c_i^2 \text{Var}[Y_i] = \frac{1}{S_{XX}^2} \sum_{i=1}^{n} (x_i - \bar{x})^2 \sigma^2$$

$$= \frac{S_{XX} \sigma^2}{S_{XX}^2} = \frac{\sigma^2}{S_{XX}}$$

Note also that, since the Y_i are independent:

$$\text{Var}[\bar{Y}] = \text{Var}\left[\frac{1}{n} \sum_{i=1}^{n} Y_i \right] = \frac{1}{n^2} \sum_{i=1}^{n} \text{Var}[Y_i] = \frac{\sigma^2}{n},$$

a familiar result. Thus:

$$\text{Var}[A] = \text{Var}[\bar{Y} - xB] = \text{Var}[\bar{Y}] - 2x\,\text{Cov}[\bar{Y}, B] + x^2 \text{Var}[B]$$

$$= \frac{\sigma^2}{n} + \frac{\bar{x}^2 \sigma^2}{S_{XX}} = \left(\frac{1}{n} + \frac{\bar{x}^2}{S_{XX}} \right) \sigma^2$$

which can also be written

$$\text{Var}\,[A] = \left(\frac{S_{XX} + n\bar{x}^2}{S_{XX}}\right)\frac{\sigma^2}{n} = \left(\frac{\sum\limits_{i=1}^{n} x_i^2}{\sum\limits_{i=1}^{n}(x_i - \bar{x})^2}\right)\frac{\sigma^2}{n}$$

Finally:

$$\text{Cov}\,[A, B] = \text{Cov}\,[\bar{Y} - \bar{x}B, B] = \text{Cov}\,[\bar{Y}, B] - \bar{x}\,\text{Var}\,[B]$$

$$= -\frac{\bar{x}\sigma^2}{S_{XX}}$$

To determine the expectation of the RSS

The definition of the residual sum of squares given earlier is:

$$\text{RSS} = \sum_{i=1}^{n} \hat{E}_i^2$$

where

$$\hat{E}_i = Y_i - A - x_i B = (Y_i - \bar{Y}) - (x_i - \bar{x})B$$

The variables $\hat{E}_i$ have means:

$$E[\hat{E}_i] = E[(Y_i - \hat{Y}) - (x_i - \bar{x})B] = E[Y_i] - E[\bar{Y}] - (x_i - \bar{x})E[B]$$

$$= (\alpha + \beta x_i) - (\alpha + \beta\bar{x}) - (x_i - \bar{x})\beta = 0$$

To determine the variances of these variables, recall the results from above:

$$\text{Var}\,[Y_i] = \sigma^2, \qquad \text{Var}\,[\bar{Y}] = \frac{\sigma^2}{n}, \qquad \text{Var}\,[B] = \frac{\sigma^2}{S_{XX}}$$

$$\text{Cov}\,[Y_i, \bar{Y}] = \frac{\sigma^2}{n}, \qquad \text{Cov}\,[Y_i, B] = \frac{(x_i - \bar{x})\sigma^2}{S_{XX}}, \qquad \text{Cov}\,[\bar{Y}, B] = 0$$

Therefore:

$$\text{Var}\,[\hat{E}_i] = \text{Var}\,[Y_i - \bar{Y} - (x_i - \bar{x})B]$$

$$= \text{Var}\,[Y_i] + \text{Var}\,[\bar{Y}] + (x_i - \bar{x})^2\,\text{Var}\,[B] - 2\,\text{Cov}\,[Y_i, \bar{Y}]$$

$$\quad - 2(x_i - \bar{x})\,\text{Cov}\,[Y_i, B] + 2(x_i - \bar{x})\,\text{Cov}\,[\bar{Y}, B]$$

$$= \sigma^2 + \frac{\sigma^2}{n} + (x_i - \bar{x})^2\frac{\sigma^2}{S_{XX}} - 2\frac{\sigma^2}{n} - 2(x_i - \bar{x})\frac{(x_i - \bar{x})\sigma^2}{S_{XX}}$$

$$= \sigma^2 - \frac{\sigma^2}{n} - (x_i - \bar{x})^2\frac{\sigma^2}{S_{XX}}$$

Note that because $E[\hat{E}_i] = 0$, $E[\hat{E}_i^2] = \text{Var}\,[\hat{E}_i]$, so that:

$$E[RSS] = E\left[\sum_{i=1}^{n} \hat{E}_i^2\right] = \sum_{i=1}^{n} E[\hat{E}_i^2] = \sum_{i=1}^{n} \text{Var}\,[\hat{E}_i]$$

$$= \sum_{i=1}^{n}\left(\sigma^2 - \frac{\sigma^2}{n} - (x_i - \bar{x})^2\,\frac{\sigma^2}{S_{XX}}\right)$$

$$= n\left(\sigma^2 - \frac{\sigma^2}{n}\right) - \frac{\sigma^2}{S_{XX}}\sum_{i=1}^{n}(x_i - \bar{x})^2$$

$$= (n-1)\sigma^2 - \frac{\sigma^2}{S_{XX}}S_{XX} = (n-2)\sigma^2$$

Exercise 10D

In Exercise 10A Question 4 you investigated the model with zero intercept:

$$Y = \beta x + E$$

(i) If:

$$B = \frac{\displaystyle\sum_{i=1}^{n} x_i Y_i}{\displaystyle\sum_{i=1}^{n} x_i^2}$$

is the estimator of β which you derived there, based on a sample of size n, show that:

$$B \sim N\left(\beta, \frac{\sigma^2}{\displaystyle\sum_{i=1}^{n} x_i^2}\right)$$

and that the residual sum of square has the property:

$$E[RSS] = (n-1)\sigma^2,$$

so that an unbiased estimate of the common variance of the E_i is:

$$\hat{\sigma}^2 = \frac{RSS}{n-1} = \frac{\displaystyle\sum_{i=1}^{n} y_i^2 - b^2 \sum_{i=1}^{n} x_i^2}{n-1}$$

(ii) Find this estimate in the case of the rate-of-reaction data given in the earlier question.

Non-linear models

Figure 10.6 reproduces the scatter diagram of cost against number of rooms, together with the straight line graph corresponding to the linear model whose parameters we estimated at the start of this chapter. Below this is a plot of the estimated residuals – the values of $y_i - a - bx_i$, for each x_i.

The shape of the residual plot, which shows a tendency for the residuals to be negative at each end of the x range and positive in the centre of this range, suggests that a straight line model is not entirely appropriate for these data. This is confirmed by looking at the original scatter diagram.

When the analyst discussed this problem with his supervisor, he explained that, based on past experience, the company has previously assumed that the variable cost of building a hotel is actually proportional to the square root of the number of rooms because of the economies of scale available in larger buildings. The analyst therefore decided to remodel the data generating process as:

$$Y = \alpha + \beta\sqrt{x} + E$$

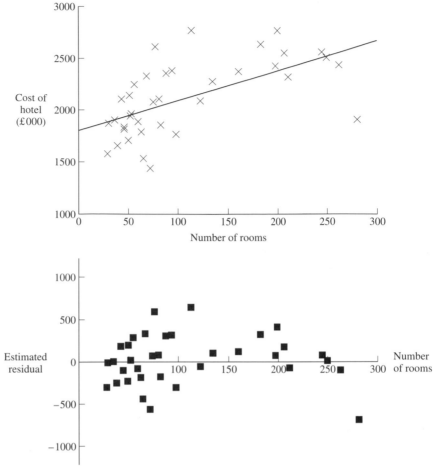

Figure 10.6

where, as before, Y is the cost of a hotel, x is the number of rooms in the hotel and α and β are two unknown parameters of the model. E is again a Normal random variable with mean zero.

The analyst then needed to use the data he had to estimate α and β.

For Discussion

Why is it important that the analyst obtained his revised model from the company's past experience and not from his inspection of the scatter graph?

Fortunately, by defining a new variable, $x' = \sqrt{x}$, this problem reduces to the one we have already analysed in detail. The model is linear in x':

$$Y = \alpha + \beta x' + E$$

and all the results of the previous sections hold, with x replaced by x' throughout.

The table below shows the hotel data, with each x_i replaced by $x_i' = \sqrt{x_i}$

	Sq root of no of rooms	Building cost (£000)		Sq root of no of rooms	Building cost (£000)		Sq root of no of rooms	Building cost (£000)
1	9.0000	2095	14	11.0454	2076	27	14.0357	2420
2	9.8995	1758	15	14.3527	2545	28	7.0711	1701
3	15.6205	2558	16	10.6302	2762	29	7.2801	1954
4	8.4853	1492	17	9.0554	1843	30	8.2462	2316
5	16.1864	2433	18	14.1067	2762	31	7.2111	1931
6	8.0623	1526	19	6.7823	1819	32	5.4772	1862
7	6.2450	1649	20	8.7750	2605	33	7.9373	1780
8	6.0000	1894	21	14.4914	2310	34	15.7797	2506
9	9.3808	2344	22	5.3852	1569	35	7.7460	1880
10	6.5574	2094	23	7.4833	2235	36	11.5758	2263
11	16.7332	1902	24	9.6954	2371	37	9.1104	1848
12	8.6603	2068	25	13.4907	2631	38	7.1414	2129
13	12.6491	2362	26	6.7823	1807			

Figure 10.7 shows a scatter graph of y against $x' = \sqrt{x}$: a linear model does look appropriate here.

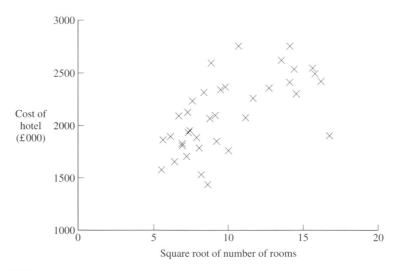

Figure 10.7

For these data, we have:

$$\bar{x}' = \frac{1}{38} \sum_{i=1}^{38} x' = 9.8465, \qquad \bar{y} = \frac{1}{38} \sum_{i=1}^{38} y = 2106.2368,$$

$$S'_{XX} = \sum_{i=1}^{38} x'^2 - 38 \cdot \bar{x}'^2 = 410.7503, \qquad S_{YY} = \sum_{i=1}^{38} y^2 - 38 \cdot \bar{y}^2 = 4\,712\,151.2,$$

$$S'_{XY} = \sum_{i=1}^{38} x'y - 38 \cdot \bar{x}'\bar{y} = 27\,899.943.$$

NOTE

These figures have to be recalculated from scratch: for instance $\bar{x}'$ is the mean of the square roots of the numbers of rooms, which is not equal to the square root of the mean number of rooms $= \sqrt{\bar{x}}$.

Thus:

$$b = \frac{S'_{XY}}{S'_{XX}} = 67.9243$$

$$a = \bar{y} - b\bar{x}' = 1437.4202$$

and the coefficient of determination is:

$$r^2 = \frac{S'^2_{XY}}{S'_{XX} \cdot S_{YY}} = 0.4022$$

so that about 40% of the variation in y is explained by the new model.

You should be very clear that this increase in the percentage of the variation in y explained does *not* mean that this is a better model than the linear one. The exercise we have undertaken is not a 'curve fitting' problem but one that estimates the parameters of a model once that model has been proposed on the basis of some prior understanding of the situation being modelled. The coefficient of determination tells you how much of the variation in y is explained by that prior understanding, and thus how much is still unexplained – the part that has been modelled by randomness. Whether the linear or square-root model is *better* depends on the underlying cost structure which affects the construction of hotel rooms: that is, whether the model used correctly captures a connection which exists in the real world between the x and Y variables.

Of course, it is perfectly possible to use the method of least squares to fit a curve to a set of points, but this is not a statistical process and it would be meaningless to discuss, for instance, the distributions of a and b in such a context.

Figure 10.8 repeats the scatter graph of y against x', adding the estimated regression line:

$$y = 1437.4 + 67.924x'$$

Figure 10.9 shows the scatter graph of y against x, with the corresponding curve which gives the estimated deterministic part of the model:

$$y = 1437.4 + 67.924\sqrt{x}$$

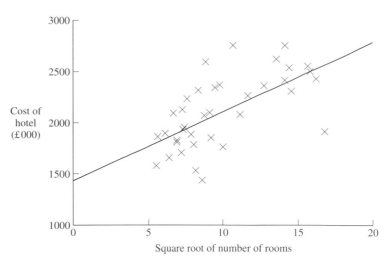

Figure 10.8

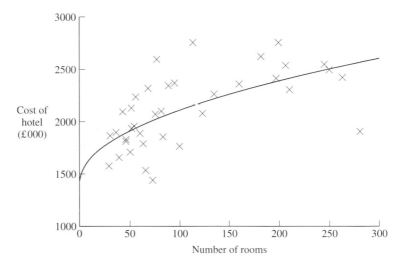

Figure 10.9

The sum of the squares of the estimated residuals is:

$$\text{RSS} = \sum_{i=1}^{38} \hat{e}_i^2 = S_{YY}(1 - r^2) = 2\,871\,066.0$$

so that an unbiased estimate of the variance of the E_i is:

$$\hat{\sigma}^2 = \frac{\text{RSS}}{38 - 2} = 78\,251.833$$

The random variables:

$$B = \frac{\displaystyle\sum_{i=1}^{n}(x_i' - \bar{x}')}{\displaystyle\sum_{i=1}^{n}(x_i' - \bar{x}')^2} \quad \text{and} \quad A = \bar{Y} - \bar{x}'B$$

are unbiased and have variances:

$$\text{Var}\,[B] = \frac{\sigma^2}{S'_{XX}} \quad \text{and} \quad \text{Var}\,[A] = \left(\frac{1}{38} + \frac{\bar{x}'^2}{S'_{XX}}\right)\sigma^2$$

This means that:

$$\frac{B - \beta}{\sqrt{\dfrac{\hat{\sigma}^2}{S'_{XX}}}} \quad \text{and} \quad \frac{A - \alpha}{\sqrt{\hat{\sigma}^2\left(\dfrac{1}{38} + \dfrac{\bar{x}'^2}{S'_{XX}}\right)}}$$

both have t-distributions with 36 degrees of freedom. Thus, as the 5% two-sided critical value for the t-distribution is 2.032 (by interpolation), 95% confidence intervals for α and β are:

$$b - 2.032\hat{\sigma}\sqrt{\frac{1}{S'_{XX}}} < \beta < b + 2.032\hat{\sigma}\sqrt{\frac{1}{S'_{XX}}}$$

$$a - 2.023\hat{\sigma}\sqrt{\frac{1}{38} + \frac{\bar{x}'^2}{S'_{XX}}} < \alpha < a + 2.032\hat{\sigma}\sqrt{\frac{1}{38} + \frac{\bar{x}'^2}{S'_{XX}}}$$

or, substituting the values for these data:

$$39.88 < \beta < 95.97$$

$$1146.3 < \alpha < 1728.6$$

EXAMPLE

It is thought that the depth, D metres, of the water at a measurement point in a tidal estuary depends on the time, t hours, after high water according to the model:

$$D = \delta + \varepsilon \cos(0.506t) + E$$

where E is a Normal variable with zero mean. It is claimed that the mean water depth at this point is at least 15 m: that is, the hypotheses to be tested are:

$$\text{H}_0: \quad \delta = 15;$$
$$\text{H}_1: \quad \delta < 15.$$

The following data have been collected.

Time, t hours, after high water	Measured water depth, D metres
0.0	22.4
0.9	19.0
1.8	14.8
3.1	12.4
4.2	10.9
5.0	8.1
6.3	5.0
7.1	7.1
8.3	11.3
9.4	14.1
10.7	17.3
11.8	19.6

The first step is to rewrite these data, with the independent variable transformed from t to $x' = \cos(0.506t)$.

$x' = \cos(0.506t)$	Measured water depth, D metres
1.000	22.4
0.898	19.0
0.613	14.8
0.002	12.4
−0.526	10.9
−0.819	8.1
−0.999	5.0
−0.900	7.1
−0.490	11.3
0.044	14.1
0.646	17.3
0.952	19.6

These data are summarised by:

$$S_{x'} = 0.420, \qquad S_h = 162.0,$$
$$S_{x'x'} = 6.488, \qquad S_{hh} = 318.3,$$
$$S'_{x'h} = 44.04.$$

Therefore, an unbiased estimate of the variance σ^2 of E is:

$$\hat{\sigma}^2 = \frac{S_{hh} - \dfrac{(S_{x'h})^2}{S_{x'x'}}}{12 - 2} = 1.936$$

The estimates e and d of ε and δ are:

$$e = \frac{S_{x'h}}{S_{x'x'}} = 6.788$$

$$d = \tfrac{1}{12} S_h - e \cdot \tfrac{1}{12} S_{x'} = 13.26$$

Thus the test statistic is:

$$\frac{13.26 - 15}{\sqrt{\dfrac{1.936}{12}}} = -4.33$$

The one-tailed 1% significance level for the t-distribution with $12 - 2 = 10$ degrees of freedom is -2.764, so the null hypothesis is rejected, even at this level of significance, and we conclude that the water is shallower than suggested.

Summary

The work above applies equally well to any model of the form:

$$Y = \alpha + \beta f(x) + E$$

where f is any function, and E is, as usual, a Normal random variable with zero mean.

By defining $x' = f(x)$, the model reduces to a linear model and all the results we obtained in the first part of this chapter apply, with x replaced by x' throughout.

Exercise 10E

1. The van der Waals equation states that the volume, v, in litres, and pressure, p, in atmospheres of a fixed mass of a gas are related by the equation:

$$v = \alpha + \frac{\kappa}{p}$$

where α and κ are unknown constants. The values of p can be fixed precisely but measurements of v are subject to a random error with zero mean.

(i) Write down a suitable model for this process which generates the measured values, V, of the volume and state the assumptions you are making.

(ii) Use the data given below:

(a) to estimate α and κ;

(b) to test the hypothesis that $\alpha = 0$.

(iii) Plot a scatter graph and add to it a curve showing the estimated deterministic part of the model.

Pressure, p, atmospheres	Volume, v, litres
80	0.318
100	0.270
120	0.196
140	0.168
160	0.171
180	0.143
200	0.134
220	0.137
240	0.101
260	0.103
280	0.104
300	0.083
320	0.085
340	0.122

2. The birth weights, B, in grams, of 40 babies with varying gestational ages, x, in days, are measured. The relationship between these variables is thought to be modelled by:

$$B = \alpha + \beta \log x + E$$

The data is summarised by:

$$\sum_{i=1}^{40} \log x_i = 96.882, \qquad \sum_{i=1}^{40} (\log x_i)^2 = 234.713;$$

$$\sum_{i=1}^{40} b_i = 123\,644, \qquad \sum_{i=1}^{40} b_i^2 = 390\,626\,000;$$

$$\sum_{i=1}^{40} \log x_i b_i = 300\,153.$$

Find 95% confidence limits on α and β.

3. The inflation rate, $R\%$, in an economy is expected to be related to the proportion, $p\%$, of the workforce which is employed, by the model:

$$R = \alpha + \beta p^3 + E$$

Before 1980, the values of α and β were taken as:

$$\alpha = -10.1, \qquad \beta = 3.81 \times 10^{-5}$$

and E was taken to have the distribution $N(0, 8.72)$.

In the 1980s the inflation rates and proportions of the workforce employed were:

Year	Proportion, $p\%$, of workforce employed	Inflation rate $R\%$
1980	88	8.6
1981	84	9.6
1982	79	3.7
1983	80	3.0
1984	83	4.8
1985	86	9.1
1986	91	18.4
1987	92	10.0
1988	84	6.7
1989	83	7.7

10

Statistics 6

Assuming that the distribution of the random variable E is unchanged in the 1980s, test the (separate) hypotheses that the values of α and β remain unchanged.

4. The expected value of the percentage, $M\%$, of a consignment of bananas which is of merchandisable quality is linearly related to the $\frac{3}{2}$th power of the amount t (parts per million) of a particular toxin in a sample of the banana skins.

   (i) Write down a suitable model for the random variable, M, in terms of t, stating clearly any assumptions you are making.

   (ii) Use the data below to:

   (a) test the hypothesis that, if there is none of the toxin present, 100% of the consignment will be of merchandisable quality;

   (b) give a 90% confidence interval for the constant of proportionality between M and $t^{\frac{3}{2}}$.

   (iii) Plot a scatter diagram and make any

calculations you think appropriate. Discuss whether a straightforward linear relationship between M and t would be equally appropriate.

Concentration of toxin, t (ppm)	Proportion of bananas of merchandisable quality, $M\%$
0.6	95.2
1.1	93.6
1.9	92.8
2.8	90.0
3.4	91.6
5.8	86.3
6.2	86.8
7.3	78.0
7.8	71.2
8.2	73.2
8.7	68.7
9.0	75.2
9.4	67.0

Bilinear models

The analyst tried to refine his model of hotel building costs further. After talking to the company's contractors, he suspected that another factor affecting the cost of building a hotel would be its location, because of different local wages and materials' prices; that the highest cost will occur near London and that the reduction in cost elsewhere is approximately proportional to the distance of the hotel from London. He accordingly collected data giving each hotel's distance from London in kilometres, which are added to the original data on cost in the table on the next page.

	Number of rooms	Sq root of no of rooms	Distance from London	Building cost (£000)
1	81	9.0000	296	2095
2	98	9.8995	368	1758
3	244	15.6205	328	2558
4	72	8.4853	295	1492
5	262	16.1864	393	2433
6	65	8.0623	330	1526
7	39	6.2450	149	1649
8	36	6.0000	336	1894
9	88	9.3808	189	2344
10	43	6.5574	246	2094
11	280	16.7332	263	1902
12	75	8.6603	228	2068
13	160	12.6491	222	2362
14	122	11.0454	300	2076
15	206	14.3527	143	2545
16	113	10.6302	254	2762
17	82	9.0554	380	1843
18	199	14.1067	215	2762
19	46	6.7823	259	1819
20	77	8.7750	223	2605
21	210	14.4914	300	2310
22	29	5.3852	299	1569
23	56	7.4833	166	2235
24	94	9.6954	64	2371
25	182	13.4907	144	2631
26	46	6.7823	179	1807
27	197	14.0357	239	2420
28	50	7.0711	324	1701
29	53	7.2801	258	1954
30	68	8.2462	205	2316
31	52	7.2111	308	1931
32	30	5.4772	283	1862
33	63	7.9373	245	1780
34	249	15.7797	105	2506
35	60	7.7460	301	1880
36	134	11.5758	283	2263
37	83	9.1104	348	1848
38	51	7.1414	204	2129

The analyst's new model is that the cost of building a hotel, Y, is a random variable given by:

$$Y = \alpha + \beta x + \gamma z + E$$

where x is now the square root of the number of rooms, z is the distance from London and E is a Normal random variable with zero mean. The numbers α, β and γ are unknown parameters of the model (and, in particular, the value of γ is expected to be negative).

The sample of hotels in the data collected is represented by the set of random variables:

$$Y_i = \alpha + \beta x_i + \gamma z_i + E_i \qquad (i = 1, \ldots, 38)$$

where the E_i are identically distributed and independent of each other.

Since the E_i have zero mean, each Y_i has expected value $\alpha + \beta x_i + \gamma z_i$, so the residuals are $e_i = y_i - \alpha - \beta x_i - \gamma z_i$. The least squares strategy then tells you to choose estimates a, b and c of α, β and γ to minimise the sum of the squares of the estimated residuals: that is, choose a, b and c to minimise:

$$R[a, b, c] = \sum_{i=1}^{n} (y_i - a - bx_i - cz_i)^2$$

Differentiating R with respect to a, b and c separately, holding the other two constant, gives:

$$\frac{\partial R}{\partial a} = \sum_{i=1}^{n} -2(y_i - a - bx_i - cz_i) = 0$$

$$\frac{\partial R}{\partial b} = \sum_{i=1}^{n} -2x_i(y_i - a - bx_i - cz_i) = 0$$

$$\frac{\partial R}{\partial c} = \sum_{i=1}^{n} -2z_i(y_i - a - bx_i - cz_i) = 0$$

The normal equations:

$$\sum_{i=1}^{n} y_i - an - b\sum_{i=1}^{n} x_i - c\sum_{i=1}^{n} z_i = 0$$

$$\sum_{i=1}^{n} x_i y_i - a\sum_{i=1}^{n} x_i - b\sum_{i=1}^{n} x_i^2 - c\sum_{i=1}^{n} x_i z_i = 0$$

$$\sum_{i=1}^{n} y_i z_i - a\sum_{i=1}^{n} z_i - b\sum_{i=1}^{n} x_i z_i - c\sum_{i=1}^{n} z_i^2 = 0$$

follow immediately from these.

Note carefully the form of these equations: the first says that the sum of the estimated residuals is zero; the second and third that the sum of the estimated residuals, each multiplied by the appropriate value of the independent variables x and z, is zero. Thought of in this way, these equations are not too hard to remember. The first of the equations gives:

$$a = \bar{y} - b\bar{x} - c\bar{z}$$

and substituting into the other two equations produces:

$$S_{XX}b + S_{XZ}c = S_{XY}$$
$$S_{XZ}b + S_{ZZ}c = S_{YZ}$$
$$(*)$$

where:

$$S_{XX} = \sum_{i=1}^{n} x_i^2 - n\bar{x}^2 = \sum_{i=1}^{n} (x_i - \bar{x})^2$$

$$S_{XY} = \sum_{i=1}^{n} x_i y_i - n\bar{x}\bar{y} = \sum_{i=1}^{n} (x_i - \bar{x})(y_i - \bar{y})$$

and similarly for S_{ZZ}, S_{XZ} and S_{YZ}.

The simultaneous solution of these equations gives the estimates:

$$b = \frac{S_{ZZ} S_{XY} - S_{XZ} S_{YZ}}{S_{XX} S_{ZZ} - S_{XZ}^2}$$

$$c = \frac{S_{XX} S_{YZ} - S_{XZ} S_{XY}}{S_{XX} S_{ZZ} - S_{XZ}^2}$$

For the data here, the summary figures are:

$$\bar{x} = 9.8465, \qquad \bar{z} = 254.5263, \qquad \bar{y} = 2106.2368$$

$$S_{XX} = 410.7503, \qquad S_{ZZ} = 217\,319.47, \qquad S_{YY} = 4\,712\,151.2,$$

$$S_{XY} = 27\,899.943, \qquad S_{YZ} = -413\,051.74, \qquad S_{XZ} = -711.7504,$$

so that:

$$b = 64.9997$$

$$c = -1.6878$$

and:

$$a = 1895.8009$$

In practice, it is probably easiest not to try to remember the equations for b and c, but to know how to obtain the results $(*)$ above and substitute directly into these, obtaining the numerical simultaneous equations:

$$410.7503b - 711.7504c = 27\,899.943$$

$$-711.7504b + 217\,319.47c = -413\,051.74$$

which can be solved reasonably easily for b and c.

As in the single variable cases we have considered, we now need to determine to what extent the model explains the variation in the data. To this end, we need to consider the residual sum of squares (RSS) defined as the minimum value of R, so that:

$$\text{RSS} = \sum_{i=1}^{n} \hat{E}_i^2 = \sum_{i=1}^{n} (Y_i - A - Bx_i - Cz_i)^2,$$

where A, B and C are the estimators corresponding to the estimates a, b and c, given by:

$$B = (S_{XX} S_{ZZ} - S_{XZ}^2)^{-1} \left\{ S_{ZZ} \sum_{i=1}^{n} (x_i - \bar{x})(Y_i - \bar{Y}) - S_{XZ} \sum_{i=1}^{n} (z_i - \bar{z})(Y_i - \bar{Y}) \right\}$$

$$C = (S_{XX} S_{ZZ} - S_{XZ}^2)^{-1} \left\{ S_{XX} \sum_{i=1}^{n} (z_i - \bar{z})(Y_i - \bar{Y}) - S_{XZ} \sum_{i=1}^{n} (x_i - \bar{x})(Y_i - \bar{Y}) \right\}$$

and:

$$A = \bar{Y} - \bar{x}B - \bar{z}C.$$

These estimates are all unbiased estimates of the respective parameters. One of the exercises at the end of the chapter asks you to prove this.

The following results, analogous to those derived in the two-variable case, hold for the RSS.

1. $\hat{\sigma}^2 = \dfrac{\text{RSS}}{n-3}$ is an unbiased estimator of the variance of the error terms E_i in the model.

   Note the denominator: the $n - 3$ is the number of degrees of freedom in the variance estimate, 3 degrees of freedom having been used up in estimating α, β and γ.

2.
$$\sum_{i=1}^{n} (Y_i - \bar{Y})^2 = \sum_{i=1}^{n} (Y_i - A - Bx_i - Cz_i)^2 + \sum_{i=1}^{n} (A + Bx_i + Cz_i - \bar{Y})^2$$

   That is:

   $$\text{TSS} = \text{RSS} + \text{ESS}$$

   so that the coefficient of determination:

   $$r^2 = \frac{\text{ESS}}{\text{TSS}} = 1 - \frac{\text{RSS}}{\text{TSS}} = 1 - \frac{\displaystyle\sum_{i=1}^{n} \hat{e}_i^2}{\displaystyle\sum_{i=1}^{n} (y_i - \bar{y})^2} \qquad \text{(where } \hat{e}_i = y_i - a - bx_i - cz_i\text{)}$$

   measures the proportion of variance explained by the model.

   An alternative, and often more convenient formula for the RSS, because it does not involve calculating each residual, is:

   $$\text{RSS} = S_{YY} - (b^2 S_{XX} + 2bc S_{XZ} + c^2 S_{ZZ})$$

   or:

   $$r^2 = \frac{b^2 S_{XX} + 2bc S_{XZ} + c^2 S_{ZZ}}{S_{YY}}$$

Here:

$$\text{RSS} = 2\,102\,102.22$$

so:

$$\hat{\sigma}^2 = \frac{\text{RSS}}{35} = 60\,060.06$$

and:

$$r^2 = 1 - \frac{\text{RSS}}{S_{YY}} = 0.553\,90$$

This value is larger than that obtained in either of our single variable analyses, so a greater proportion of the variation of the Y_i in the sample is being explained by the model. However, the warning from the previous section should be repeated here even more strongly: when an additional variable is added to a model, as has been done here with z, the value of r will always be larger (the additional unknown parameter gives an extra degree of freedom in fitting the model) so that the increased r cannot be taken as evidence that this three-variable model is better than the two-variable ones we studied earlier.

EXAMPLE

On page 192, we considered an example modelling the dependence of the water depth in an estuary on the cosine of a multiple of the time from high water. An unrealistic aspect of this modelling was that it required us to know the time of high water. We are now in a position to estimate this parameter as well. The model to be adopted here is one which includes as its deterministic part a sinusoidal oscillation of arbitrary amplitude and phase:

$$D = \delta + \beta \cos (0.506t) + \gamma \sin (0.506t) + E$$

where t is the time in hours after midnight and D the depth in metres at a measurement point.

The data giving values of t and d for this measurement point are given below, together with corresponding values of:

$$x = \cos (0.506t)$$

$$z = \sin (0.506t)$$

Time after midnight, t (hours)	$x = \cos (0.506t)$	$z = \sin (0.506t)$	Depth of water, d (metres)
0	1	0	17.8
1	0.875	0.485	15.6
2	0.530	0.848	18.7
3	0.053	0.999	12.9
4	−0.438	0.899	9.9
5	−0.819	0.574	7.9
6	−0.994	0.105	7.5
7	−0.921	−0.390	12.0
8	−0.617	−0.787	15.6
9	−0.158	−0.987	16.6
10	0.341	−0.940	20.3
11	0.754	−0.657	23.1
12	0.978	−0.210	20.5
13	0.957	0.291	16.1

These data are summarised by:

$$\bar{x} = 0.110, \qquad \bar{z} = 0.016, \qquad \bar{v} = 15.3;$$

$$S_{XX} = 7.539, \qquad S_{ZZ} = 6.288, \qquad S_{XZ} = 0.190;$$

$$S_{XY} = 36.57, \qquad S_{YZ} = -20.14$$

The simultaneous equations derived from the normal equations are therefore:

$$7.539b + 0.190c = 36.57$$
$$0.190b + 6.288c = -20.14$$

which leads to:

$$b = 4.94, \qquad c = -3.35$$

This, finally, gives:

$$a = 15.3 - 0.110b - 0.016c = 14.8$$

Figure 10.10 shows the experimental points, and the fitted curve.

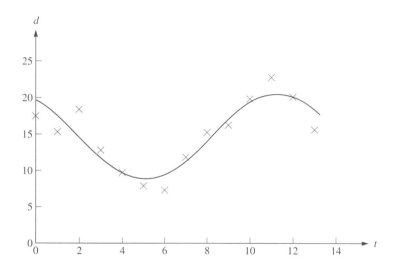

Figure 10.10

As this example illustrates, the two-variable model can also be used to fit models of the form:

$$Y = \alpha + \beta f(t) + \gamma g(t) + E$$

for any functions, f and g, of a single independent variable, t, by defining x = f(t), y = g(t) and using the formulae derived for the two-variable linear model.

Investigation

A food technologist investigating taste enhancing chemicals A and B found ten yogurts containing different amounts of A and B. Two panels of experienced tasters then rated the strength of flavour in each yogurt.

Investigation continued

The results were as follows.

Amount of A (mg per 100 g)	Amount of B (mg per 100 g)	Rating of panel 1 (scale 1–10)	Rating of panel 2 (scale 1–10)
12	16	3.5	3.5
7	9	2.0	2.0
15	20	4.4	4.4
22	29	6.4	6.4
34	45	9.9	9.9
16	21	4.6	4.5
11	15	3.2	3.3
5	7	1.5	1.6
24	32	7.0	7.1
33	44	9.6	9.7

(i) Use the model:

$$R = \alpha + \beta x + \gamma z + E$$

where R is the panel rating, x is the amount of A and z is the amount of B. Estimate α, β and γ using the data from panel 1 and (separately) the data from panel 2.

(ii) Explain why apparently very similar ratings differ so greatly in their estimates of the effect of A and B on the taste: you may find it helpful to plot a scatter graph of x against z.

(iii) What could the food technologist do to assess the separate effects of the two flavour enhancers?

Investigation

In a road research laboratory, the distance, $D\,(\text{m})$, in which cars stop is measured. One model for the way in which D depends on the speed, $v\,(\text{ms}^{-1})$, of the car is:

$$D = \alpha v + \beta v^2 + E$$

(i)   Use the method of least squares to derive formulae for estimates a and b of α and β respectively.

An alternative model for the dependence of the stopping distance per unit speed, $\left(\dfrac{D}{v}\right)$, on speed is

$$\frac{D}{v} = \alpha + \beta v + E$$

(ii) Write down expressions for ordinary least squares estimates of α and β, using values of $\dfrac{d}{v}$ as y values and values of v as x values.

Investigation continued

(iii) Use the data below to find both sets of estimates of α and β.

Speed, v (ms^{-1})	Stopping distance (m)
3	2.48
6	5.90
9	16.03
12	22.65
15	30.74
18	43.74
21	52.50
24	65.34
27	84.35
30	92.42

(iv) Discuss your results.

   Some questions you might consider are given below:

   • Why do the methods not give the same estimates?

   • Do the two equations describe the same statistical model?

   • Do both estimators give unbiased estimates of α and β?

   • Are you making the same assumptions in each case?

Exercise 10F

1. When assessing the air quality in a city, monitoring scientists measure the amount X in parts per million (ppm) of a particular oxide. This is believed to depend linearly on the temperature t, in °C, and the humidity, $h\%$, at the time of measurement, as well as on other factors which are represented by a random variable E, with zero mean, so that the amount of oxide is modelled by

the equation

$$X = \alpha + \beta t + \gamma h + E$$

The monitoring scientists gather the data summarised below.

$$n = 30, \quad \sum_{i=1}^{30} t_i = 287, \quad \sum_{i=1}^{30} h_i = 1700,$$

$$\sum_{i=1}^{30} X_i = 2755, \quad \sum_{i=1}^{30} t_i^2 = 3631, \quad \sum_{i=1}^{30} h_i^2 = 113\,264,$$

$$\sum_{i=1}^{30} t_i h_i = 17\,451, \quad \sum_{i=1}^{30} t_i x_i = 29\,497,$$

$$\sum_{i=1}^{30} h_i x_i = 169\,115, \quad \sum_{i=1}^{30} x_i^2 = 276\,003$$

(a) Calculate estimates of α, β, and γ using this data.

(b) Calculate r^2. What is the significance of this value?

2. The daily growth rate of rice plants is believed to be linearly related to both the number of hours of sunshine received in the day and to the concentration of a particular nutrient in the soil. The table shows the daily growth rate of plants in different environments.

Amount of sunshine, s (hours/day)	Concentration of nutrient, n (mg/litre)	Growth rate, g (cm/day)
0	5	3.3
2	11	6.1
2	19	7.3
3.5	2	8.2
4	7	10.0
5.5	3	7.1
6	11	6.1
7	10	8.6
8.5	16	15.7
8.5	4	7.0
12	7	9.9
12	11	15.7
12	15	16.5

(i) (a) Write down a suitable model for the process which generates the values of G, the daily growth, and state the assumptions that you are making.

(b) Use the data to estimate the coefficients of this model.

(c) Determine the value of r^2.

(ii) (a) Now take the coefficient of n to be zero, so that the model is no longer a bilinear one. Write down a suitable model for the process which generates the values of G, in this case. Are the assumptions the same as in (i) (a)?

(b) Use the data to estimate the coefficients of this model.

(c) Determine the value of r^2.

(iii) Compare the results of the two analyses.

3. Two variables x and y are thought to be related by the equation

$$y = Ax^r(1 - x)^s$$

When an experiment is conducted to determine the coefficients in this relationship, x can be determined exactly, but y is subject to measurement error, and the process generating measured values Y is modelled by the equation

$$\log Y = \log A + r \log x + s \log (1 - x) + E$$

where E is a Normal random variable with zero mean.

(i) Use the data summarised below to estimate A, r and s,

$$n = 49, \quad \sum_{i=1}^{49} \log x_i = \sum_{i=1}^{49} \log (1 - x_i) = -20.465,$$

$$\sum_{i=1}^{49} \log y_i = -16.114,$$

$$\sum_{i=1}^{49} (\log x_i)^2 = \sum_{i=1}^{49} (\log (1 - x_i))^2 = 15.683,$$

$$\sum_{i=1}^{49} (\log x_i(\log (1 - x_i)) = 3.3448,$$

$$\sum_{i=1}^{49} (\log x_i)(\log y_i) = 34\,700,$$

$$\sum_{i=1}^{49} (\log (1 - x_i))(\log y_i) = 12.169,$$

$$\sum_{i=1}^{49} (\log y_i)^2 = 12.943$$

(ii) It is thought, on theoretical grounds, by another researcher that $r + s = 1$.

(a) Explain why he should use the model

$$\log \frac{Y}{1 - x} = \log A + r \log \frac{x}{1 - x} + E.$$

(b) Explain why

$$\sum_{i=1}^{49} \log \frac{y_i}{1 - x_i} = \sum_{i=1}^{49} \log y_i - \sum_{i=1}^{49} \log (1 - x_i)$$

and

$$\sum_{i=1}^{49} \left(\log \left(\frac{y_i}{1 - x_i} \right) \right)^2$$

$$= \sum_{i=1}^{49} (\log y_i)^2 - 2 \sum_{i=1}^{49} (\log (1 - x_i))(\log y_i)$$

$$+ \sum_{i=1}^{49} (\log (1 - x_i))^2$$

and derive similar expressions for

$$\sum_{i=1}^{49} \log \frac{x_i}{1 - x_i} \quad \text{and} \quad \sum_{i=1}^{49} \left(\log \left(\frac{x_i}{1 - x_i} \right) \right)^2.$$

(c) Determine estimates of r and A for this model.

(iii) Comment on your estimates in (i) and (ii).

4. In a chemical reaction, the concetration m in moles per litre of reagent S in the mixture is thought to obey the equation

$$m = \alpha + \beta e^{-(t/10)} + \gamma e^{-(t/4)}$$

where t is the time in seconds from the start of the reaction.

(i) (a) If measurement of m is subject to a random error, write down a suitable model for the value of M, the measured value of the concentration of S.

(b) Use the data tabulated and summarised below to estimate values of α, β and γ.

t (seconds)	m (moles/litre)
0	0.049306
0.5	0.243388
1.0	0.42797
1.5	0.610533
2.0	0.645428
3.0	0.826058
4.0	0.960657
5.0	0.963602
6.0	1.096277
8.0	1.016695
10.0	0.92592
12.0	0.778161
14.0	0.742894
16.0	0.703204
18.0	0.588661
20.0	0.488587
25.0	0.321562
30.0	0.178949
35.0	0.234523
40.0	0.111801

$$n = 20, \quad \sum_{i=1}^{20} e^{-t/10} = 9.1499, \quad \sum_{i=1}^{20} \theta^{t/4} = 5.6513,$$

$$\sum_{i=1}^{20} m_i = 11.914, \quad \sum_{i=1}^{20} (e^{-(t/10)})^2 = 6.3875,$$

$$\sum_{i=1}^{20} (e^{-(t/4)})^2 = 3.7449,$$

$$\sum_{i=1}^{49} (e^{-(t/10)})(e^{-(t/4)}) = 4.6451$$

$$\sum_{i=1}^{20} (e^{-(t/10)})m_i = 5.7289, \quad \sum_{i=1}^{20} (e^{t/4})m_i = 2.9710,$$

$$\sum_{i=1}^{20} m_i^2 = 9.1008$$

(ii) (a) In the case where α is known to be zero, and M is modelled by

$$M = \beta e^{t/10} + \gamma e^{-t/4} + E$$

where E is a Normal random variable with zero mean, derive estimators for β and γ using the method of least squares.

(b) Find the corresponding estimates for β and γ using the data above.

(iii) Plot the data points on a graph of m against t and, on the same axes, draw the curves given by the regressions carried out in (i) and (ii). Give two possible reasons why the curve given by the regression in (ii) does not apparently fit the data points as well as that derived from the regression in (i).

5. Show that the least squares estimators A, B and C, derived in the text, are all unbiased.

Answers

Exercise 1A

1. P(2 or fewer not roadworthy if $p = 40\%$) = 0.0271; two-tailed: not significant at 5% level
3. P(3 or more left-handed if $p = 0.05$) = 0.0665; one-tailed: not significant at 5% level
6. P(9 or fewer overweight if $p = 70\%$) = 0.0596; one-tailed: significant at 10% level, not significant at 5% level

Exercise 1B

1. test statistic $= -2.191 < -1.96$ (2-tailed, 5% level) so reject H_0
2. (i) $0.5487 < \pi < 0.7967$
3. test statistic $= -2.833 < -2.326$ (1-tailed, 1% level) so reject H_0
4. (i) $\pi < 0.001\,903$
5. (i) test statistic $= -1.772 > -1.96$ (2-tailed, 5% level) so accept H_0
   (ii) $0.3969 < \pi < 0.5049$

Exercise 1C

1. test statistic $= -1.010 > -1.96$ (2-tailed, 5% level) so accept H_0
2. $0.0312 < \pi_C \quad \pi_B < 0.0854$
3. test statistic $= 2.570 > 2.326$ (1-tailed, 1% level) so reject H_0
4. $\pi_B - \pi_W > 0.0180$
5. test statistic $= 0.8239 < 1.96$ (2-tailed, 5% level) so accept H_0
6. $0.3922 < \pi_C - \pi_L < 0.5789$

Exercise 2A

1. $\chi^2_{15} = 28.89 > 27.49$ conclude variance is not 14.8
2. $\chi^2_9 = 4.86 > 3.325$ conclude variance is 2
3. $\chi^2_8 = 17.5 < 17.53$ conclude variance is 0.08
4. $\chi^2_7 = 4.18 > 1.690$ conclude variance is 9.3
5. (i) $\chi^2_9 = 3.99 > 3.325$ conclude variance has not reduced
   (ii) Assumes that the number of passengers is distributed Normally.
6. (i) $\chi^2_{13} = 23.70 < 24.74$ conclude variance is 2
   (ii) $\chi^2_{13} = 23.70 > 22.36$ conclude variance is >2
7. (i) $S^2 = 6.67$
   (ii) (a) $\chi^2_{22} = 14.68 > 10.98$ conclude variance is 10
       (b) $\chi^2_{22} = 36.69 < 36.78$ conclude variance is 4

Exercise 2B

1. (i) $7.29 < \sigma^2 < 20.78$ (ii) $6.73 < \sigma^2 < 23.39$
2. $0.096 < \sigma^2 < 0.673$
3. (i) $0.090 < \sigma^2 < 0.512$ (ii) $0.300 < \sigma < 0.716$
4. $26.84 < \sigma^2 < 136.58$
5. (i) $33.14 < \sigma^2 < 233.48$ (ii) The standard deviation is no longer 18.4
6. (i) $H_0: \sigma^2 = 6.8^2$, $H_1: \sigma^2 \neq 6.8^2$, $\chi^2_9 = 21.94 > 19.02$ conclude variance has changed
   (ii) $59.96 < \sigma^2 < 305.11$ (iii) Journey times are Normally distributed.

Exercise 2C

1. $F_{24,19} = 1.32 < 2.45$ conclude variances are equal
2. $F_{7,9} = 1.92 < 5.61$ conclude variances are equal
3. $S^2 < 12.49$ or $S^2 > 64.38$
4. $\dfrac{S_B^2}{S_A^2} = 4.74$ but $F_{24,24}(\text{critical}) = 1.98 \Rightarrow F_{59,59}(\text{critical}) < 1.98$ hence B is less consistent
5. (i) $F_{4,5} = 1.164 < 7.39$ conclude variances are equal
   (ii) Samples are independent and random and reaction times are Normally distributed.
6. (i) $F_{6,5} = 1.23 < 6.98$ conclude variances are equal
        $t_{11} = 0.626 < 2.201$ conclude no significant difference in the means at 5% level
   (ii) Samples are independent and random and egg masses are Normally distributed.
7. (i) $F_{10,7} = 2.901 < 4.76$ conclude variances are equal
   (ii) $t_{17} = 1.779 > 1.742$ conclude the new treatment has a higher mean
   (iii) Samples are independent and random and the time taken to rust is Normally distributed.
         The test in (ii) assumes the two distributions have equal variances.
8. (i) $0.103 < \sigma^2 < 0.480$ this assumes that the population is Normal
   (ii) (a) $F_{8,14} = 1.943 < 2.70$ conclude variances are equal
         (b) $H_0: \sigma_s^2 = \sigma_w^2$ $H_1: \sigma_s^2 > \sigma_w^2$
         (c) Samples are independent.
9. (i) $F_{7,9} = 1.385 < 4.20$ conclude variances are equal
   (ii) The underlying populations are Normal.
   (iii) Yes – the unpaired t-test requires equal variances.
10. (i) $F_{7,9} = 2.13 < 4.20$ conclude variances are equal
    (ii) $235.4 < \sigma^2 < 829.2$
    (iii) The probability that σ^2 lies between l and u is either 0 or 1. If a large number of such intervals were constructed, then σ^2 would lie within about 80% of them.

Exercise 3A

1. (i)   critical region is $\{x \leqslant 5\} \cup \{x \geqslant 15\}$; $\alpha = 0.0414$
2. (iii) $\rho \geqslant 0.596$
3. (i)   significance level $= \frac{1}{13}$ (iii) significance level $= \frac{1}{8}$
4. (i) $\alpha = 0.2759$, $\beta = 0.1844$ (ii) $\alpha = 0.0086$, $\beta = 0.0335$
5. (i) $r = 0.11$ (ii) probability of type II error $= 0.412$
6. (ii) (a) $I_{\text{crit}} = m_0 \alpha^{1/n}$, (b) $\text{OC}(m) = 1 - \alpha \left(\dfrac{m_0}{m} \right)^n$
7. (i) $H_0: \mu = 0$; $H_1: \mu > 0$ (ii) $\bar{d} > 0.26 \hat{\sigma}$
9. (i) $\alpha = 0.1587$, $\beta = 0.0668$ (ii) $k = 2.645$, $\beta = 0.7405$ (iii) $k = 1.5$, $n = 61$

Exercise 4A

1. $G(t) = \frac{1}{36}t^2 + \frac{2}{36}t^3 + \frac{3}{36}t^4 + \frac{4}{36}t^5 + \frac{5}{36}t^6 + \frac{6}{36}t^7 + \frac{5}{36}t^8 + \frac{4}{36}t^9 + \frac{3}{36}t^{10} + \frac{2}{36}t^{11} + \frac{1}{36}t^{12}$
2. $G(t) = \frac{1}{6} + \frac{5}{18}t + \frac{2}{9}t^2 + \frac{1}{6}t^3 + \frac{1}{9}t^4 + \frac{1}{18}t^5$
3. $G(t) = \frac{1}{8} + \frac{3}{8}t + \frac{3}{8}t^2 + \frac{1}{8}t^3$
4. $G(t) = \frac{3}{5}t + \frac{3}{10}t^2 + \frac{1}{10}t^3$
5. $G(t) = \frac{3}{5}t + \frac{2}{5} \times \frac{3}{5}t^2 + \left(\frac{2}{5} \right)^2 \times \frac{3}{5}t^3 + \left(\frac{2}{5} \right)^3 \times \frac{3}{5}t^4 + \cdots + \left(\frac{2}{5} \right)^{n-1} \times \frac{3}{5}t^n + \cdots = \dfrac{3t}{5 - 2t}$
6. $k = \frac{1}{153}$; $G(t) = \frac{1}{153}t + \frac{2}{153}t^2 + \frac{6}{153}t^3 + \frac{24}{153}t^4 + \frac{120}{153}t^5$
7. $G(t) = \frac{1}{3} + \frac{1}{2}t + \frac{1}{6}t^3$
8. $G(t) = \frac{12}{35} + \frac{18}{35}t + \frac{1}{7}t^2$

Exercise 4B

1. $E(X) = 2\frac{1}{6}$; $\text{Var}(X) = 2\frac{23}{36}$ 2. $E(X) = 2\frac{2}{3}$; $\text{Var}(X) = \frac{8}{9}$.
3. $E(X) = 3\frac{1}{2}$; $\text{Var}(X) = 2\frac{11}{12}$ 4. $E(X) = 1\frac{1}{2}$; $\text{Var}(X) = \frac{3}{4}$.
5. $\text{Var}(X) = na(1-a)$ 6. $G(t) = \left(\frac{12}{13} + \frac{1}{13}t \right)^4$; $E(X) = \frac{4}{13}$; $\text{Var}(X) = \frac{48}{169}$.

8. $a = \frac{1}{3}$, $b = \frac{1}{6}$, $c = \frac{1}{2}$.

9. $G(t) = \frac{1}{36}t + \frac{3}{36}t^2 + \frac{5}{36}t^3 + \frac{7}{36}t^4 + \frac{9}{36}t^5 + \frac{11}{36}t^6$; $E(X) = 4\frac{17}{36}$; $Var(X) = 1.97$.

Exercise 4C

1. (ii) $G(t) = \left(\dfrac{t}{6 - 5t}\right)^2$ (iii) $E(X) = 12$; $Var(X) = 60$

2. (i) $G_X(t) = t(0.6 + 0.4t)$; $G_Y(t) = t(0.2 + 0.5t + 0.3t^2)$;
$G(t) = G_X(t) \times G_Y(t) = t(0.6 + 0.4t) \times t(0.2 + 0.5t + 0.3t^2)$
(ii) $E(X + Y) = E(X) + E(Y) = 3.5$; $Var(X + Y) = Var(X) + Var(Y) = 0.73$

3. (i) Pgf for constant c is $G_c(t) = t^c$
Since X and c are independent: $G_Y(t) = G_{X+c}(t) = G_X(t) G_c(t) = t^c G_X(t)$
(ii) $E(c) = c$ and $Var(c) = 0$; results follow from independence of X and c

4. (i) $G_X(t) = e^{3.4(t-1)}$, $G_Y(t) = e^{4.8(t-1)}$ (ii) $G_{X+Y}(t) = e^{12.2(t-1)}$

5. (i) $\frac{1}{6}t + \frac{1}{3}t^2 + \frac{1}{2}t^3$; $G_X(t) = \left(\frac{1}{6}t + \frac{1}{3}t^2 + \frac{1}{2}t^3\right)^5$ (ii) $E(X) = 11\frac{2}{3}$; $Var(X) = 2\frac{7}{9}$

6. $G_z(t) = G_X(t) \cdot G_Y(t) = \dfrac{t(1 - t^6)}{6(1 - t)} \times \dfrac{t(1 - t^4)}{4(1 - t)}$

Exercise 4D

1. (i) *Hint*: Let $G(t) = p_1 t + p_2 t^2 + p_3 t^3 + \cdots$ and find $G(1) + G(-1)$.
(ii) (a) 0.5;   (b) 0.25.

2. (i) $\frac{1}{6}$ (ii) $\frac{1}{6}$ (iii) $\frac{2}{3}$. $E(R) = 3\frac{1}{3}$.

3. (a) $P(X = r) = e^{-\lambda} \dfrac{\lambda^r}{r!}$; $G_X(t) = e^{\lambda(t-1)}$, (b) $k = \dfrac{1}{1 - e^{-\lambda}}$.

4. $3\frac{6}{7}$.

5. (i) $P(X = x) = pq^{x-1}$, $x \geqslant 1$ (ii) $E(X) = \dfrac{1}{p}$; $Var(X) = \dfrac{q}{p^2}$,

(iii) $G_Y(t) = [G(t)]^k = \left(\dfrac{pt}{1 - qt}\right)^k = \dfrac{p^k t^k}{(1 - qt)^k}$

6. $P(X = x) = e^{-\theta_1} \dfrac{\theta_1^x}{x!}$; $P(Y = y) = e^{-\theta_2} \dfrac{\theta_2^y}{y!}$; $P(X + Y = z) = e^{-(\theta_1 + \theta_2)} \dfrac{(\theta_1 + \theta_2)^z}{z!}$.

$G_X(t) = e^{\theta_1(t-1)}$; $G_Y(t) = e^{\theta_2(t-1)}$; $G_{X+Y}(t) = e^{(\theta_1 + \theta_2)(t-1)}$

(i) $P(X + Y = z) = e^{-(\theta_1 + \theta_2)} \dfrac{(\theta_1 + \theta_2)^z}{z!}$ (ii) $\theta_1 + \theta_2$ (iii) $\theta_1 + \theta_2$.

7. (i) e^{-2}, e^{-2}, $\frac{3}{2}e^{-2}$, $\frac{7}{6}e^{-2}$, $\frac{25}{24}e^{-2}$ (ii) 3   (iii) 5   (iv) 3

8. (iii) $P_n = (2p - 1)^{n-1}(\theta - 0.5) + 0.5$

9. (i) $q_j = \dfrac{j - 1}{N}$, $p_j = \dfrac{N - j + 1}{N}$ (ii) $G(t) = \dfrac{p_j t}{1 - q_j t}$, $E(X_j) = \dfrac{N}{N - j + 1}$;

(iv) $Var(X) = N\left(N - 1 + \dfrac{N - 2}{2^2} + \dfrac{N - 3}{3^2} + \cdots + \dfrac{1}{(N - 1)^2}\right)$

10. (i) $G_X(t) = \frac{2}{3} + \frac{1}{3}t$ (ii) $G_Y(t) = \frac{1}{2} + \frac{1}{2}t$ (iii) $E(S) = \frac{11}{6}$, $Var(S) = \frac{17}{36}$

Exercise 5A

1. $\mu_3 = 0$ **3.** (ii) $\mu_3 = -\frac{1}{160}$ **4.** $\mu_3 = \frac{1}{160}$

Exercise 5B

1.   mgf of $B(n, p)$ is $(q + pe^\theta)^n$ (i) mgf of Y is $(q + pe^\theta)^{n_1 + n_2 + \dots + n_k}$

2.   mgf of Poisson(m) is $e^{-m}e^{me^\theta}$;
(i) mgf of Y is $e^{-M}e^{Me^\theta}$ where $M = m_1 + m_2 + \dots + m_n$
(ii) Distribution of Y is Poisson(M).

3. mean $= np$, variance $= npq$

4. (ii) mgf of Y is $\{\lambda/(\lambda - t)\}^{nk+n}$;
mean $= (nk + n)/\lambda$, variance $= (nk + n)/\lambda^2$
(iii) pdf of Y is $\lambda^{nk+n} y^{nk+n-1} e^{-\lambda y}/(nk + n - 1)!$

5. (ii) mgf of $N(0,1)$ is $e^{t^2/2}$ (iii) mgf of $N(\mu, \sigma^2)$ is $e^{\mu t + \sigma^2 t^2/2}$
(iv) means are $2\mu, 0$; variances are $2\sigma^2, 2\sigma^2$

6. (iii) $\mu, \mu, \mu + 3\mu^2$ (iv) 3

7. (i) $M(\theta) = (1 - 2\theta)^{-n/2}$

8. (i) X has distribution function $1 - e^{-0.001x}$ and pdf $0.001 e^{-0.001x}$ (iv) Option 2

9. (ii) $\dfrac{\alpha}{\alpha - \theta} \cdot \dfrac{\beta}{\beta - \theta}$ (iii) mgf of Z is $\dfrac{\alpha}{\alpha - \theta} \cdot \dfrac{\beta}{\beta - \theta}$ (iv) $\dfrac{1}{\alpha} + \dfrac{1}{\beta}$

10. (i) mgf is $\lambda/(\lambda - \theta)$, mean $1/\lambda$, variance $1/\lambda^2$
(ii) S_n is time to arrival of nth car; mgf is $\lambda^n/(\lambda - \theta)^n$
(iii) $\lambda^n/(\lambda - \theta)^n$ (iv) same as pdf of Y

Exercise 6A

1. (i) $\hat{\lambda} = \dfrac{a + b + c}{20}$ **2.** $\hat{\rho} = \dfrac{2a + b}{2n}$ **3.** $\hat{\rho} = \frac{1}{4}$

4. (i) $L = \dfrac{(a + b + c)!}{a! \, b! \, c!} p^{4a + 3b} (1 - p)^{b + 2c} (1 + 2p + 3p^2)^c$
(ii) $12(a + b + c) p^3 = (4a + b) p^2 + (4a + 2b) p + (4a + 3b)$

5. (i) $(m + 2n) \hat{p}^8 + (m - a) \hat{p}^4 - (a + 2b) = 0$ (ii) $\hat{p} = 0.9474$

6. (i) (a) $6\hat{\mu}^3 + (1320 - (a + b + c)) \hat{\mu}^2 + 20(4320 - (5a + 8b + 9c)) \hat{\mu} + 2400(720 - (a + 2b + 3c)) = 0$
(b) $120(3\hat{\lambda}^3 + 2\hat{\lambda}^2 + \hat{\lambda}) - (a + 2b + 3c) = 0$
(ii) (a) $\hat{\mu} = 47.41$ (b) $\hat{\lambda} = 1.314$

8. $\hat{\beta} = \dfrac{\sqrt{t_1} + \sqrt{t_2} + \ldots + \sqrt{t_r} + (n - r)\sqrt{\tau}}{r}$

9. (i) $f(x) = \dfrac{\delta}{\pi(\delta^2 + x^2)}$ (ii) $\displaystyle\sum_{i=1}^{n} \dfrac{2}{\hat{\delta}^2 + x_i^2} = \dfrac{n}{\hat{\delta}^2}$

(iii) $f(x) = \dfrac{\delta}{2\alpha(\delta)(\delta^2 + x^2)}$, $\displaystyle\sum_{i=1}^{n} \dfrac{2}{\hat{\delta}^2 + x_i^2} = \dfrac{n}{\hat{\delta}^2} + \dfrac{nH}{\hat{\delta}\alpha(\hat{\delta})(H^2 + \hat{\delta}^2)}$, where $\alpha(\delta) = \arctan\left(\dfrac{H}{\delta}\right)$

(iv) $\displaystyle\sum_{i=1}^{n} \dfrac{2(x_i - \hat{\xi})}{\hat{\delta}^2 + (x_i - \hat{\xi})^2} = 0$

10. (i) $\hat{\beta} = 31$ (ii) $\hat{\alpha} = \frac{7}{64}$

11. (i) $\ln(x_1 x_2 \ldots x_n) \hat{\kappa}^2 + (2n + \ln(x_1 x_2 \ldots x_n)) \hat{\kappa} + n = 0$

(ii) $\hat{\kappa} = \dfrac{(2 - s) + \sqrt{4 + s^2}}{2s}$ (iii) $\hat{\kappa} = 4.375$

12. $\displaystyle\sum_{i=1}^{n} y_i - n\hat{\alpha} - \hat{\beta} \sum_{i=1}^{n} x_i = 0$, $\displaystyle\sum_{i=1}^{n} y_i x_i - \hat{\alpha} \sum_{i=1}^{n} x_i - \hat{\beta} \sum_{i=1}^{n} x_i^2 = 0$

Exercise 7A

1. (i) 0.3, 0.5, 0.2; 0.2, 0.4, 0.4; (iii) (a) 0.3, (b) 0.6, (c) 0.2 (iv) 0.9, 1.2;
(v) (a) 2.1, (b) 7.5, (c) 3.3

2. (ii) $P(X = r) = P(Y = r) = \frac{1}{4}$, $r = 1, 2, 3, 4$;

(iii)

$x + y$	2	3	4	5	6	7	8
$P(X + Y = x + y)$	0	$\frac{1}{6}$	$\frac{1}{6}$	$\frac{1}{3}$	$\frac{1}{6}$	$\frac{1}{6}$	0

(iv) both $= 5$

3. (ii) $2\frac{1}{3}, 3, \frac{5}{9}, 1$;

(iii)

$x + y$	2	3	4	5	6	7
$P(X + Y = x + y)$	$\frac{1}{60}$	$\frac{1}{15}$	$\frac{1}{6}$	$\frac{4}{15}$	$\frac{17}{60}$	$\frac{1}{5}$

(iv) both $= 5\frac{1}{3}$, both $= 1\frac{5}{9}$;

(v)

xy	1	2	3	4	6	8	9	12
$P(XY = xy)$	$\frac{1}{60}$	$\frac{1}{60}$	$\frac{1}{10}$	$\frac{2}{15}$	$\frac{1}{5}$	$\frac{2}{15}$	$\frac{3}{20}$	$\frac{1}{5}$

(vi) both $= 7$

4. (i) $\frac{6}{28}, \frac{1}{28}, \frac{9}{28}, \frac{6}{28}, \frac{3}{28}$ (ii) $\frac{10}{28}, \frac{15}{28}, \frac{3}{28}, \frac{15}{28}, \frac{12}{28}, \frac{1}{28}$ (iii) $\frac{10}{28}$ (iv) 0.75, 0.5, 1.25

5. (i)

x	1	2	3	4	5	6
$P(X=x)$	$\frac{11}{36}$	$\frac{9}{36}$	$\frac{7}{36}$	$\frac{5}{36}$	$\frac{3}{36}$	$\frac{1}{36}$;

y	0	1	2	3	4	5
$P(Y=y)$	$\frac{3}{18}$	$\frac{5}{18}$	$\frac{4}{18}$	$\frac{3}{18}$	$\frac{2}{18}$	$\frac{1}{18}$;

(iii) (a) $\frac16$, (b) $\frac13$, (v) $\frac{91}{36}, \frac{35}{18}, \frac{7}{12}$

6. (i) $a+0.21, b+0.24, c+0.2; b+0.11, a+0.13, c+0.41;$
(ii) 0.1, 0.2, 0.05

7. (i) $\frac{3}{64}, \frac{3}{64}, \frac{3}{32}, \frac{3}{16}, \frac{3}{32}, \frac{3}{16}, \frac{3}{16}$ (ii) $\frac18, \frac38, \frac38, \frac18; \frac{27}{64}, \frac{27}{64}, \frac{9}{64}, \frac{1}{64};$
(iv) 1.5, 0.75; 0.75, 0.5625 (v) 2.25, 0.75

8. (iii) $\frac{1}{216}, \frac{7}{216}, \frac{19}{216}, \frac{37}{216}, \frac{61}{216}, \frac{91}{216}; \frac{91}{216}, \frac{61}{216}, \frac{37}{216}, \frac{19}{216}, \frac{7}{216}, \frac{1}{216};$
(iv) 4.96, 2.04 (v) 7, 2.92

Exercise 7B

1. (ii) 0.30, 0.34, 0.36; 0.38, 0.34, 0.28 (iii) 1.06, 0.9;
(iv) 0.263, 0.353, 0.429; X and Y not independent.

3. (i) $^4C_2 = 6; \frac16, 0, \frac16, \frac16, 0, \frac16, \frac16, \frac16; \frac13, \frac12, \frac12, \frac13, \frac16;$
(ii) *not* independent, e.g. $P(X=2, Y=3) = 0 \neq \frac16 \times \frac16 = P(X=2) \times P(Y=3)$

4. (ii) $\frac{1}{120}, \frac{3}{40}, \frac{3}{40}, \frac{1}{120}, \frac{1}{10}, \frac{1}{10}, \frac{3}{20}, \frac{3}{20}, \frac{1}{30}$ (iii) $\frac16, \frac12, \frac{3}{10}, \frac{1}{30}; \frac{7}{24}, \frac{21}{40}, \frac{3}{40}, \frac{1}{120};$
(iv) $\frac{1}{35}, \frac{12}{35}, \frac{18}{35}, \frac{4}{35}; \frac17, \frac47, \frac27, 0; \frac37, \frac47, 0, 0; 1, 0, 0, 0$

5. (i)

x	1	2	3	4	5	6
$P(X=x)$	$\frac{1}{36}$	$\frac{3}{36}$	$\frac{5}{36}$	$\frac{7}{36}$	$\frac{9}{36}$	$\frac{11}{36}$;

y	0	1	2	3	4	5
$P(Y=y)$	$\frac{3}{18}$	$\frac{5}{18}$	$\frac{4}{18}$	$\frac{3}{18}$	$\frac{2}{18}$	$\frac{1}{18}$;

(iv) $\frac{1}{36}, \frac{2}{36}, \frac{2}{36}, \frac{2}{36}, 0, 0$; no

6. (ii)

x	0	1	2	3
$P(X=x)$	$\frac18$	$\frac38$	$\frac38$	$\frac18$;

y	1	2	3
$P(Y=y)$	$\frac14$	$\frac12$	$\frac14$;

$1\frac12$; 2;

(iii) no; e.g. $P(X=1, Y=2) = \frac14 \neq \frac38 \times \frac12 = P(X=1) \times P(Y=2)$

7. (i)

x	1	2	3
$P(X=x)$	$\frac12$	$\frac14$	$\frac14$;

y	1	2	3
$P(Y=y)$	$\frac58$	$\frac13$	$\frac{1}{24}$;

$1\frac34$; $1\frac{5}{12}$;

(ii) $\frac25, \frac25, \frac15; \frac34, \frac14, 0; 0, 1, 0$ (iii) no, each conditional distribution is different;
(iv) 2, $1\frac14$, 2; $2 \times \frac58 + 1\frac14 \times \frac13 + 2 \times \frac{1}{24} = 1\frac34$

6. (ii)

x	1	2	3
$P(X=x)$	0.35	0.35	0.30;

y	1	2	3
$P(Y=y)$	0.4	0.4	0.2;

1.95; 1.8;

(ii) no; e.g. $P(X=3, Y=1) = 0.15 \neq 0.3 \times 0.4 = P(X=3) \times P(Y=1)$;

(iii) (a)

$x+y$	2	3	4	5	6
$P(X+Y=x+y)$	0.20	0.15	0.40	0.20	0.05

(b)

$x-y$	-2	-1	0	1	2
$P(X-Y=x-y)$	0.05	0.20	0.45	0.15	0.15

(c)

xy	1	2	3	4	6	9
$P(XY=xy)$	0.20	0.15	0.20	0.20	0.20	0.05

(iv) (a) true, (b) true, (c) false: $E(XY) = 3.55; E(X) \times E(Y) = 3.51$

9. (i) $\frac78, \frac{31}{56}$ (ii) $\frac78, \frac27, \frac14$ (iii) no; e.g. $P(X=0, Y=1) = \frac{3}{56} \neq \frac18 \times \frac{31}{56} = P(X=0) \times P(Y=1)$

Exercise 7C

1. (i)

x	1	2	3
$P(X=x)$	$\frac{3}{8}$	$\frac{3}{8}$	$\frac{1}{4}$;

y	1	2	3
$P(Y=y)$	$\frac{3}{8}$	$\frac{1}{3}$	$\frac{7}{24}$;

$1\frac{7}{8}; \frac{39}{64};$

(ii) $\frac{2}{3}, \frac{1}{3}, 0; 0, \frac{3}{4}, \frac{1}{4}; \frac{3}{7}, 0, \frac{4}{7};$

(iii) no; e.g. $P(X=1, Y=0) = 0 \neq \frac{3}{8} \times \frac{1}{3} = P(X=1) \times P(Y=0)$ (iv) $\frac{9}{32}$

2. (i) no; e.g. $P(X=1, Y=1) = 0 \neq 2p^2 = P(X=1) \times P(Y=1)$

(iii) $\frac{1}{6}, \frac{1}{12};$

(iv) $\frac{2}{5}, \frac{1}{5}, \frac{2}{5}; 0, 1, 0; \frac{2}{5}, \frac{1}{5}, \frac{2}{5}$

3. (ii) e.g. $P(X=1, Y=2) = 0.25 \neq 0.25 \times 0.5 = P(X=1) \times P(Y=2); 0$

4. (i) $\frac{13}{18}$

(ii)

x	-1	0	1
$P(X=x)$	$\frac{5}{18}$	$\frac{5}{12}$	$\frac{11}{36}$;

y	1	2	3
$P(Y=y)$	$\frac{2}{9}$	$\frac{5}{12}$	$\frac{13}{36}$;

$\frac{1}{36}, \frac{755}{1296}, 2\frac{5}{36};$

(iii) $\frac{1}{2}, 0, \frac{1}{2}; \frac{2}{5}, \frac{3}{5}, 0; 0, \frac{6}{13}, \frac{7}{13}$ (iv) no   (v) $\frac{247}{1296}$

5. (i) $P(X=x, Y=y) = P(X=x) \times P(Y=y)$ for all x, y (ii) 2, 1.02   (iv) 0.51

6. (i) $\frac{19}{32}$ (ii) $\frac{3}{16}, \frac{1}{4}, \frac{1}{4}, \frac{5}{16}; -\frac{5}{16}, \frac{311}{256}, \frac{3}{8}, \frac{3}{32}, \frac{5}{32}, \frac{3}{8};$

(iii) e.g. $P(X=1, Y=4) = 0 \neq \frac{5}{16} \times \frac{3}{32};$ (iv) $\frac{1}{6}, \frac{1}{4}, \frac{1}{6}, \frac{5}{12}$ (v) 0.028

7. (i) $P(X=x) = \frac{1}{6}, x = 1, 2, 3, 4, 5, 6; 3\frac{1}{2}, 15\frac{1}{6}$ (ii) 0;

(iii) $P(U=3) = \frac{1}{18} \neq \frac{1}{5} = P(U=3 \mid V=1)$

Exercise 7D

1. (i) 1   (ii) 9   (iii) 4   (iv) 25   (vi) 2

2. (ii) (a) 4.2, (b) 2.6, (c) 1.84

3. (i)

x	2	3	4	5
$P(X=x)$	0.1	0.2	0.3	0.4;

y	1	2	3	4
$P(Y=y)$	0.4	0.3	0.2	0.1;

(ii) 3, 1;   (iii) no; $\text{Cov}(X, Y) \neq 0$

4. (ii)

x	0	1	2	3	4
$P(X=x)$	$\frac{1}{16}$	$\frac{4}{16}$	$\frac{6}{16}$	$\frac{4}{16}$	$\frac{1}{16}$

y	1	2	3	4
$P(Y=y)$	$\frac{1}{8}$	$\frac{3}{8}$	$\frac{3}{8}$	$\frac{1}{8}$;

$2, 2.5;$

(iii) 1.75; no; e.g. $P(X=2, Y=3) = \frac{1}{8} \neq \frac{3}{8} \times \frac{3}{8} = P(X=2) \times P(Y=3)$, although $\text{Cov}(X, Y) = 0$

5. (i) $E(X) + E(Y) + E(Z)$;

$\text{Var}(X) + \text{Var}(Y) + \text{Var}(Z) + 2\,\text{Cov}(X, Y) + 2\,\text{Cov}(X, Z) + 2\,\text{Cov}(Y, Z)$;

(ii) (a) 10.5, (b) 8.75

6. (ii) $\text{Cov}(X, Y) \div \text{Var}(Y)$ (iii) 0.555, not significant at 5% level

7. $(ac + bd)\sigma^2$ **8.** (iii) $\dfrac{1}{\sqrt{n}}$ **9.** 0

Exercise 8A

1. (i) $\begin{bmatrix} \frac{43}{64} & \frac{21}{64} \\ \frac{21}{32} & \frac{11}{32} \end{bmatrix}$, $\begin{bmatrix} \frac{341}{512} & \frac{171}{512} \\ \frac{171}{256} & \frac{85}{256} \end{bmatrix}$, $\begin{bmatrix} \frac{2731}{4096} & \frac{1365}{4096} \\ \frac{1365}{2048} & \frac{883}{2048} \end{bmatrix}$ (ii) $\begin{bmatrix} \frac{11}{18} & \frac{7}{18} \\ \frac{7}{16} & \frac{9}{16} \end{bmatrix}$, $\begin{bmatrix} \frac{107}{216} & \frac{109}{216} \\ \frac{109}{192} & \frac{83}{192} \end{bmatrix}$, $\begin{bmatrix} \frac{1409}{2592} & \frac{1183}{2592} \\ \frac{1183}{2304} & \frac{1121}{2304} \end{bmatrix}$

(iii) $\begin{bmatrix} \frac{13}{18} & \frac{5}{18} \\ \frac{5}{18} & \frac{13}{18} \end{bmatrix}$, $\begin{bmatrix} \frac{19}{54} & \frac{35}{54} \\ \frac{35}{54} & \frac{19}{54} \end{bmatrix}$, $\begin{bmatrix} \frac{97}{162} & \frac{65}{162} \\ \frac{65}{162} & \frac{97}{162} \end{bmatrix}$ (iv) $\begin{bmatrix} 0.52 & 0.48 \\ 0.16 & 0.84 \end{bmatrix}$, $\begin{bmatrix} 0.412 & 0.588 \\ 0.196 & 0.804 \end{bmatrix}$, $\begin{bmatrix} 0.347 & 0.653 \\ 0.218 & 0.782 \end{bmatrix}$

2. (i)

	sunny	cloudy
sunny	0.7	0.3
cloudy	0.2	0.8

(ii) (a) 0.55, (b) 0.525, (c) 0.4375

3. (i)

	Dem	Rep
Dem	$\frac{8}{15}$	$\frac{7}{15}$
Rep	$\frac{3}{10}$	$\frac{7}{10}$

(ii) $\frac{7}{15}$ (iii) $\frac{191}{450}$

4. (i)
$$\begin{array}{cc} & \text{disco} \quad \text{cinema} \\ \begin{array}{c}\text{disco} \\ \text{cinema}\end{array} & \begin{bmatrix} 0.5 & 0.5 \\ 0.75 & 0.25 \end{bmatrix}\end{array}$$

(ii) (a) 0.625, (b) 0.40625   (iii) 0.5977 *or* 0.6006

5. (i)
$$\begin{array}{cc} & \text{fore} \quad \text{back} \\ \begin{array}{c}\text{forehand} \\ \text{backhand}\end{array} & \begin{bmatrix} \frac{1}{5} & \frac{4}{5} \\ \frac{1}{3} & \frac{2}{3} \end{bmatrix}\end{array}$$
(ii) $\frac{32}{45} \approx 0.711$ (iii) (a) $\frac{476}{665} \approx 0.705$, (b) $\frac{796}{1125} \approx 0.708$

6. (i)
$$\begin{array}{cc} & \text{Oxf} \quad \text{Cam} \\ \begin{array}{c}\text{Oxf} \\ \text{Cam}\end{array} & \begin{bmatrix} \frac{3}{5} & \frac{2}{5} \\ \frac{1}{3} & \frac{2}{3} \end{bmatrix}\end{array}$$

(ii) Oxford won last year: Oxf $\frac{37}{75}$, Cam $\frac{38}{75}$
Cambridge won last year: Oxf $\frac{19}{45}$, Cam $\frac{26}{45}$

7. (i)
$$\begin{array}{cc} & \text{L} \qquad \text{OT} \\ \begin{array}{c}\text{L} \\ \text{OT}\end{array} & \begin{bmatrix} 0.25 & 0.75 \\ 0.5 & 0.5 \end{bmatrix}\end{array}$$
(ii) (a) 0.625, (b) 0.602 (3 s.f.)

8. (i) $a + b = 1$, $c + d = 1$ (ii) $\begin{bmatrix} a^2 + bc & ab + bd \\ ac + cd & bc + d^2 \end{bmatrix}$

Exercise 8B

1. (i) $\begin{bmatrix} 0.792 & 0 & 0.208 \\ 0.208 & 0.375 & 0.417 \\ 0.139 & 0.417 & 0.444 \end{bmatrix}$, $\begin{bmatrix} 0.174 & 0.396 & 0.431 \\ 0.628 & 0.104 & 0.267 \\ 0.683 & 0.069 & 0.248 \end{bmatrix}$, $\begin{bmatrix} 0.656 & 0.087 & 0.258 \\ 0.301 & 0.314 & 0.385 \\ 0.258 & 0.341 & 0.400 \end{bmatrix}$;

(ii) $\begin{bmatrix} 0.378 & 0.465 & 0.158 \\ 0.325 & 0.438 & 0.238 \\ 0.345 & 0.405 & 0.250 \end{bmatrix}$, $\begin{bmatrix} 0.352 & 0.450 & 0.198 \\ 0.343 & 0.436 & 0.221 \\ 0.349 & 0.433 & 0.218 \end{bmatrix}$, $\begin{bmatrix} 0.348 & 0.443 & 0.209 \\ 0.347 & 0.439 & 0.214 \\ 0.348 & 0.439 & 0.213 \end{bmatrix}$;

(iii) $\begin{bmatrix} 0.389 & 0.333 & 0.278 \\ 0.333 & 0.333 & 0.333 \\ 0.278 & 0.333 & 0.389 \end{bmatrix}$, $\begin{bmatrix} 0.352 & 0.333 & 0.315 \\ 0.333 & 0.333 & 0.333 \\ 0.315 & 0.333 & 0.352 \end{bmatrix}$, $\begin{bmatrix} 0.340 & 0.333 & 0.327 \\ 0.333 & 0.333 & 0.333 \\ 0.327 & 0.333 & 0.340 \end{bmatrix}$

2. (i)
$$\begin{array}{cc} & \text{camping} \quad \text{city} \quad \text{winter} \\ \begin{array}{c}\text{camping} \\ \text{city} \\ \text{winter}\end{array} & \begin{bmatrix} 0 & 0.5 & 0.5 \\ 0.5 & 0 & 0.5 \\ 0.5 & 0.5 & 0 \end{bmatrix}\end{array}$$
(ii) (a) 0.5, (b) 0.25, (c) 0.375

3. (i)
$$\begin{array}{cc} & \text{H} \quad T \quad G \\ \begin{array}{c}\text{Herald} \\ \text{Tribune} \\ \text{Gazette}\end{array} & \begin{bmatrix} \frac{7}{8} & \frac{1}{8} & 0 \\ \frac{3}{4} & \frac{1}{12} & \frac{1}{6} \\ \frac{1}{2} & \frac{1}{6} & \frac{1}{3} \end{bmatrix}\end{array}$$
(ii) (a) $\frac{1}{6}$, (b) $\frac{27}{288} \approx 0.128$, (c) 0.122

4. (i)
$$\begin{array}{cc} & A \quad C \quad T \\ \begin{array}{c}A \\ C \\ T\end{array} & \begin{bmatrix} 0 & \frac{3}{5} & \frac{2}{5} \\ \frac{1}{6} & \frac{1}{3} & \frac{1}{2} \\ \frac{1}{2} & \frac{1}{4} & \frac{1}{4} \end{bmatrix}\end{array}$$
(ii) (a) 0.3, 0.3, 0.4, (b) 0.25, 0.38, 0.37

5. (i) C   (ii) A: 2921, B: 2578, C: 2501

6. (i) $a + b + c = 1$, $d + e + f = 1$, $g + h + i = 1$,

(ii) $\begin{bmatrix} a^2 + bd + cg & ab + be + ch & ac + bf + ci \\ ad + de + fg & bd + e^2 + fh & cd + ef + fi \\ ag + dh + gi & bg + eh + hi & cg + fh + i^2 \end{bmatrix}$

7. (i)
$$\begin{array}{cc} & S_0 \quad S_1 \quad S_2 \quad S_3 \\ \begin{array}{c}S_0 \\ S_1 \\ S_2 \\ S_3\end{array} & \begin{bmatrix} q & p & 0 & 0 \\ q & 0 & p & 0 \\ q & 0 & 0 & p \\ 0 & 0 & 0 & 1 \end{bmatrix}\end{array}$$
(ii) $f_1 = f_2 = f_3 = q$, $f_1 = q^2(q^2 - 3q + 3)$

Exercise 8C

1. *Equilibrium probabilities*
   Ex. A: q.1:
   (i) $\frac{2}{3}, \frac{1}{3}$ (ii) $\frac{9}{17}, \frac{8}{17}$ (iii) $\frac{1}{2}, \frac{1}{2}$ (iv) 0.25, 0.75;
   q.2: 0.4, 0.6   q.3: 0.6, 0.4   q.4: $\frac{9}{23}, \frac{14}{23}$ q.5: $\frac{5}{17}, \frac{12}{17}$.
   Ex. B: q.1:
   (i) $\frac{4}{9}, \frac{2}{9}, \frac{1}{3}$ (ii) 0.3475, 0.4402, 0.02124   (iii) $\frac{1}{3}, \frac{1}{3}, \frac{1}{3}$.
   q.2: $\frac{1}{3}, \frac{1}{3}, \frac{1}{3}$ q.3: $\frac{28}{33}, \frac{4}{33}, \frac{1}{33}$.

2.
$$\begin{array}{c} \\ city \\ suburbs \end{array}\begin{array}{c} city \quad suburbs \\ \begin{bmatrix} 0.95 & 0.05 \\ 0.02 & 0.98 \end{bmatrix} \end{array}; \frac{2}{7}, \frac{5}{7}.$$

3.
$$\begin{array}{c} \\ A \\ B \\ C \end{array}\begin{array}{c} A \quad B \quad C \\ \begin{bmatrix} 0.5 & 0.25 & 0.25 \\ 0.25 & 0.5 & 0.25 \\ 0.25 & 0.25 & 0.5 \end{bmatrix} \end{array}; \frac{1}{3}, \frac{1}{3}, \frac{1}{3}.$$

4. (i)
$$\begin{array}{c} \\ A \\ B \\ main \end{array}\begin{array}{c} A \quad\ B \quad\ main \\ \begin{bmatrix} \frac{1}{2} & \frac{1}{3} & \frac{1}{6} \\ \frac{2}{3} & \frac{1}{4} & \frac{1}{12} \\ \frac{1}{2} & \frac{1}{2} & 0 \end{bmatrix} \end{array}$$
   (ii) $\frac{13}{24}, \frac{47}{144}, \frac{19}{144}$ (iii) $\frac{51}{92}, \frac{15}{46}, \frac{11}{92}$

6. (i)
$$\begin{array}{c} \\ A \\ B \\ C \end{array}\begin{array}{c} A \quad B \quad C \\ \begin{bmatrix} \frac{1}{4} & \frac{3}{4} & 0 \\ \frac{1}{3} & 0 & \frac{2}{3} \\ 0 & \frac{1}{2} & \frac{1}{2} \end{bmatrix} \end{array}$$
   (ii) $\frac{3}{8}$ (iii) $\frac{4}{25}, \frac{9}{25}, \frac{12}{25}$

7. (i)
$$\begin{array}{c} \\ T \\ Co \\ Ch \end{array}\begin{array}{c} T \quad\ Co \quad\ Ch \\ \begin{bmatrix} 0.2 & 0.4 & 0.4 \\ 0.2 & 0.4 & 0.4 \\ 0.2 & 0.2 & 0.6 \end{bmatrix} \end{array}$$
   (ii) 160   (iii) row vectors approximately equal

8. (i)
$$\begin{array}{c} \\ Work \\ Rep \\ Wait \end{array}\begin{array}{c} Work \quad Rep \quad Wait \\ \begin{bmatrix} 0.8 & 0.125 & 0.075 \\ 0.5 & 0.5 & 0 \\ 0.9 & 0 & 0.1 \end{bmatrix} \end{array}$$
   (ii) 0.3125   (iii) 0.8   (iv) 0.75, 0.1875, 0.0625

9. (i)
$$\begin{array}{c} \\ 1 \\ 2 \\ 3 \\ 4 \\ 5 \\ 6 \end{array}\begin{array}{c} 1 \ \ 2 \ \ 3 \ \ 4 \ \ 5 \ \ 6 \\ \begin{bmatrix} 0 & p & 0 & 0 & 0 & q \\ q & 0 & p & 0 & 0 & 0 \\ 0 & q & 0 & p & 0 & 0 \\ 0 & 0 & q & 0 & p & 0 \\ 0 & 0 & 0 & q & 0 & p \\ p & 0 & 0 & 0 & q & 0 \end{bmatrix} \end{array}$$

   (ii)
$$\begin{array}{c} \\ 1 \\ 3 \\ 5 \end{array}\begin{array}{c} 1 \quad\ 3 \quad\ 5 \\ \begin{bmatrix} 2pq & p^2 & q^2 \\ q^2 & 2pq & p^2 \\ p^2 & q^2 & 2pq \end{bmatrix} \end{array}$$

10. (i)
$$\begin{array}{c} \\ A \\ B \\ C \\ D \end{array}\begin{array}{c} A \quad\ B \quad\ C \quad\ D \\ \begin{bmatrix} 0 & \frac{4}{7} & \frac{3}{7} & 0 \\ \frac{2}{3} & 0 & 0 & \frac{1}{3} \\ \frac{1}{2} & 0 & 0 & \frac{1}{2} \\ 0 & \frac{2}{5} & \frac{3}{5} & 0 \end{bmatrix} \end{array}$$
   (ii) Robert: $A \frac{25}{42}$, $D \frac{12}{42}$; Daniel: $B \frac{18}{35}$, $C \frac{17}{35}$

11. (i)
$$\begin{array}{c} \\ A \\ B \end{array}\begin{array}{c} A \qquad\quad B \\ \begin{bmatrix} 1 - p_1 & p_1 \\ p_2 & 1 - p_2 \end{bmatrix} \end{array}$$
   (iii) $\dfrac{p_2}{p_1 + p_2}, \dfrac{p_1}{p_1 + p_2}$

Exercise 8D

1. (i) $2\frac{1}{3}$ (ii) 4 (iii) 1 (iv) $\frac{1}{3}$ (v) 2 (vi) $\frac{1}{4}$ (vii) $\frac{1}{11}$ (viii) 7 (ix) $\frac{1}{2}$ (x) $\frac{1}{3}$

2. (i)

	MB	IP	R1
MB	$\frac{1}{3}$	$\frac{1}{3}$	$\frac{1}{3}$
IP	$\frac{2}{3}$	$\frac{1}{6}$	$\frac{1}{6}$
R1	$\frac{1}{3}$	$\frac{2}{3}$	0

(ii) (a) $\frac{2}{9}$, (b) $\frac{2}{9}$, (c) $\frac{11}{27}$, (d) $\frac{16}{81}$;

(iii) $\frac{13}{29}, \frac{10}{29}, \frac{6}{29}$ (iv) $\frac{1}{5}$

3. (i)

	A	B	SB
A	0.6	0.15	0.25
B	0.3	0.6	0.1
SB	0.5	0.5	0

(ii) Tues: 0, 0.5, 0.5; Wed: 0.175, 0.45, 0.375 (iii) 1.5

4. (i)

	B	C	main
A	0.6	0.15	0.25
B	0.3	0.6	0.1
SB	0.5	0.5	0

(ii) Thur: 0, $\frac{3}{5}, \frac{2}{5}$; Wed: $\frac{7}{30}, \frac{1}{2}, \frac{4}{15}; \frac{5}{27}, \frac{14}{27}, \frac{8}{27}$ (iii) $\frac{1}{5}$

5. (i)

	D	W
D	0.75	0.25
W	0.338	0.662

(ii) 0.57483, 0.42517;

(iii) $\mathbf{P}^{10} = \begin{bmatrix} 0.57489 & 0.42511 \\ 0.57475 & 0.42575 \end{bmatrix}$

(iv) 2.96, 4; $2.96 + 4 \approx 7$

6. (i)

	Work	Minor	Major
Work	0.8	0.1	0.1
Minor	0.6	0.2	0.2
Major	0.3	0.3	0.4

(ii) 0.73, 0.13, 0.14 (iii) $\frac{42}{61}, \frac{9}{61}, \frac{10}{61}$ (iv) $P(N = n) = 0.2 \times 0.8^n$; 4

7. $\begin{bmatrix} 0.82 & 0 & 0.18 \\ 0.375 & 0.25 & 0.375 \\ 0.18 & 0 & 0.82 \end{bmatrix}$, $\begin{bmatrix} 0.756 & 0 & 0.244 \\ 0.4375 & 0.125 & 0.4375 \\ 0.244 & 0 & 0.756 \end{bmatrix}$; 0.4375, 0.125, 0.4375; 0.5, 0, 0.5

(i) (a) stays in state 1,
(b) moves to states 1, 2 or 3 with probabilities 0.25, 0.5, 0.25,
(c) stays in state 3
(ii) eventually moves to states 1 or 3 with probability 0.5

Exercise 9A

1. (i) $H_0: \mu_1 = \mu_2 = \mu_3 = \mu_4 = \mu_5$, H_1: not all μ_i equal

(ii)

Method	1	2	3	4	5	Overall
Sample size	4	4	4	4	4	20
Sample mean	21.75	26.75	19.25	19.75	24	22.2
Sample variance	6.92	3.58	4.25	3.58	6	12.16

(iii)

Source of variation	SS	DF	VE
Between samples	158.2	4	39.55
Within samples	73	15	4.87

(iv) $F = 8.13$ (v) Reject H_0

2. $s_b^2 = 195$; $s_w^2 = 23$; $F = 8.48$; C.V. $= 3.89$; reject H_0

3. $s_b^2 = 122.9$; $s_w^2 = 23$; $F = 3.21$;
(i) C.V. $= 3.24$; accept H_0 (ii) C.V. $= 5.29$; accept H_0

4. $s_b^2 = 37.5$; $s_w^2 = 13.94$; $F = 2.69$; C.V. $= 4.07$; accept H_0
5. $s_b^2 = 147.5$; $s_w^2 = 290.2$; $F = 0.51$; C.V. $= 4.26$; accept H_0
6. $s_b^2 \approx 97.4$; $s_w^2 = 24.3$; $F = 4.01$;
   (i) C.V. $= 2.96$; reject H_0 (ii) C.V. $= 4.67$; accept H_0

Exercise 9B

1. (i) 21   (ii) 7   (iii) $s_b^2 = 18.95$; $s_w^2 = 4.2$; $F = 4.51$; C.V. $= 3.55$; reject H_0.

2. (i)

Method of storage	1	2	3	Overall
Sample size	5	3	6	14
Sample mean	7.4	6.067	5.7	6.386
Sample variance	0.58	0.536	0.697	1.211

   (ii)

Source of variation	SS	DF	VE
Between samples	8.27	2	4.14
Within samples	8.69	11	0.79

   (iii) $F = 5.234$; C.V. $= 3.98$; reject H_0
3. (i) $s_b^2 = 1626.7$; $s_w^2 = 127.3$; $F = 12.8$; C.V. $= 5.04$; reject H_0
   (ii) mean $= 48.25$ hours; standard error $= 5.64$ hours.
4. (i) $s_b^2 = 27.75$; $s_w^2 = 50.31$; $F = 0.55$; C.V. $= 4.26$; accept H_0;
   (ii) e.g. day of week, comfort, cost
5. (i) $s_b^2 = 281.3$; $s_w^2 = 50.6$; $F = 5.56$;
   (ii) H_0: $\mu_1 = \mu_2 = \mu_3$, H_1: not all μ_i equal; C.V. $= 3.63$;
   (iii) reject H_0
6. (ii) (a) $s_b^2 = 1.655$; $s_w^2 = 0.262$; $F = 6.32$; C.V. $= 3.49$;
   (iii) reject H_0
7. (ii) $s_b^2 = 11.08$; $s_w^2 = 3.52$; $F = 3.15$; C.V. $= 3.34$; accept H_0;
   (iii) $t = -2.156$; C.V. $= -2.145$; just significant
8. (ii) $s_b^2 = 0.153$; $s_w^2 = 0.0205$; $F = 7.44$; C.V. $= 8.02$; accept H_0
9. (i) $s_b^2 = 17.78$; $s_w^2 = 0.3975$; $F = 44.7$; C.V. $= 10.8$; accept H_0
10. (i) $s_b^2 = 31.84$; $s_w^2 = 2.01$; $F = 15.8$; C.V. $= 6.22$; reject H_0

Exercise 10A

1. (i) $\hat{\alpha} = 68.76$, $\hat{\beta} = 0.5549$ (ii) $r = -0.5660$
2. (i) $\hat{\alpha} = 323.9$, $\hat{\beta} = 14.51$ (ii) $r^2 = -0.5660$
3. $c = \bar{y}$, $m = \dfrac{\displaystyle\sum_{i=1}^{n} (x_i - \bar{x})(y_i - \bar{y})}{\displaystyle\sum_{i=1}^{n} (x_i - \bar{x})^2}$
4. (iii) $b = 0.2935$ (iv) $a = 0.001933$, $b = 0.2797$
   (v) $(\alpha \equiv 0)$ RSS $= 4.651 \times 10^{-5}$, $(\alpha$ estimated) RSS $= 3.850 \times 10^{-5}$

Exercise 10C

1. test statistic $= 2.017 > 1.96$ (2-tailed, 5% level) so reject H_0
2. (i) $40.35 < \alpha < 67.82$, $9.597 < \beta < 15.85$ (ii) Normal, mean zero
3. test statistic $= 6.689 > 1.761$ (1-tailed, 5% level, $\nu = 14$) so reject H_0
4. (i) $L = \alpha + \beta c + E$, $E \sim N(0, 0.085)$ (ii) $12.0340 < \alpha < 12.5049$
5. (i) $Y = \alpha + \beta n + E$, $E \sim N(0, \sigma^2)$
   (ii) test statistic $= 1.141 < 1.833$ (1-tailed, 5% level, $\nu = 9$) so accept H_0

6. (i) $P = \alpha + \beta h + E$, $E \sim N(0, \sigma^2)$ (ii) $-0.01772 < \beta < -0.00624$

7. $A + 18B \sim N\left(\alpha + 18\beta, \dfrac{\sigma^2}{S_{XX}}\left\{\dfrac{1}{n}\sum_{i=1}^{n} x_i^2 - 36\bar{x} + 324\right\}\right)$

test statistic $= 1.468 < 2.05$ (2-tailed, 5% level, $\nu = 28$) so reject H_0

Exercise 10E

1. (i) $V = \alpha + \kappa\dfrac{1}{\rho} + E$, $E \sim N(0, \sigma^2)$

(ii) (a) $\hat{\alpha} = 0.01691$, $\hat{\beta} = 23.63$

(b) test statistic $= 1.769 < 2.179$ (2-tailed, 5% level, $\nu = 12$) so accept H_0

2. $-27135 < \alpha < -21712$, $10241 < \beta < 12480$

3. (α changed) test statistic $= -0.7298 > -1.96$ (2-tailed, 5% level) so accept H_0

(β unchanged) test statistic $= -0.0884 > -1.96$ (2-tailed, 5% level) so accept H_0

4. (i) $M = \alpha + \beta t^{3/2} + E$, $E \sim N(0, \sigma^2)$

(ii) (a) test statistic $= -2.639 < -1.812$ (1-tailed, 5% level, $\nu = 10$) so reject H_0

(b) $-1.084 < \beta < -0.7466$

Exercise 10F

1. (a) $a = 32.79$, $b = 2.779$, $c = 0.5728$

(b) $r^2 = 0.7032$, gives the proportion of the variance in oxide content within the sample explained by the estimated model.

2. (i) (a) $G = \alpha + \beta s + \gamma n + E$, where E is a random variable with mean zero

(b) $a = 1.662$, $b = 0.6946$, $c = 0.3016$, (c) $r^2 = 0.6345$

(ii) (a) $G - \alpha + \beta s + E'$, where E' is a random variable with mean zero, which is not the same assumption, (b) $a = 4.267$, $b = 0.7168$, (c) $r^2 = 0.4702$

3. (i) $A = 1.386$, $r = 0.2110$, $s = 0.9160$ (ii) (c) $A = 1.227$, $r = 0.1475$

4. (i) (a) $M = \alpha + \beta e^{-(t/10)} + \gamma e^{-(t/4)} + E$, where E is a random variable with zero mean

(b) $a = 0.09970$, $b = 2.923$, $c = -2.983$

(ii) (b) $b = 3.266$, $c = -3.258$

(iii) reason 1: the mean concentration does not in fact tend to zero as t increases, ie the deterministic part of the model reflects reality better in (i)

reason 2: the mean concentration does in fact tend to zero as t increases, but a systematic measurement error leads to a positive value for the mean error ie the deterministic part of the model reflects reality better in (ii), but the assumptions underlying the statistical parts of the models are invalid.